Theatrical Translation and Film Adaptation

TOPICS IN TRANSLATION
Series Editors: Susan Bassnett, *University of Warwick, UK*
Edwin Gentzler, *University of Massachusetts, Amherst, USA*
Editor for Translation in the Commercial Environment:
Geoffrey Samuelsson-Brown, University of Surrey, UK

For more details of these or any other of our publications, please contact:
Multilingual Matters, Frankfurt Lodge, Clevedon Hall,
Victoria Road, Clevedon, BS21 7HH, England
http://www.multilingual-matters.com

TOPICS IN TRANSLATION 29
Series Editors: Susan Bassnett, *University of Warwick*
and Edwin Gentzler, *University of Massachusetts, Amherst*

Theatrical Translation and Film Adaptation
A Practitioner's View

Phyllis Zatlin

MULTILINGUAL MATTERS LTD
Clevedon • Buffalo • Toronto

Library of Congress Cataloging in Publication Data
A catalog record for this book is available from the Library of Congress.

British Library Cataloguing in Publication Data
A catalogue entry for this book is available from the British Library.

ISBN 1-85359-833-X / EAN 978-1-85359-833-3 (hbk)
ISBN 1-85359-832-1 / EAN 978-1-85359-832-6 (pbk)

Multilingual Matters Ltd
UK: Frankfurt Lodge, Clevedon Hall, Victoria Road, Clevedon BS21 7HH.
USA: UTP, 2250 Military Road, Tonawanda, NY 14150, USA.
Canada: UTP, 5201 Dufferin Street, North York, Ontario M3H 5T8, Canada.

Typeset by Techset Ltd.
Printed and bound in Great Britain by MPG Books Ltd.

Contents

Preface

When Robert Wechsler wrote his highly acclaimed study on literary translation, *Performing Without a Stage* (Wechsler, 1998), he was not specifically thinking of theatre. He speaks of actors interpreting the work of the playwright and of singers interpreting the work of the songwriter, thus establishing through performance that their own work is an art. 'The translator's problem is that he is a performer without a stage, an artist whose performance looks just like the original, just like a play or a song or a composition, nothing but ink on a page' (Wechsler, 1998: 7). It is my belief, however, that theatrical translation should be intended precisely for performance. If a play translation is nothing but ink on a page, it is not theatre (performance text). If it is published and read, it may be considered drama (literary text), and Wechsler's excellent observations on literary translation will apply. Even if the translator's contribution to the production remains invisible to some observers, theatrical translators, like playwrights, need to perform *with* a stage. Marion Peter Holt, the foremost translator of contemporary Spanish theatre in the United States, affirms that performability has been the prime aim of every play he has translated, with publication perhaps coming after performance (Holt, 2002, personal communication).

In *Performing Without a Stage*, Wechsler makes one reference to Molière and several to Shakespeare, but he generally concentrates on the translation of novel and poetry. In this respect, his book is similar to the vast majority of studies in the field. Theory of literary translation has centered on these genres. In *Translating Literature: Practice and Theory in a Comparative Literature Context* (Lefevere, 1992), André Lefevere includes 374 books and articles in his 'Suggestions for Further Reading'; in only six of these titles is drama specifically mentioned. Prefacing her discussion of the subject in the first edition of her *Translation Studies* (Bassnett-McGuire, 1980: 120), Susan Bassnett identifies theatre as 'one of the most neglected areas'; given her own strong interest in the subject, she gives to theatre some 12 pages of her 53-page chapter on literary translation. In the third edition of her groundbreaking book, she appends a select bibliography of works published in English from 1980 onward (Bassnett, 2002: 149–64). Her list includes 210 books and 47 articles; only six of these books and three of the articles refer to theatre. It is therefore understandable that in *Literary Translation. A Practical Guide*, Clifford E. Landers (2001) dedicates only two and a half pages to translating for the theatre. Brigitte Schultze theorizes that much less has been written on the translation of drama because with narrative fiction and poetry one has to deal only with written text. 'Drama translation, in contrast, implies simultaneous transfer into two forms of communication: monomedial literature (reading) and polymedial theatre (performance)' (Schultze, 1998: 177).

The tendency to bypass theatre in translation studies is one of the reasons for the defensive tone that I have adopted in Chapter 1: 'In Theatrical Translation, There is No Lack of Conflict'. Of course the relative lack of such studies is also the primary impetus for this book.

Despite the traditional emphasis in translation studies on narrative and poetry, there is a growing bibliography on theatre. From the period 1980–1989, we find three interesting anthologies in English containing the perspectives of theatrical translators from various countries: two volumes edited by Ortrun Zuber-Skerritt, *The Languages of Theatre. Problems in the Translation and Transposition of Drama* (Zuber, 1980) and *Page to Stage. Theatre as Translation* (Zuber-Skerritt, 1984); and *The Play Out of Context. Transferring Plays from Culture to Culture*, edited by Hanna Scolnicov and Peter Holland (1989). More recent publications include *Stages of Translation* (1996), an anthology of essays and interviews that discuss theatrical translation in practice, edited by David Johnston; *Moving Target. Theatre Translation and Cultural Relocation* (2000), edited by Carole-Anne Upton; and *Time-Sharing on Stage. Drama Translation in Theatre and Society* (2000), a theoretical work by Sirkku Aaltonen. The present book, like Aaltonen's, is a unified study by a single author, but in spirit it is closer to the diversified array of the several anthologies and to the approach taken in Landers' practical guide.

As a professor of Spanish literature for 40 years, my principal area of specialization has always been contemporary theatre. Initially I examined texts as literature only, but over time, in both my teaching and writing, I began to focus on plays in performance. In 1987, I was unexpectedly cast as coordinator of my department's certificate and masters programmes in translation. I therefore also assumed the role of a translator, and it was natural for me to turn to plays as source texts. Among translations from Spanish and French that I have created, ten works have been performed by professional or university groups. My practical experience also extends to close association with the work of others. Among the masters theses in translation that I have directed, there are more than 20 in the field of theatre; several of these translated plays have been staged or published. I have been actively involved since its founding in 1992 with ESTRENO Plays, an ongoing collection of translations of contemporary Spanish theatre, and have been general editor of the series since 1998. Most of the translations published by ESTRENO Plays have been performed at some level.

In preparing this book I have consulted published studies but have drawn as well upon personal interviews and correspondence with translators and other theatre professionals in the United States and Europe. I have been fortunate in receiving thoughtful responses to a written questionnaire from an international selection of theatrical translators. The results of the survey and the names of the participants are found in Chapter 2: 'Out of the Shadows: The Translators Speak for Themselves'. An outgrowth of the questionnaire, along with interviews during a sabbatical trip to Europe in 2003, is Chapter 3: 'Networking: Collaborative Ventures'. Additional references to the questionnaires are incorporated in various places within the text, and the survey form appears as an appendix. Quotes given throughout the book without specific source references have been taken from the questionnaire responses.

Although my expertise is concentrated in contemporary Spanish theatre and I work from Spanish and French into English, I have deliberately reached out to include translation into English from other languages, and, to a lesser degree, other language combinations: from English or Spanish to French, for example. Readers will discover a disproportionate concentration on Hispanic texts but the goal throughout has been to elaborate concepts that are not language specific.

This book is intended as a point of departure, not an all-inclusive study of a complex subject. Absent here, for example, are separate chapters on such topics as translation of opera libretti, adaptation of stage plays as musical comedies, intralingual translation (that is, the modernization of classic texts), or translation of drama written in verse, although these are all subjects that crop up frequently the more one explores the general issue of theatrical translation and adaptation. In his thoughtful introduction to the 1985 modernization of José Zorrilla's *Don Juan Tenorio*, Andrés Amorós clarifies his position on adapting that 19th-century verse drama for contemporary audiences. Rejecting both total fidelity and radical change, he affirms:

> I believe one must 'dust it off': suppress repetitions, eliminate what today sounds ridiculous to us or distances us too much. Of course it is necessary to keep the classic rhyme and stanzas. That requires

delicate adaptation work, because changing one word almost always means revising the line or the whole stanza. (Amorós, 1985: 19)

Amorós succinctly identifies here not only the basic problem for all theatrical translation of how to reach the target audience but also the special difficulties posed by poetry.

It is no doubt true that to translate poetry one must be a poet. Not being a poet myself, I would never tackle verse drama; nevertheless, theatrical translators often find they must confront occasional passages of poetry or song lyrics. The subject is thus among those dealt with in Chapter 4: 'Practical Approaches to Translating Theatre'.

This book includes a separate chapter on the translation of bilingual play texts because I have had to confront that problem several times myself as translator, editor, or teacher. To my knowledge, Chapter 5: 'Variations on the Bilingual Play Text', is the first published effort at providing a general analysis of the subject.

As the hybrid title indicates, my study is not limited to play translation per se. Chapter 6: 'Titling and Dubbing for Stage and Screen' was originally suggested by Tommi Grover of Multilingual Matters. I anticipated that my exploration of the topic would lead to just a few pages but soon learned that this, too, is a complex issue. Very little has been written about the use of these forms of translation to make theatre performance accessible to spectators who do not understand the language of the play. With respect to film, I found a number of published studies but from my travels discovered that previous articles, labeling certain countries as strongly preferring dubbing to subtitling, are either out of date or were based on prime-time television rather than movies.

The chapter on subtitling and dubbing presents a transition between my examination of theatre and my commentary on film adaptation of plays. In 1992, when I first taught a graduate seminar, 'Literature into Film', I was struck by the similarities between translation and adaptation/transformation theory. The strategies and conventions of film are often described as a language. At the fidelity end of the scale, the goal in translating a play to a second natural language or transforming it for the screen is to carry the source text over into that other language with dynamic equivalence. Thus I have routinely mentioned the parallels with translation when teaching film adaptation and with film adaptation when teaching literary translation. I am, of course, not alone in observing this connection.

As is true of translation theory, adaptation theory concentrates on the novel and tends to bypass theatre. The annotated bibliography in James

Naremore's *Film Adaptation* (2000) cites 38 books and articles; in their titles, only three of them refer directly to theatre, and two of those are to Shakespeare, the 'literary' playwright par excellence. What is more, studies in the field often disparage theatre and its influence on movies. Chapter 7, 'On and Off the Screen: The Many Faces of Adaptation', traces that debate while establishing that adaptation of stage plays has been and continues to be an important part of film history.

Chapter 8, 'From Stage to Screen: Strategies for Film Adaptation', in parallel with Chapter 4 on theatrical translation, presents specific suggestions for transforming a play into a movie. These suggestions are developed from a number of concrete examples that are primarily, but not exclusively, based on American and Spanish films.

In the process of preparing this book, I have received encouragement, guidance, recommendations, and information from a large number of people. Without their collective assistance, this book could not have been written. I have recognized their contributions within the text and in notes; I would like to express my continuing gratitude to them all. I am also deeply appreciative for the insights I have gained from the playwrights whose works I have translated, from colleagues who have collaborated in one way or another in the work of ESTRENO Plays, from those who have organized and participated in various panels on theatrial translation or film transformation at conferences in Jaén and Madrid, Spain, and at annual meetings of the American Literary Translators Association, and from my students of translation studies and film adaptation over the years. My special thanks to Patricia W. O'Connor, founding editor of *Estreno*; Martha T. Halsey, founding editor of ESTRENO Plays; Iride Lamartina-Lens of Pace University, and Geneviève and Pierre Ulmann for urging me to undertake my first play translations from Spanish and French; to Marion Peter Holt, for his boundless generosity in sharing his knowledge and expertise with me and my students; and to Maria Delgado, for facilitating my research in the United Kingdom in numerous ways. I would also like to acknowledge the benefit I derived from directing the research of several students who helped clarify my understanding of their subjects: Patricia Santoro and Asun Gómez, on film adaptation; Ellen Bay, on subtitling; and Kerri Allen, on theatrical translation.

References

Aaltonen, S. *Time-sharing on Stage. Drama Translation in Theatre and Society.* Clevedon: Multilingual Matters, Topics in Translation 17, 2000.

Amorós, A. '*Don Juan Tenorio*, mito teatral.' Introduction. In J. Zorrilla, *Don Juan Tenorio*, Versión de Andrés Amorós. Madrid: La Avispa, Colección Teatro 12, 1985.

Bassnett, S. *Translation Studies*, 3rd edn. London and New York: Routledge, 2002. Reprinted 2003.

Bassnett-McGuire, S. *Translation Studies*, 1st edn. London and New York: Methuen, 1980.

Holt, M. P. E-mail to Megan Fuller Pérez, 7 September 2002.

Johnson, D., ed. *Stages of Translation*. Bath, England: Absolute Classics, 1996.

Landers, C.E. *Literary Translation. A Practical Guide.* Clevedon: Multilingual Matters, Topics in Translation 22, 2001.

Lefevere, A. *Translating Literature: Practice and Theory in a Comparative Literature Context.* New York: The Modern Language Association of America, 1992.

Naremore, J., ed. *Film Adaptation.* New Brunswick, NJ: Rutgers University Press, 2000.

Schultze, B. 'Highways, byways, and blind alleys in translating drama: Historical and systematic aspects of a cultural technique.' In K. Mueller-Vollmer and M. Irmscher, eds, *Translating Literatures. Translating Cultures. New Vistas and Approaches in Literary Studies*. Berlin: Erich Schmidt Verlag, 1998, 177–96.

Scolnicov, H. and Holland, P., eds. *The Play Out of Context. Transferring Plays from Culture to Culture.* Cambridge: Cambridge University Press, 1989.

Upton, C.-A., ed. *Moving Target. Theatre Translation and Cultural Relocation.* Manchester, UK and Northampton, MA: St. Jerome Publishing, 2000.

Wechsler, R. *Performing Without a Stage. The Art of Literary Translation.* New Haven, CT: Catbird Press, 1998.

Zuber, O. *The Languages of Theatre. Problems in the Translation and Transposition of Drama.* Oxford and New York: Pergamon Press, 1980.

Zuber-Skerritt, O., ed. *Page to Stage. Theatre as Translation.* Amsterdam: Rodopi, 1984.

Chapter 1

In Theatrical Translation, There is No Lack of Conflict

Nothing is more difficult and less appreciated than a good translation
Paul Claudel[1]

Drama, by definition, is the story of conflict. No conflict, no drama. In that respect, the practice of literary translation presupposes dramatic action, for translators may anticipate from the outset the conflict stemming from the widely held belief that they are traitors who invariably betray the source text. With the old adage, *traduttore, traditore*, the translator is cast as Iago.

We can, of course, object to such a negative view by citing innumerable examples of fine translations that capture well the meaning and style of their source texts. In theatrical translation, however, some betrayal is a necessity. As Ortrun Zuber succinctly observes, 'a play is dependent on the immediacy of the impact on the audience' (Zuber, 1980: 92). Readers who are committed to learning more about another culture may have no problem with translated novels that offer explanations in footnotes or that inspire them to research unfamiliar references. Spectators in the theatre must grasp immediately the sense of the dialogue. Readers may delight in the recreation of antiquated language within a narrative text, but, as Hamlet maintains, actors on stage must be able to speak the speech 'trippingly on the tongue'. Clifford Landers correctly states: 'Even style, which is by no means unimportant in dramatic translation, sometimes must yield to the reality that actors have to be able to deliver the lines in a convincing and natural manner' (Landers, 2001: 104). To achieve speakable dialogue, theatrical translators can and do adapt.

I am not making new discoveries here. Previous essays on translating for the stage repeatedly establish these points. Robert W. Corrigan affirmed that theatrical translators, like playwrights, must know how writing for the theatre differs from literature and must be trained in the practice of theatre: 'Without such training the tendency will be to translate words and their meanings. This practice will never produce performable translations, and that is, after all, the purpose of doing the job in the first place' (Corrigan, 1961: 100). Two decades later, George Wellwarth (1981) insisted on the importance of style with this warning: 'No audience will give its full attention to a play whose dialogue is stilted' (Wellwarth, 1981: 142). Rick Hite (1999: 304) advised theatrical translators to become actors and listen to their work so that they may perceive 'the problems of translating from spoken text to spoken text' and 'become more sensitive to the vocal idiosyncrasies of both languages, of their inherent rhythms, patterns, and stress'.

Corrigan, Wellwarth and Hite refer specifically to the modern American stage. Their comments could be applied equally well to the British, French and Spanish stages but are not necessarily universal today nor applicable to earlier periods. Geneviève Ulmann, who has for many years headed an international literary agency in Paris, states that in Belgium, Germany, and the Scandinavian countries, spectators accept translations that sound like translations.[2] In France translations are not considered stageworthy unless they flow like original texts.

It is this latter goal, of producing texts that flow, that we shall have in mind throughout this book. That goal is consistent with a final declaration on minimal requirements for theatrical translators that was issued in January 1998 by the Ariane Literary Network, a project of the European Union. Those requirements encompass linguistic competency, theatrical experience, and writing talent (European Union, 1998).

In the early decades of the 20th century, American audiences apparently were as amenable to stilted dialogue as Ullmann believes contemporary Belgian, German and Scandinavian spectators are still. A number of plays by Nobel prize winner Jacinto Benavente and other Spanish authors reached the Broadway stage with ease in translations by John Garrett Underhill that today we might kindly call 'wooden'. Underhill's absolute fidelity to his source, coupled with his failure to recognize idiomatic expressions, resulted in the kinds of passages that give translators a bad name. Consider, for example, this one sentence spoken by the Captain in an early scene of Benavente's internationally acclaimed metatheatrical farce, *The Bonds of Interest*:

> Because we were defeated in the late wars – more through these base traffickers who govern us and send us to defend their interests without enthusiasm and without arms, than through any power of the enemy, as if a man could fight with his whole heart for what he

did not love – defeated by these traffickers who did not contribute so much as a single soldier to our ranks or lend one single penny to the cause but upon good interest and yet better security; who, as soon as they scented danger and saw their pockets in jeopardy, threatened to make common cause with the enemy – now they blame us, they abuse us and despise us, and seek to economize out of our martial misery, which is the little pay that they give us, and would dismiss us if they dared, if they were not afraid that some day all those whom they have oppressed by their tyranny and their greed would rise up and turn against them. (Benavente, 1929: 50)

The original Spanish – believe it or not – has comic flair. A good translation would allow us to 'hear' the voice of a talented comic actor delivering this monologue. But with Underhill's language, any bonds of interest that a potential director today might feel up to this point in the script would rapidly unravel. No wonder Lorenzo Mans decided to do a new translation of Benavente's *Los intereses creados* (*The Art of Swindling*) for the 1996 staging in Atlanta.

Poor translation is a serious matter if one is trying to get a play staged. Theatrical directors are not likely to go beyond the title and the opening pages if those lack 'sparkle'. In my experience, directors tend either to love a play on first sight or to reject it with the same speed. This is so in large part because even the smallest professional theatre is likely to be inundated with hundreds of unsolicited manuscripts a year. Well-established, large theatres are likely to reject all unsolicited manuscripts automatically and let literary agents do their initial screening for them.

Why are Underhill's translations no longer acceptable? In general the approach to translation has changed radically in the post Chomsky era.[3] Comparative linguistics has provided a framework for translation theory, and the new theory has inspired more dynamic recreations of source texts. We are now aware that each language has its own stylistics and that theatre conventions vary from country to country. A wise translator takes those differences into account.

In making the adjustments to a dramatic text that today we find essential, translators are by no means alone in adapting and interpreting their source. From the perspective of theatre practitioners, staging a play always involves translation of many kinds. Reba Gostand notes:

Drama, as an art-form, is a constant process of translation: from original concept to script (when there is one), to producer/director's interpretation, to contribution by designer and actor/actress, to visual and/or aural images to audience response ... there may be a number of subsidiary processes of translation at work. (Gostand, 1980: 1)

Spanish playwright and director Ernesto Caballero similarly states that the process of staging a play, particularly one that is not a contemporary work from the same country, is a process of translation that inevitably implies betrayal because it is impossible to take a literal approach to a 'text that belongs to another period or another culture' (Caballero, 2001: 68).[4]

Zuber affirms that translators, like playwrights, should write for actors. In an ideal arrangement, 'the translator's manuscript would first be tried out on the stage and discussed and changed in rehearsals, and only then published for future performances – or for readers' (Zuber, 1980: 93). Because the required transformation from page to stage is complex, most experienced theatrical translators wish to be involved in the dynamics of rehearsals, standing in as the author's surrogate. But far too frequently, the translator is shunted aside. Even the role of Iago, the villain, is better than being written totally out of the script: of being forgotten not only in the process but also in programme credits and play reviews.

In her book on drama translation, Sirkku Aaltonen (2000) titles one of her chapters 'The Translator in the Attic.' The intertextual reference to Sandra Gilbert and Susan Gubar's *The Madwoman in the Attic* (1979) is provocative: like the monstrous women characters hidden away in such 19th-century novels as Charlotte Brontë's *Jane Eyre*, the translator could be described as 'the *author's* double, an image of her own anxiety and rage', a mad creature who reflects 'uniquely female feelings of fragmentation' (Gilbert & Gubar, 1979: 78). Should we view the author–translator relationship as conflictive aspects of a split personality?

Perhaps this comparison to a psychotic, socially unacceptable character from a Gothic novel is a bit melodramatic, but it is often true that translators, rather than getting equal billing with the authors, may be invisible.[5] In 1996, I was delighted that *The New York Times* chose to review Ubu Repertory's staging of Eduardo Manet's *Lady Strass*; if you read D.J.R. Bruckner's positive criticism (Bruckner, 1996), you will learn the names of the director and the actors, but you will not discover that the translation of the French play was mine. I have at hand four reviews from an April 2003 staging in Madrid of Michael Frayn's *Copenhagen*; only one of the critics makes any reference to the quality of Charo Solanas's Castilian version of the British play (Críticas Copenhague, 2003). One can readily find other examples of this phenomenon. The translators' attic is a crowded place.

Aaltonen with reason wants to move translators from the attic to stage centre. She therefore agrees with Lawrence Venuti that literary translators should share copyright with the original authors: 'Venuti's proposal is particularly justifiable in theatre translation, where adaptation ties the translation even more closely and visibly to the target society' (Aaltonen, 2000: 110). We shall deal further with the question of royalties in the next chapter.

If they are involved in the rehearsal process, the translators' contribution may be similar to that of a dramaturg: a consultant to a theatre company who knows the text well and can clarify details for the actors and director. André Ernotte, the director of *Lady Strass*, in fact invited me to go to New York and attend a rehearsal. I found nothing to clarify; the reading that Susanne Wasson, Paul Albe, and Robert Jimenez were giving the text coincided completely with my own. When I expressed amazement at this coincidence, I was told that the theatre's artistic director, Françoise Kourilsky, had given them copies of my detailed scene-by-scene notes on the play's action.

Before translating Manet's play, I had prepared those notes at the request of a potential director. The project fell through. Some years later, I found that analysis in my file and sent it on to Ubu Repertory without giving the matter any thought. More months passed, and by the time I got to the rehearsal, I had forgotten about the notes. The experience at Ubu showed me that a translator–dramaturg, even a forgetful one who does not live in the same city, can participate productively in the process. Unwittingly, I had fulfilled the role that Patrice Pavis has outlined: 'The translator is a dramaturg who must first of all effect a *macrotextual* translation, that is, a dramaturgical analysis of the fiction conveyed by the text' (Pavis, 1989: 27); that analysis should provide 'a coherent reading of the plot as well as the spatio-temporal indications contained in the text' and stage directions (Pavis, 1989: 28). The reviewer for *The New York Times* may have been oblivious to my existence, but the director and actors were not, thanks to my pre-translation analysis.

There is another cure for the psychological fragmentation that theatrical translators may suffer. How can one simultaneously be true to the author and yet reach the target audience? The following comment by Louis G. Kelly provides us with a way out of the attic: 'Fidelity will mean either collaboration or servitude' (Kelly, 1979: 207). The servitude of total fidelity is undesirable for all concerned: even if it were possible, it would yield unstageworthy results. Collaboration with living authors is not always easy: the give and take of any interpersonal relationship may be complicated by an author's unwillingness to accept modification to a beloved text. But if the author respects the translator's judgement and open dialogue is possible, collaboration is ideal.

In my contact with authors as editor and translator, I have invariably found a willingness to work for viable solutions to problems the translator has identified. Such problems have ranged from the title of the play to the names of the characters and to intertextual references to movies, songs, and other items of cultural significance. Did the author have an alternate working title that might translate more gracefully? Could a character's name be changed to one that is more easily pronounced by our actors and/or does not carry an undesirable connotation? Are there other movies or songs, better known to our target audience, that would serve as well? How can we fill a particular cultural gap most effectively? The authors have quickly supplied an answer they already had contemplated, or have thought the problem through and come up with a workable idea, or have given the translator and/or editor carte blanche for coming up with something original. Perhaps the secret to assuring collaboration is to couch the problem as a question.

Playwright José Luis Alonso de Santos, who recently headed the National Company for Classic Theatre in Madrid, has prepared or directed a number of modernized adaptations and understands well the translator's role. From its beginning, this theatre has set out 'to connect with the sensibilities of today's spectator' (Cuadernos de Teatro Clásico 16, 2002: 21). In his programme notes on adapting a Golden Age play by Agustín Moreto, Alonso de Santos explicitly suggests that he collaborated with the long-deceased dramatist: 'Taking the liberty of reincarnating myself for a while in the 17th century, I asked the author for advice about my questions' (Cuadernos de Teatro Clásico 16, 2002: 38). Alonso de Santos' comment echoes Pavis' assertion that 'in order to find out what the source text means, I have to bombard it with questions from the target language's point of view' (Pavis, 1989: 26).

American playwright and translator Caridad Svich speaks of her relationship with Federico García Lorca, who died decades before she was born, in terms similar to those of Alonso de Santos: 'It is a rare treat to train under another writer's guidance' (Svich, personal communication, 2002). Spaniard Fernando Savater describes the experience of translating Molière's *Le Misanthrope* as being the opportunity 'to spend several months in the company of one of liveliest and most scathing minds of European culture' (Cuadernos de Teatro Clásico 16, 2002: 141). Many translators of dead authors assert that, by putting themselves into the spirit of their source, they have determined what a particular writer would have said were he living today in the target culture.

French theorist Patrice Pavis pursues this thought when he describes the paradox of Shakespeare being easier to understand today in French or German translation than in the original English precisely because the translation has been prepared for the target audience, by 'adapting the text to the current situation of enunication' (Pavis, 1989: 28). Franz Link asks whether the translation of a classic text should be modernized or if the spectator should be asked to travel into another time (Link, 1980: 25); ultimately he responds: 'As the author uses the language of his own time, so does the translator of the play into another language' (Link, 1980: 30).

Translators of living authors do not have to fictionalize their source's thought patterns: they can call or send an e-mail. When Bethany Korp was working through problems in translating Catalan playwright Beth Escudé i Gallès's *El color del gos quan fuig* for ESTRENO Plays, the author and the translator had the opportunity to meet and talk for hours. In the process, the meaningless literal translation of the title, 'The Color of the Fleeing Dog', was transformed into *Killing Time*, to the satisfaction of all. Had Korp, as translator, or I, as editor, decided to impose an English title on Escudé's play, we would surely have had on-going conflict with the author. Spanish playwright Ignacio del Moral relates that he quickly authorized the Swedish translator of his *La mirada del hombre oscuro* to soften certain speeches once he understood how unacceptable the father's verbal treatment of his son would be for the target audience (personal interview, 2003). Imposing that change, without explanation, might have evoked a less cordial reaction.

Editors can be the bane of both author and translator for, as Marion P. Holt observes, 'External influences introduced by editing must be weighed against the language of the translation as a whole and its fidelity to the original text' (quoted in Boyd & Boyd, 1987: 3). One of the first plays I translated was Alonso de Santos's box-office hit, *Bajarse al moro* (*Going Down to Marrakesh*), a script featuring young characters who use colloquial language and, starting with the title, drug slang. I did not find my own idiolect reflected in the cast, so in the process of recreating the language of the various characters, I consulted young people: my children and my students. The language patterns they suggested were those of the East Coast. Patricia W. O'Connor, my editor who lives in the more conservative Midwest, was far less satisfied than I with the result. She sent me a copy editor's version that removed all of the offensive language – and hence, in my opinion, distanced itself considerably from the source text. Our peaceful resolution to the battle was a return to my translation but with this explanatory note:

> The original Spanish text makes frequent use of Madrid slang of the 1980s. The equivalent language in the translation is drawn from the New York metropolitan area. Colloquial expression of young people, in any language, not only changes rapidly but varies widely from region to region. Directors, in consultation with the translator, are invited to update the slang in this American version as appropriate for their productions. (Alonso de Santos, 1992: 314)

Francis Cullinan, who directed *Going Down to Marrakesh* at the University of Missouri–Kansas City in March 1992, did not alter the slang. Perhaps he should have. I understand that the theatre was barraged with phone calls from outraged people at local churches; they objected to colourful references to the use of bodily orifices for smuggling drugs. Kansas City, linguistically and otherwise, is a more conservative place than Madrid. But, surprisingly enough, so is New York. A friendly contact at a non-profit theatre in New York City told me he liked Alonso de Santos' comedy but would not touch it. He feared that if Jesse Helms heard anything about the play, the theatre's future funding from the National Endowment for the Arts would be in jeopardy. Helms, an influential and conservative US Senator from the South, had recently expressed impassioned opposition to 'culture' he considered erotic or sacrilegious. And First Lady Nancy Reagan had popularized her 'Just say no to drugs' solution to a social crisis. For *Going Down to Marrakesh*, censorship in the United States was alive and well.

Despite my experiences as a translator, I am not necessarily the ideal editor from the viewpoint of other translators. Rick Hite has not forgotten our disagreement over the translation of the protagonist's name in Paloma Pedrero's *Una estrella*. The author typically invents character names that have meaning and then plays on that meaning within the dialogue; her names thus require great care. 'Estrella', which means 'star', is not an uncommon name in Spanish. On the other hand, 'Star' is an unusual name in English and the Spanish 'Estrella' is both difficult to pronounce and meaningless for most audience members. Hite settled on 'Estelle' while I preferred 'Stella' (and its association with 'stellar' and 'Stella by Starlight'). I doubted that spectators would connect 'Estelle' with 'star'. Hite, on the other hand, not only associated 'Stella' with *A Streetcar Named Desire* but specifically with Marlon Brando yelling at his wife in the movie version of Tennessee Williams's play. The solution, once again, was an explanatory note:

> Translator's note: While 'Estelle' is the translator's choice for 'Estrella' [Star], of the original Spanish, either 'Stella' or 'Estrella' might be substituted should the director so choose. (Pedrero, 2001: 2)

The consideration of connotations evoked by names or of regional reactions to slang, vulgar or otherwise, moves us from purely linguistic to cultural concerns. To the minimal requirements for theatrical translators proposed by the Ariane Literary Network – linguistic competency, theatrical experience, and writing talent – we would be wise to include a thorough grounding in both cultures. As Alan Thomas says, 'It is evident cultural borders, as much as language, form barriers to successful translation' (Thomas, 1998: 3). Pavis similarly observes: 'We cannot simply translate a text linguistically; rather we confront and communicate heterogenous cultures and situations of enunciation that are separated in space and time' (Pavis, 1989: 25). However desirable from the perspective of potential directors, such cultural adaptation can prove to be treacherous ground.

Prestigious foreign texts have frequently been adapted both by those in power in order to reinforce their ideology and by those opposed to repressive regimes as a means of subverting censorship. *Fuenteovejuna*, the Spanish Golden Age history drama by Lope de Vega, was staged with the government's approval in the Soviet Union because it exalts the power of the people; to get the desired effect, the final scene of the source text, which praises the king, had to be deleted. In East Germany, under communist rule, a production of Shakespeare's *Julius Caesar* became a commentary against those in power when the actor who played the title character wore a mask that looked like Party Secretary Honnecker (Meech, 2000: 129).

Tinkering with classical plays, while perhaps dangerous for political reasons, is not the same as adapting living authors. Zuber recounts a court case between Williams and a Berlin theatre group that cast a black actor as Stanley in *A Streetcar Named Desire* and portrayed Blanche not as a rape victim but as a willing sex partner of her brother-in-law. Through his agent in Germany, Williams prevented the production from opening. The case confirmed judicial limitations that apply to translating a play, transferring it to a new cultural setting, and, in this case, imposing a German interpretation of American race relations. The German court found in Williams's favour, even while acknowledging the need for some degree of cultural adaptation:

> [T]he message of the original and the dramatist's intention [should] be adhered to as closely as possible and be rendered, linguistically and

artistically, into a form which takes into account the different traditional, cultural and socio-political background of the recipient
country. (Zuber, 1980: 95)

As translator and editor I know that any liberties taken with the source
text should be made with the knowledge and approval of a living playwright. The more famous the playwright, the more likely there will be
serious conflicts if the translator or the director decides on radical
changes. Playwrights assuredly have the right to protect the integrity of
their intellectual property. Translators, like directors, are therefore
limited in their freedom to make changes to works that are still under
copyright. As another famous lawsuit affirmed, the author owns both
the dialogue and the stage directions: Samuel Beckett successfully prevented the action of his *Happy Days* from being moved into a New York
subway station. Theatrical translators may well discover that they are
limited in their freedom in many other ways as well.

The United States prides itself on being the home of free expression, a
nation that rejects censorship, but theatrical translators quickly discover
that free expression is a myth. In practice, there are always varieties of
censorship, or attempted censorship, in every country of the world, for
economic if not political reasons. Editors (myself included) may try to
impose their views on translators. Theatre directors may decide that a
play should be silenced because it will not attract sufficient spectators.
Religious and political leaders may vocally protest that particular
works are offensive.

In 2001, Larry Life, chair of the Theatre Department at Indiana
University, Purdue University at Fort Wayne (UPFW), a state university,
became a hero to both the American Association of University Professors
(defender of academic freedom) and the American Civil Liberties Union
(defender of constitutional rights) when he stood up to the Indiana legis-
lature and refused to remove Terrence McNally's *Corpus Christi* from
the theatre's summer schedule. Deeply upset because McNally's controversial play depicts Jesus and some of his disciples as gay men, 21 state
legislators filed suit in federal court. On 20 July 2001, US District Judge
William C. Lee ruled against the plaintiffs, finding that they 'failed to
show how the production would violate the establishment clause of the
Constitution, which requires a separation of church and state' (National
Coalition Against Censorship Website: 1).

In this case, freedom of expression won, but all too frequently censorship prevails, often to the detriment of translated theatre. In March–April
2002, UPFW staged my translation of Paloma Pedrero's *The Color of*

August, including its climactic scene in which two women artists paint each other's nude bodies. The Indiana legislators made no comment; no lawsuits were filed; the sky did not fall. That may only prove that Pedrero's play is not yet well known in the Midwest. By contrast, McNally's text had met with controversy across the country and its reputation had preceded it. But the Theatre Department at nearby Ohio Wesleyan University – a church-affiliated college where *Estreno* was sponsoring an international theatre symposium with Pedrero in attendance – said they could not invite the UPFW production to their campus precisely because of the female nudity. They were not concerned that the conference participants might see the revealing scene, but they had to protect the potential audience of college students – all of whom are doubtless old enough to see R- and X-rated movies, but not with college sponsorship.

The decision at Ohio Wesleyan is not the first time that *The Color of August* has run into censorship problems in the United States. Russian-born director Timur Djordjadze felt obliged to delete the climactic scene when he gave the play its American university premiere in 1991 at Pace University in Manhattan. Critic William García lamented that self-censorship had eliminated a scene that 'if not the most important' in the play is 'extremely relevant due to its metaphoric value linked to the theme of women's creativity (body as text, painting)' (García, 1993: 156). Djordjadze, without mentioning the deleted scene, in his notes on Pedrero's theatre cited an essential difference between American attitudes and audience reaction in other countries:

> It is true that Ms Pedrero sometimes describes sexual acts and body parts in graphic terms that a segment of the American audience – in contrast to the Europeans – might find risqué, even offensive. But one must note that the language is never tasteless or vulgar, is always justifiable in terms of character development and relationships. (Djordjadze, 1999: 56)

Despite the obvious lessons from *Going Down to Marrakesh* and *The Color of August*, I am a slow learner. When I later translated Itziar Pascual's *Meowless*, I expected it to be a runaway hit with area high schools. The play is short, can be done with bare stage, and requires only simple props and costumes. The four cast members – two humans and two cats played by human actors – are young roles. This delightful little play has been well received in Spain at amateur and university theatres. I photocopied my translation and distributed it to my graduate students who are teachers. One by one they told me that the play was inappropriate for performance at their respective high schools because it openly implies that the male and female cats might be sexually attracted to each other. In New Jersey, a relatively liberal state by American standards, one may speak to teenagers about the birds and bees but apparently not about cats and dogs.

Among the conflicts translators will face is the discrepancy between acceptable subjects in the source and target cultures. Whoever chooses a play to be translated or staged is always exercising the right to exclude other texts. Theatre directors will understandably exclude texts that might cause trouble with funding agencies or governmental authorities or that might be boycotted by their audiences. Economic censorship is a powerful force. Directors may also impose their ideas of what kind of theatre will play well in the United States. Anglo-American realism/ naturalism will often get absolute preference over the varieties of more imaginative theatre that come from other cultures in the same way that Hollywood-style movies will dominate over European art films.

Audience receptivity to foreign plays or films varies from country to country, with the United States being among the least open to other cultures. In her 1988 essay, 'Exposing the Translation Gap', Felicia Hardison Londré documents the enormous resistance of the American stage to any drama not written originally in English (Londré, 1988). In the words of noted critic Clive Barnes, 'The English-speaking theatre takes an extraordinarily shuttered and blinkered view of world theatre' (quoted in Londré, 1988: 48).

Londré reacted to Barnes' observation by tabulating the production lists from 1981 to 1986 of non-profit theatres across the country that are associated with the Theatre Communications Group (TCG): 'The results were amazingly – and dishearteningly – consistent' (Londré, 1988: 48). Only about 10% of the 6596 productions she tallied were foreign plays in English translation, and most of those were of 'classic' authors, such as Molière, Chekhov, and Ibsen. She found only 2.25% of the total productions to be works by still-living foreign-language authors. My follow-up study of TCG theatres in the mid-1990s revealed virtually identical statistics.[6]

Londré offers several possible explanations for the abysmal situation for foreign plays in general but emphasizes the matter of translation quality. She maintains that many staged translations, from all languages, have been haphazard, uncredited, out-moded, or cut-and-paste jobs done by directors trying to avoid paying royalties (Londré, 1988: 49).

Londré's thought is echoed by playwright and translator Paul Schmidt, who debunks the widespread idea that it is easy to translate Chekhov: 'All someone has to do – and directors do it depressingly often – is simply read all the available translations, and then write some sort of a paraphrase' (Schmidt, 1997: 18). Never mind that they had no understanding of the source text. Even good translators, who do understand, will produce inferior results if they are pressured to work in haste. Tony Harrison says it took two years for Racine to write his Phaedra tragedy, so logically it took him two years to translate it (Harrison, 1989: 101).

If contemporary playwrights from around the world are excluded from regional TCG theatres, there is little likelihood that their plays will reach the commercial Broadway stage. Only once in a while does a contemporary play in translation become a box-office hit in the United States. A recent, outstanding example is Yasmina Reza's *Art*, translated from the French by British playwright Christopher Hampton. That play's enormous international success gives hope to playwrights and translators alike, but it is an exception.

The overly enthusiastic Spanish press has been known to proclaim that certain Spanish playwrights have 'conquered Manhattan' (Boo, 1996), but some of us might refer to those same Spanish-language productions as under-under-off-off Broadway. Certainly few of them are noted in the mainstream, English-language press. In New York City, Washington, DC, Miami, California and Texas, there are many small Hispanic theatres. Generally run by Latin Americans, these playhouses tend to prefer Latin American and Latino texts that speak directly to their audiences to Spanish ones and, in any event, are seldom a venue for theatrical translations.

Although the United Kingdom is not so receptive to translation as other European countries, the situation there is somewhat more encouraging than in the United States.[7] According to criticism appearing in *Theatre Record*, in 1998 one in eight of the professional productions that were reviewed in Great Britain's national press were translations. They included 73 (12.63%) of the productions in London and 33 (14.4%) of the regional productions (Hale & Upton, 2000: 1). Moreover, as we shall note in the chapter on networking, there are theatres in London, like the Gate and Royal Court, that visibly promote foreign theatre in translation. Fortunately, the uphill battle of American theatrical translators is not a universal experience.

Theatrical translators in the English language, along with editors of their play translations, share problems that arise from the relative invisibility of theatre among scholars and the reading public. *The Oxford Guide to Literature in English Translation* (France, 2000) does not consistently consider theatre to be literature: there are no sections on either contemporary French or Latin American drama. The section on 20th-century Spanish drama, prepared by British translator David Johnston, generally bypasses living playwrights and translations published in the United States.[8] The major gateway journals to American library acquisitions – *Publishers Weekly, Choice*, and *Library Journal* – either exclude play editions entirely or review them only sporadically.

Drama shelves in chain bookstores in the United States – and in my local library – primarily feature Shakespeare, Ibsen, Chekhov and perhaps a handful of living, English-language authors. The assumption is that no one reads drama, but one wonders to what extent that is true because the books have become increasingly inaccessible. With the exception of a few places such as the Drama Book Shop in New York City and Offstage Theatre and Film Bookshop in London, theatre bookstores in the United States and the United Kingdom are not interested in carrying new series of play translations from a variety of national stages. Perhaps the solution to marketing play translations published by small presses will be the Internet site of Babel Guides. The mission of www.babelguides.com responds to this situation:

> Foreign literature has a remarkably low level of readership in the large English-speaking countries. Considering the globalizing and domineering trends of the day, now is the time to fuel the quantity and quality of literary translations into English. (Leri, 2003)

The website for world literature that Babel Guides is in the process of building includes theatre.

Difficulties for translators working into Spanish and English are compounded by the existence of countries separated by a common language. That facetious comment is usually made with reference to the United Kingdom and the United States but applies also to the Spanish-speaking world. I am indebted to playwright Jorge Díaz for making me aware of the extent of the problem.

Díaz is generally considered a Chilean author but lived for many years in Madrid, where colloquial language has absorbed expressions that in the Southern Cone would be considered offensive. The playwright thus discovered that his works written in Madrid had to be submitted to intralingual translation so that Chilean spectators would not find them shocking (Díaz, personal communication, 1987). Spain and the Caribbean countries are more open to the use of slang and obscenities than Chile and Argentina, where audiences will prefer more formal language. To see how the process worked in the opposite direction, Díaz advised me to examine the 1976 version for Spain by Alfredo Mañas of *Hablemos a calzón quitado*, by the Argentine playwright and actor Guillermo Gentile. One of the most successful productions ever of a Latin American play on the Spanish stage, *Hablemos a calzón quitado* ran for more than 600 performances in Madrid before going on tour; it was directed by the author, who also played the lead role. We can therefore assume that Gentile accepted Mañas's intralingual translation. Mañas understandably suppressed the Argentine use of *vos* for 'you' and regional words like *pibe* ('kid'). He made other predictable substitutions: a reference to returning from Europe was changed to returning from Miami Beach. Somewhat more surprising was the introduction of swear words and crude language, apparently to meet the expectations of Madrid audiences. Lines of dialogue in the version for Spain often turned out much longer than the source text because of interpolated profanity.[9]

The caveat for translators into Spanish is obvious: do not assume that your translation will be readily accepted throughout the Spanish-speaking world, particularly if it makes extensive use of colloquial, realistic language. Wellwarth correctly asserts that translation of nonpoetic texts implies 'the transference of the colloquial idiom of one language to the colloquial idiom of the other' (Wellwarth, 1981: 144). Link informs us, 'As far as non-poetic language is concerned the less it is stylized the faster it changes' (Link, 1980: 28); and the more it varies from region to region.

Original plays by the great 20th-century playwrights from Spain – García Lorca and Valle-Inclán – are performed throughout Spanish America without noticeable revision, but translators will often be denied that kind of universality. During the 1998–1999 season, Reza's *Art* was the box office hit in Madrid in a translation by Josep Maria Flotats, who also directed the production and played one of the three roles. It should be noted that Flotats was an actor in France for years, enjoys an international reputation as actor and director, and that his translation of *Art* was published immediately. Nevertheless, when *Art* successfully returned to the Madrid stage in 2002–2003 in an Argentine production (dir. Luis Romero), it featured a different translation by F. Masllorens and E. González del Pino. One might question why, if the Argentine translation worked in Madrid, the Spanish translation would not have worked equally well in Buenos Aires.

American and British translators are well aware of this kind of tension. Television series and movies travel with relative ease but theatre people have often felt the need for different versions of the same play for performance on opposite sides of the Atlantic. Thus we find rival translations of plays by Jean-Paul Sartre, published within the space of a year of each other and with different titles: _Huis clos_ is known as _In Camera_ (1946) and _No Exit_ (1947); _Les Mains sales_ became _Crime Passionnel_ in the United Kingdom (1949) and _Dirty Hands_ in the United States (1949). Albert-Reiner Glapp discusses the changes that author Brian Clark made to his script when _Whose Life is it Anyway?_ (1978) travelled from London to Broadway – even though the British English would have been understood by American audiences. Clark clarified that 'American and English have the same passive vocabulary but a vastly different active vocabulary' (quoted in Glapp, 1989: 222).

I would contend that such differences in active vocabulary relate to contemporary, colloquial language and should not affect Antonio Buero-Vallejo's _The Sleep of Reason_, a historical drama about painter Francisco de Goya. The action of Buero's play is placed in the early 19th century and the dialogue is free of dialect and slang. American translator Marion P. Holt has explicitly clarified his position on translating historical drama: 'If the original playwright has used a 19th-century tone in the play, then you should keep it that way' (quoted in Boyd & Boyd, 1987: 5). In Holt's version, _The Sleep of Reason_ has received several successful stagings in the United States and in 1991 was directed in London by Tessa Schneiderman. In his review of the London production for a theatre journal in Spain, David Johnston lambasted the English-language text for its 'American peculiarities' that made Goya sound like 'a Hollywood actor' (Johnston, 1992: 109).

Whether the distant translator or the London performer made Goya sound like 'a Hollywood actor' is a debatable point. The reference appears to be to acting style rather than to some quality of the written dialogue. In 1997, when my translation of Alonso de Santos's _La estanquera de Vallecas_ (_Hostages in the Barrio_) was given a staged reading in Miami Beach, an enthusiastic member of the audience in the discussion that followed asked how much time the author had spent in South Florida. She felt that he had faithfully captured the tone of working-class Cuban immigrants in nearby Hialeah. To my knowledge, the author has never visited Florida and the English text was mine, not his. More to the point, it was the actors – especially Manny Fernandez in the role of Tocho – who had creatively brought the dialogue to life and given it that special local flavour.

Although the translator may be credited or blamed with the transposition of a text for a given target audience, in truth many factors are involved in the context of a performance that are beyond the translator's control. In her insightful study of Sabina Berman, Francine A'ness analyses the reception of the Mexican playwright's *Between Pancho Villa and a Naked Woman* by critics and audiences in the United States and Canada. A'ness notes that in the English-language performances that Berman has attended, the author has 'yet to see a Pancho Villa that she approved of' (A'ness, 2001: 228). The historic figure outside of Mexico is 'emptied of significance and resemantified to become a caricatured "made-in-America" symbol of what it means to be Mexican' (A'ness, 2001: 236). In essence, Berman's play is appropriated by foreign theatre groups and audiences:

> When a play travels (in time and/or space) beyond the culture for which it was originally conceived, it is a new interpretive community with different values and cultural assumptions, memories and associations that receives and interprets the text. (A'ness, 2001: 227)

A'ness discovers 'border anxiety' no matter who translates the play. The first American staging of Berman's *Between Pancho Villa and a Naked Woman* was in an adaptation by Ruben Garfia, who both directed the production and played one of the roles. Garfia shifted the action from Mexico to Los Angeles and changed the characters into Mexican-Americans. When the play has been performed in the more faithful translation by Shelley Tepperman, Berman's official translator, Pancho Villa on stage has still been perceived as a 'gun-slinging folk hero', that is, the stereotypical 'Latin-American macho man' (Calgary review, quoted in A'ness, 2001: 232).

By now the reader may believe that theatrical translators are invariably caught in the middle and begin to wonder if anyone besides confirmed masochists would want to translate plays at all. Despite the frustrations and conflicts, there is a great deal of satisfaction to be derived from translating for the stage. In the next chapter, we will look at responses to a questionnaire sent to a selection of theatrical translators in several countries.[10] Comparative comments from those who have also translated other kinds of texts are illuminating. David Ball generally translates poetry, but with reference to the play *Ubu roi* recalls: 'I enjoyed translating Jarry more than anything else I've done.' Anne Alice Barlind points out that technical translation allows one to eat but is boring. Jörn Cambreleng finds that, in contrast, translating a novel is a long-distance race. Holt similarly observes that his experiments in translating prose taught him that he lacks 'the enthusiasm (and patience) for non-dramatic writing.' For some translators, the similarities between translating drama and poetry or drama and narrative may outweigh the differences, but many theatrical translators are completely committed to their art.

Notes

1. Quoted by Cobos Castro (1995: 51).
2. Franz Link (1980: 33), a professor of English in Freiburg, Germany, wonders if the playbill or the introduction of a narrator might be used to fill cultural gaps. From Ulmann's comments, I suspect that such strategies would be accepted more readily in Germany than in the United States.
3. American linguist Noam Chomsky (b. 1928) developed influential theories of generative grammar and transformational rules.
4. Throughout this book, unless otherwise noted, all translations are my own.
5. Lawrence Venuti has specifically highlighted this aspect in the title of his history of translation, *The Translator's Invisibility* (Venuti, 1995).
6. For an article I published in *Theatre Survey*, the editors asked me to update Londré's study. I analysed three seasons at TCG theatres from 1996–1997 through 1998–1999 (Zatlin, 2001: 74).
7. The percentage of translations for theatrical productions in the United Kingdom is considerably higher than the percentage for published books. Figures reported by Hale and Upton indicate that the translation rate for books in the United Kingdom, like that of the United States, is only about 2%. Numbers they report for other countries are: Germany, 14%; France, 18%; Spain, 24%; Italy, 26% (Hale & Upton, 2000: 1).
8. Another shortcoming I observed was the omission of all women writers from David Callahan's section on 19th- and 20th-century prose fiction of Spain. I reported my analysis of *The Oxford Guide to Literature in English Translation* in a panel discussion at the annual meeting of American Translators Association on 8 November 2002.
9. Here is an extreme example.
   Gentile's original text:
   Claro que me enojo! Basta! Terminen de hacerse los payasos! Hasta ahora me callé la boca porque creí que era mejor no decir nada.
   Mañas's translation for Spain:
   ¡No, si no me cabreo! Digo, qué coño, claro que sí que me cabreo ¡Faltaría más! ¡C'est fini! ¡Stop! ¡Basta! ¿Vamos a terminar de hacer los payasos de una puñeterísima vez...? ¡Jesús! Hasta ahora he tenido mis labios sellados porque he creído conveniente no decir ni pío...
10. More specific information on the questionnaire is provided in the next chapter. The questionnaire itself appears as an appendix.

References

Aaltonen, S. *Time-Sharing on Stage. Drama Translation in Theatre and Society.* Clevedon: Multilingual Matters, Topics in Translation 17, 2000.
Alonso de Santos, J. L. *Going Down to Marrakesh.* In P. W. O'Connor, ed., *Plays of the New Democratic Spain (1975–1990)* (trans. P. Zatin). Lanham, MD, and London: University Press of America, 1992, 313–79.
Alonso de Santos, J. L. *Hostages in the Barrio* (trans. P. Zatlin). Staged reading directed by Steve Wise. The Bridge Theater, Miami Beach Women's Club, 24 October 1997.
A'ness, F. The production of a national playwright: Sabina Berman, her audience, and the changing Mexico City stage. PhD dissertation, University of California, Berkeley, 2001.

Benavente, J. *The Bonds of Interest,* translated with a preface by John Garrett Underhill. New York: Charles Scribner's Sons, 1929.

Boo, J. V. 'El teatro hispano conquista el gran Manhattan and "Entre tinieblas", de Pedro Almodóvar, sube a los escenarios'. *ABC,* 6 May 1996: 105.

Boyd, L. A. and Boyd, G. N. The translator's voice: an interview with Marion Peter Holt. *Translation Review* 23 (1987): 3–7.

Bruckner, D. J. R. Review of *Lady Strass,* by Eduardo Manet. *The New York Times,* 14 October 1996: C16.

Caballero, E. Una traición leal: los límites de la representación calderoniana. In J. Mayorga, ed., Pedro Calderón de la Barca, *El monstruo de los jardines.* Madrid: Fundamentos/Clásicos RESAD, 2001, 67–73.

Cobos Castro, E. *Teatro y traducción en el siglo XIX: El papel evaluador de la crítica teatral. Estudios de Investigación Franco-Española* 12 (1995): 11–52.

Corrigan, R. W. Translating for actors. In W. Arrowsmith & R. Shattuck, eds, *The Craft & Context of Translation.* Austin: University of Texas Press (for Humanities Research Center), 1961, 95–106.

Críticas Copenhague. E-mail from copenhagueteatro@copenhagueteatro.com, 15 May 2003.

Cuadernos de Teatro Clásico 16. *La Compañía Nacional de Teatro Clásico 1986–2002.* Madrid: Compañía de Teatro Clásico, 2002.

del Moral, I. Personal interview, 6 March 2003.

Díaz, J. Personal interview, 22 May 1987.

Djordjadze, T. Directing Paloma Pedrero. In Paloma Pedrero's *Parting Gestures with A Night in the Subway* (trans. P. Zatlin. Rev. ed.) New Brunswick, NJ: ESTRENO Plays, Estreno Contemporary Spanish Plays 6, 1999, 55–57.

European Union. Déclaration finale. Colloque 'Écriture et traduction théâtrales'. Projet de l'Union Européenne 'Ariane Literary Network'. 2–4 January 1998. Château de Seneffe, Belgium.

France, P. (ed.) *The Oxford Guide to Literature in English Translation.* Oxford and New York: Oxford University Press, 2000.

García, W. Review of three one-act plays by Paloma Pedrero. Dir. Timur Djordjadze. *Gestos* 8.15 (April 1993): 155–57.

Gentile, G. *Hablemos a calzón quitado.* Argentine edition. No date.

Gentile, G. *Hablemos a calzón quitado.* Version by Alfredo Mañas. Unpublished manuscript.

Gilbert, S. M. and Gubar, S. *The Madwoman in the Attic. The Woman Writer and the Nineteenth-Century Literary Imagination.* New Haven and London: Yale University Press, 1979.

Glapp, A.-R. *Whose Life is it Anyway?* in London and on Broadway: a contrastive analysis of the British and American versions of Brian Clark's play. In H. Scolnicov and P. Holland, eds, *The Play Out of Context. Transferring Plays from Culture to Culture,* 1989, 214–23.

Gostand, R. Verbal and non-verbal communication: Drama as translation. In O. Zuber, ed., *The Languages of Theatre. Problems in the Translation and Transposition of Drama,* 1980, 1–9.

Hale, T. and Upton, C.-A. Introduction. In C.-A. Upton, ed., *Moving Target. Theatre Translation and Cultural Relocation,* 2000, 1–13.

Harrison, T. Phaedra Britannica. In R. Warren, ed., *The Art of Translation. Voices from the Field,* 1989, 101–19.

Hite, R. 'Speak the speech, I pray you...' Translating for Actors and Audience. In M. T. Halsey and P. Zatlin, eds, *Entre Actos: Diálogos sobre teatro español entre siglos*. University Park, PA: ESTRENO, 1999, 303–307.

Johnston, D. Buero en Londres. *El Público* 88 (Jan–Feb 1992): 108–109.

Johnston, D. Valle-Inclán: The Mirroring of Esperpento. *Modern Drama* 41.1 (Spring 1998): 30–48.

Kelly, L. G. *The True Interpreter. A History of Translation Theory and Practice in the West.* Oxford: Blackwell, 1979.

Landers C. E. *Literary Translation. A Practical Guide.* Clevedon: Multilingual Matters, Topics in Translation 22, 2001.

Leri, D. E-mail to ESTRENO Plays, for babelguides.com, 2 August 2003.

Link, F. H. Translation, adaptation and interpretation of dramatic texts. In O. Zuber, ed., *The Languages of Theatre. Problems in the Translation and Transposition of Drama*, 1980, 24–50.

Londré, F. H. Exposing the translation gap. *American Theatre* 5.2 (1988): 48–50.

Meech, A. The irrepressible in pursuit of the impossible: Translating the theatre of the GDR. In C.-A. Upton, ed., *Moving Target. Theatre Translation and Cultural Relocation*, 2000, 127–37.

Pavis, P. Problems of translation for the stage: interculturalism and post-modern theatre. In H. Scolnicov and P. Holland, eds, *The Play Out of Context. Transferring Plays from Culture to Culture* (trans. L. Kruger). Cambridge: Cambridge University Press, 1989, 25–44.

Pedrero, P. *First Star and The Railing* (trans. R. Hite). New Brunswick, NJ: ESTRENO Plays, 2001.

Schmidt, P. Translating Chekhov all over again. *Dramatists Guild Quarterly* 33.4 (Winter 1997): 18–23.

Scolnicov, H. and Holland, P. eds, *The Play Out of Context. Transferring Plays from Culture to Culture.* Cambridge: Cambridge University Press, 1989.

Svich, C. E-mail, 8 September 2002.

Thomas, A. Introduction. *Modern Drama* 41.1 (Spring 1998). Special Issue: Translations, A. Thomas and D. Blostein, eds, 1–5.

Ulmann, G. Personal interview, 5 May 2003.

Upton, C.-A., ed. *Moving Target. Theatre Translation and Cultural Relocation.* Manchester, UK & Northampton, MA: St. Jerome Publishing, 2000.

Venuti, L. *The Translator's Invisibility: A History of Translation.* London: Routledge, 1995.

Warren, R., ed. *The Art of Translation. Voices from the Field.* Boston: Northeastern University Press, 1989.

Wellwarth, G. E. Special considerations in drama translation. *Translation Spectrum. Essays in Theory and Practice.* In M. G. Rose, ed., Albany: State University of New York Press, 1981, 140–46.

www.babelguides.com (literary website for world literature).

www.ncac.org/issues/corpuschristi.html (website of the National Coalition Against Censorship).

Zatlin, P. Twentieth-century Spanish theatre on the American stage. *Theatre Survey* 42:1 (May 2001): 69–84.

Zuber, O. *The Languages of Theatre. Problems in the Translation and Transposition of Drama.* Oxford and New York: Pergamon Press, 1980.

Chapter 2

Out of the Shadows: The Translators Speak for Themselves

'Whose play is it anyway?' asks an article on 'the war of the translators' in a March 2003 issue of *The Guardian* (Logan, 2003). In his feature on the subject, Brian Logan cites the time-honoured belief that the best theatrical translators were 'invisible'. The more faithful they were to the original text, the more they remained in the shadows. British theatre-goers have long been familiar with such great foreign playwrights as Molière, Chekhov and García Lorca but traditionally have had no idea whose translation they were hearing. That situation has been changing in the United Kingdom and, to a lesser extent, in the United States because of what Logan calls 'the recent controversial eclipse of the academic–translator by the playwright–translator'.[1] It is not intended that a playwright–translator be invisible nor that there be a faithful translation. An author is invited to do an 'adaptation' with the thought that another famous name in the publicity will help sell the production. Often the playwright does not know the language of the original text but is given someone else's 'literal translation' as a point of departure for his or her creative work. The translator who produces that original script is now doubly invisible: generally by-passed not only on the play programme but, having been paid a flat fee, also in the distribution of royalties if the play is a hit.

Logan interviews a number of people in Great Britain on both sides of the controversy. The response he attributes to Philippe Le Moine is startling. Le Moine, who runs the National Theatre Studio's translation project, is quoted as encouraging playwrights without knowledge of foreign languages while rejecting bona fide translators.[2] Logan states that Le Moine does so because of 'commercial pressure'. Apparently spectators, who for centuries did not object to invisible translators, now demand famous adapters. This monetary explanation begs the key issue, and none of Logan's respondents forcefully challenges the underlying dichotomy between 'academic' (bad) and 'playwright' (good) translators. Yet, is it not possible to produce a stageworthy script without being a playwright per se? Does one have to be a playwright to have dramatic insight? Isn't knowing the original language essential to producing a good translation? Isn't it possible to be both a playwright and a real translator: one who knows the source language and is sensitive to the original text? And where do we place professors of theatre if we accept a split between academics and theatre practitioners?

In a recent interview, Koshi Odashima, a prolific Japanese translator of modern English-language drama, does address the issue, albeit facetiously. Daniel J. Webster asked him if there is 'a great deal of friction in Japan between "artistic" translators of drama and scholars'. Odashima responded: 'There was, but not any more. Now the relationship between those who translate for production and academics is much better, because these academics have finally actually started going to theaters!' (quoted in Webster, 2002: 4). Odashima is an academic, a university professor of English literature. He is also the son of a translator who succeeded in making Shakespeare accessible to popular Japanese audiences.

In the late 1980s when I became a translator and began teaching translation studies, I thought in terms of a range of good to bad translations, not in categories of people who would, by definition, produce translations at the extremes of the quality scale. Among the first plays I translated from Spanish was Jaime Salom's Brechtian drama about Bartolomé de las Casas, *Bonfire at Dawn*. When Salom learned that I would be spending a few days in Paris in May 1992, he arranged for me to go to the Bureau Littéraire International Marguerite Scialtiel to meet his French agent, Geneviève Ulmann, and her husband. It was, I thought, a mere courtesy call, so I was somewhat taken aback during our conversation when Pierre Ulmann commented two or three times, 'Vous n'avez rien de professeur.' What did he mean? Was he referring to my casual clothes and long ponytail? Was I making mistakes in French? Then he asked if I translated plays from French as well as Spanish, and Geneviève began to talk to me about Jean-Paul Daumas's *The Elephant Graveyard*, a poetic tragicomedy that I subsequently translated for them. The Ulmanns explained to me that professors are notoriously boring, that their translations are known to be dull, but that I had a sense of humour and for that reason did not seem like a professor. They hastened to add that not all dull translations are produced by academic translators, and they were willing to consider the possibility that an academic could produce a translation that 'sparkled'.

We are, of course, dealing with stereotypes. Professors who take up translation are thought to spend their time surrounded by books and be interested in nothing else. But perhaps we can learn from teachers. Nicole Thévenin has had considerable success as a translator of Italian theatre; her co-translation of Luigi Lunari's *Fausse adresse* has been performed throughout the Francophone world, was nominated for a Molière prize as best adapation of a foreign play, and was chosen for publication in the distinguished French theatre journal *L'Avant-Scène Théâtre*. Nonetheless, she comes to theatrical translation as an educator, not a theatre professional: 'After thirty years of teaching, I was led to translate because I loved the Italian language but, above all, my mother tongue, French. There is a real joy in carrying over to one's own language the thoughts and writing of a foreign author' (response from questionnaire).

To my mind, it is a fallacious assumption that academic–translators produce boring texts because they think only of publication and not of performance. Marion Peter Holt, a retired professor of Spanish and Theatre, affirms categorically:

> Performability has always been the prime aim of every play I've translated. Then I assume that if it's performed (or performable) it's publishable. I think the old 'performable versus publishable' has its roots in some 19th century practices. That is, certain academic specialists translated and published various classical works (Corneille, Racine, Calderón, Lope, etc.) and the published versions were seldom if ever performed. Today it seems rather meaningless. Only the rare academic isolationist would ever think of translating a play solely to put it in a book. (Or so I think.) In all, it doesn't seem a very meaningful kind of debate in the 21st century. (Holt, personal communication, 2002)

Feliu Formosa, an actor and director who has translated numerous German plays into Catalan, similarly refers to academic specialists from the past. As a young actor, he discovered inadequate translations that inspired him to become a translator himself. In disregard of performance, these published translations were 'versions of ancient and modern classic texts that were made in accord with philological criteria' (Formosa, 2002: 43).

Contrary to Holt's opinion, the controversy goes on. British playwright Pam Gems adapted García Lorca's *Yerma* for the Manchester Royal Exchange with the help of a literal translation. She affirms that academic translation was 'not drama. It was faithful and boring and C-R-A-P. It completely denied the notion that dramatic skills have any value.'

She suggests that in the 1980s, when the pattern of inviting dramatists to do creative versions began, translators became upset because 'they were losing their livelihoods' (quoted in Logan, 2003).

To be sure, Gems – at least as quoted by Logan – has created a straw man.[3] In reality, theatrical translators generally do not rely on their play translations as a significant source of income; they take dramatic skills very seriously, even if they are not playwrights; and they consider knowledge of the source language imperative, even if they are playwrights. In 2002–2003, I distributed a questionnaire to a selection of theatrical translators in several countries.[4] I received responses from the United States (11), France (9), the United Kingdom (7), Germany (4), Spain (4), and Italy (1). The translators, some of whom know multiple languages, translate from Spanish (17), French (11), English (8), Portuguese (6), Catalan (5), German (5), Italian (4), Russian (4), Hebrew (2), Polish (1), Romanian (1), and Swedish (1).[5] Including two who work both into and out of their primary language, the 36 respondents translate to English (18), French (9), German (4), Spanish (3), Catalan (1), Italian (1), Polish (1), and Swedish (1). These translators are a diversified group, including both playwrights and other theatre professionals as well as academics, but, with the exception of Spanish playwright Fermín Cabal, they speak in one voice on the need to know the source language themselves. Many of them also express their strong preference for translation, not 'adaptation'.

In general my respondents answered affirmatively, in one word, to my question: 'Do you always translate directly from a language you know well?'; but several of them added comments, prompted by the follow-up question: 'If you have ever worked through someone else's translation rather than an original play, please identify the text involved and how well you thought the process worked.' Some emphasized their yes answer to the first question by writing 'Jamais!' or 'Never' to the second. French translator and critic André Camp asserted that it is much better to know the language well. Guido Nahum, an Italian playwright and translator, rejected working through another's translation because it would be less interesting. Thévinin, who includes Nahum among the Italian playwrights she has translated into French, in turn declares that such an indirect translation is a mere product, not a profound literary work. David Tushingham, a British translator of German plays, once translated to English a German translation from Serbo-Croat: 'It was actually quite easy translating a translation – a sign I think that translations tend to have a slightly narrower linguistic range than original works.'

When I drafted my question on adaptation, I was not thinking of the polemic about literal translations being used for subsequent adaptations by famous playwrights. I had in mind the kinds of changes that translators may feel obliged to make, to varying degrees, to achieve audience understanding of the text: 'To what extent do you believe that your theatrical translations need to be adapted for your target audience in order to have them staged successfully? (In other words, how familiar is your target audience with the culture of your source text?)' Indeed my idea of a questionnaire to be distributed internationally was prompted by a dialogue, first by e-mail and then during a meeting in Paris in June 2002, with translator Hugo Paviot. For a text by José Luis Alonso de Santos, Paviot left in Spanish a song that I would have struggled to convert to an equivalent with more or less the same meaning for American spectators. How could he have taken the easy way out? I asked. His answer was illuminating: some Spanish songs are well-known in France and hence require no adaptation there; the significance of other songs can be understood from context.[6] He and I might translate the same play, but our circumstances and hence need to adapt were different. Once I realized how problematic it would be to generalize about principles of theatrical translation from the perspective of only one country or one language combination, I determined to confer with a wide range of translators.

Some of those surveyed gave thoughtful, detailed answers to the adaptation question as I initially conceived it. Several others, no doubt in tune to the debate identified by Logan, emphasized that they never adapt. Anne Alice Barlind, who translates from Swedish to French as well as French to Swedish, states that in general she is suspicious of adaptations and much prefers the word 'translation'. These translators' goal, as expressed by David Bradby, who translates from French to English, is 'to remain as close as possible to the original text' or, as Maria Delgado, who works primarily from Spanish to English, affirms, 'to retain a firm flavour of the original'. Jörn Cambreleng sees himself as a conduit who transposes culture from Germany to France but resists any adaptation that would, for example, shift the action from Stuttgart to Toulouse. In agreement, Elishéva Marciano, a French translator of English texts, wishes to retain cultural specificity. Henry Thorau, who translates Brazilian theatre to German, wants the audience to have a new experience. Translators like John Clifford, Claude Demarigny, and Paviot, who are dramatists in their own right, oppose adaptation. Clifford states that as a translator, he does not adapt. Demarigny does not adapt extensively because he strives to arouse the curiosity of his French audience for works from Latin America. Paviot leaves Spanish names untouched in his French translations: 'If I translate Juan Domínguez as Jean Dominguez, it's no longer the same character... A French (spectator) is transported to Spain just by hearing the Spanish names, without need for typical (Spanish) sets'. Sasha Dugdale, who translates Russian plays for the Royal Court Theatre, likewise prefers fidelity to the source text: 'It widens our understanding to be exposed to such different cultures. Adaptations merely limit the experience.'

I interpret answers like these as part of a collective translators' protest against the use of 'literal translation' as a stepping stone to a 'performable adaptation'. Theatre professor Delgado believes that the practice prevents theatrical translators from having their work staged:

> Theatres want 'a name' to sell a new production of a perhaps rather unknown international play. Having a writer attached to the project helps with marketing. Translators too often just serve to provide a first draft which a writer then appropriates.

Holt similarly states:

> In England and also to some extent in the U.S., theatre companies insist on commissioning a new translation for a production and, sadly, these are all too often a playwright or director's adaptation of a so-called 'literal translation'.

Sharon Carnicke is a theatre practitioner whose translations of Chekhov have been staged to acclaim in various theatres in the United States; but her translation of a contemporary play, Buravsky's *The Russian Teacher*, was made unproduceable when the playwright signed an exclusive contract with South Coast Repertory, 'which preferred a version by a resident American playwright who adapted from a commissioned "literal" translation made by a native Russian speaker.' Carnicke conjectures that the production failed because the resulting 'adaptation was less sensitive to the Russian cultural milieu from which it arose.' One might also ask what was the probability that the native Russian speaker was qualified to do any translation into English, let alone a literary one.

Playwright-adaptations are not by any means confined to contemporary or unknown works, and the practice clearly has international repercussions. Odashima, who does not know Russian, has translated Chekhov's *The Sneeze* via English. To Webster's query about translating a translation, Odashima responded that he had not really done so: 'The Chekov omnibus was a special case, because it was really more of an *adaptation* of Chekhov by Michael Frayn, rather than a pure translation.

So, in a sense, it was actually written by Frayn' (quoted in Webster, 2002: 10). Frayn, a distinguished playwright in Great Britain, does know Russian and translates directly from that language. In *The Sneeze*, he juxtaposes several short texts, and these Odashima consulted individually in their published Japanese translations. *The Sneeze* represents an atypical situation; nevertheless, Odashima's comment opens the possibility that a free adaptation in one language can become the basis for versions in other languages and that the original text will become lost in the translation of translations.

A significant piece of the problem, as Joseph Farrell noted in a round table discussion in London in 1994, is the definition of a literal translation. As a translator from Italian, Farrell has refused to prepare such a preliminary text.

> I really don't know precisely what a literal translation might mean, because at each point you must be making an interpretation; you've got to be deciding obscure points, thinking this is possibly what it means, or this is the meaning that fits into the overall context of the play, or what do we know about the overall ideas of this man and what do we pick up from the language itself? (Farrell, 1996: 284)

Any translation that does not consider such points will be defective, and those shortcomings will then become part of the playwright–adapter's product. Translator Kevin Halliwell argues that in the process audiences 'are being insulated from the original' (quoted in Logan, 2003). Ibsen translator Michael Meyer observed that perhaps there is a rationale in the case of obscure languages but having a literal translation that someone else turns into English is 'inexcusable as a device for translating from one of the world's major languages to another' (quoted in Wellwarth, 1981: 142).

Germane in this respect is an article by Eva Espasa, a translator who works from English to Catalan. She suggests that British theorist Susan Bassnett began building her argument against performability because 'the concept of "performability" has been used as a pretext so that the status of translation is considered inferior to that of theatrical writing' (Espasa, 2000: 57). The issue, again, is of commissioning the literal translation, then hiring the 'real' writer so that the translator may be pushed aside.

Those answering my questionnaire may object strongly to adaptations based on 'literal translations', but they identify legitimate reasons for consulting others' translations. Carnicke translated such Chekhov plays as *The Seagull, Three Sisters* and *The Cherry Orchard* without checking earlier English versions; after her work is drafted she does glance at published translations. Miguel Sáenz, a distinguished Spanish translator of German novels and plays, works directly from the source but sometimes finds it useful to compare his solutions with the French, English or Italian translations of the same texts. When Almuth Fricke translated María Irene Fornés's *Fefu y sus amigas* into German, she correctly took into consideration the English version as well; the Spanish-language play was the Cuban-American playwright's own translation of her original English-language play, *Fefu and Her Friends*.

While the current fad of adapting from a literal translation appears to abandon the concept of a faithful rendering of the source text, a related strategy has been used at times for precisely the opposite purpose because of political circumstances. For more than a quarter of a century in Franco's Spain, both the publication and the performance of Bertolt Brecht's theatre were officially prohibited. Travel from Spain to East Germany, where the communist dramatist resided, was also restricted. Once censorship eased in 1965, several of Brecht's plays were promptly produced, an action that hints at thorough familiarity with the forbidden texts. How did Spanish theatre professionals know these works despite the censorship? Where did the stageworthy Spanish texts come from so quickly?

To find answers, in 1986 I conducted personal and telephone interviews of the various translators. I discovered that Argentine and French translations had circulated clandestinely in Spain throughout the long period of silence, that some theatre people had gone to Paris to see the Berliner Ensemble perform there, and that a few Spanish translators and directors, like Pedro Laín Entralgo, Ricard Salvat and José Luis Gómez, in fact knew German well.

It some respects, it is true that Antonio Buero-Vallejo, one of 20th-century Spain's most admired playwrights, created his version of *Mother Courage* based on someone else's unacknowledged literal translation from German, but his goal clearly was to achieve dynamic equivalence. Buero-Vallejo learned about Brecht's anti-militaristic, anti-capitalistic play from the time of its premiere in 1949; with considerable excitement, he read it in French translation. When he set about preparing a Spanish version of *Mother Courage*, he asked for a literal translation from the German. He then painstakingly worked from the German original, bilingual dictionary in hand, while constantly consulting the literal translation to Spanish and the French version (Buero-Vallejo, telephone interview, 1986). In an article on translating drama, Philip Boehm describes the process as 'a labor of love' and speaks of 'crimes of passion' rather than 'instances of petty or high treason against the original text' (Boehm, 2001: 27). Surely Buero's dedicated rendering of Brecht's masterwork was such a labour of love.

As several of my informants in 1986 alerted me, a more likely danger than being unfaithful to Brecht's intentions was too much fidelity. Theatre people in Spain knew Brecht's theory so well and had examined photographs and descriptions of his productions in such depth that in the 1960s they ran the risk of sacrificing all freshness to their deep respect for the German dramatist. Twenty years after the successful premiere of Buero's version of *Mother Courage*, Lluís Pasqual staged a revival at the María Guerrero National Theatre. He used Buero's by then classic translation but decided to eliminate the songs. Buero and many other theatre professionals were outraged at his lack of loyalty to Brecht's dramatic concepts.

Over a period of 30 years, playwright and director Cabal has produced a gamut from faithful translations to free versions. He is known in Spain as being the theatre professional who has the greatest familiarity with contemporary American drama. His staged translations from American and British authors include plays by Christopher Durang, David Mamet, Shelagh Delaney, David Ives, and Harold Pinter. He feels a particular affinity with the style of these Anglosaxon authors, whose works he loves:

> They are authors whom I admire and with whom I identify in many respects. It's as if they were from my own family. I have had no great difficulty in translating them. And, significantly, I have not created versions of any of these texts. They are all pure translations.

Cabal translates from Romance languages as well as English, but has not hesitated to adapt works originally written in German, Russian, Greek and Latin – languages which he does not know. He collaborated closely with a 'professional translator' in preparing his version of Brecht's *La ópera de dos centavos*. In adapting a play by the Russian author Alexander Galin, he collaborated directly with the playwright of the source text in an arrangement that Cabal believes functioned very well.

The British translator Ranjit Bolt, who specializes in Molière, has taken liberties with the classic French comedies in order to reach contemporary audiences but admits that there would be trouble 'if the author was around' (quoted in Logan, 2003). Cabal knows about such trouble first-hand. In the late 1970s, he adapted Dario Fo's *Non si paga* under the title *Sopa de mijo para cenar* and moved the action from Italy to Spain. Initially Fo accepted changes made to fit Spanish political circumstances;

then Fo withdrew from the project and the play was staged as a 'collective creation'. When Cabal revised the text for a new production in 1999, Fo filed suit to prevent the staging. The Italian playwright lost his case.

To some extent, all stagings of plays, whether or not they are translations, involve adaptation to new circumstances. As Boehm observes:

> All translations are adapted to an audience during performance. The more attuned the translator is to a given production, the more finely focused the translation will be to begin with. This gives a chance for rehearsals to start from a more advanced position, which allows time for more rehearsing and less revising.

Laurence Sendrowicz, who calls for something akin to dynamic equivalence, echoes Boehm's opinion when she affirms, 'Everything is adapted.' Tushingham, who defines translating as 'adapting something to a new linguistic context', is leery of significant adaption of works by contemporary authors:

> I try to avoid plays where particular events or characters need changing. If a play by a living writer needs rewriting I'm not sure it's worth doing. Or rather: I'm not sure it's appropriate for me to do.

Translators Robert Lima and Lorenzo Mans, who have undertaken precisely that kind of adaptation, have written about their respective authors' reaction to the changes they felt necessary. Lima had to adjust Spanish playwright José Martín Recuerda's *The Inmates of the Convent of Saint Mary Egyptian* to make the text shorter and the work more suitable for the smaller stage where it was to be performed in 1980 at Penn State University. Director Manuel Duque personally took the revised text to Spain to discuss it with the playwright. Lima recalls that 'Duque returned from the meeting with great praise for the dramatist and his generosity in accepting our ideas about his work' (Lima, 2000: 7). INTAR's artistic director Max Ferrá set up a conference call to Paris to discuss changes that director Tom O'Horgan and Mans wanted to make for the 1990 production of Fernando Arrabal's *The Body-Builder's Book of Love*. Mans recalls that Arrabal agreed that 'the only way to be creative' was to give complete artistic freedom to the director and the translator. Even so, Mans was relieved when he saw the playwright and his wife Luce respond with 'unbridled enthusiasm that bordered on rowdiness' at the New York premiere (Mans, 2001: 46).

While most theatrical translators bristle at the hint they might work through others' translations, there is no reluctance to work in collaboration or to seek assistance as needed. For 11 years Thévenin worked jointly with a native speaker of Italian; she believes that because of their complementary language strengths, they avoided many errors. British translator Delgado works alone from Spanish; when she translates plays from French, she has preferred to collaborate with fluent French speakers. For example, she and Bradby together translated Bernard-Marie Koltès's _Black Battles with Dogs_, a text that has been produced at 7 Stages of Atlanta (USA) and published by Methuen. Jaume Melendres, who has translated over 30 plays to Catalan from French, Italian and English since 1972, continues to ask advice on difficulties in English texts from 'people who know [that language] better than I'. When Holt first began translating from Catalan, he found himself consulting dictionaries and, taking advantage of e-mail, asking frequent questions of the playwrights. Pascale Paugam works from Spanish with ease but has sought collaboration when preparing theatrical adaptations of narrative texts from Italian or German.

Paugam is one of several respondents to my questionnaire who arrived at translation from being an actor. Dissatisfied with the script she was given of Arthur Schnitzler's _La Ronde_, she decided to read the original German text and four different translations. In order to play a part, she says that she needs to understand it thoroughly and that her work as a translator enriches her performance as an actor. As a translator, she gives the scripts in progress to actors so that they can tell her how it sounds and can comment on surface and subtextual meaning: 'what impressions are left by certain sounds, words, phrases, responses, dialogues, etc.' Similarly, Carnicke embarked upon translation when she decided that she could do a more actor-friendly translation of Chekhov's _Three Sisters_ than the available published versions. Other actor–translators include Barlind, Sendrowicz, and Jörn Cambreleng. Co-director of a theatre company in France, Barlind began her acting career as a child in Sweden. She has performed on stage and in television in both Sweden and France and also routinely does film dubbing for two agencies in France. Sendrowicz was an actress in Israel from 1979 to 1988; she has been a playwright since 1983 and a translator since 1990. Cambreleng, who has performed at major theatres in Paris and other French cities, began his acting career in 1986, a decade before he turned to translating as well.

To the question, 'In a nutshell, what advice do you have for aspiring theatrical translators who wish to get started in the field?', the majority of my respondents gave the same basic answer. First get involved in theatre. Learn to act, make friends with theatre people or at least visit a local theatre and talk to literary managers, directors, actors or theatre critics. Carnicke specifically advises sitting in on acting classes and play rehearsals. Holt suggests analysing successful translations (such as Maurice Valency's version of Jean Giraudoux's *The Madwoman of Chaillot* or Christopher Hampton's enormously popular version of Yasmina Reza's *Art*), in comparison with the original French texts if possible. Cabal recommends that translators first write their own plays because practical stage experience can be the best teacher. In a similar vein, Paviot believes that being a playwright facilitates his translating dialogue, and Demarigny affirms that because he is a playwright he can be of greater help to the source author when he translates (Demarigny, personal interview, 2003). Camp affirms that to translate poetry, one must be a poet; to translate theatre, one must be a playwright or theatre practitioner. Tushingham similarly advises first creating theatre, as director, playwright, dramaturg, actor or set designer; he finds that translating is a skill, not a career, and that it works well in conjunction with these other activities. Thorau emphasizes that one learns to translate by translating, translating and translating.

On the other hand, several people left the advice to aspiring translators question blank or simply urged translators to find plays they really love, preferably by authors whose works they know well. Sharon Feldman, an American academic who translates from Catalan, explains:

> In order to translate any play, you must have a good grasp and profound knowledge of the work of the playwright and his/her creative trajectory, influences, models . . . It is not enough merely to be familiar with an individual play.

Margarita Vargas, an academic whose well-known anthology of seven co-translated Spanish American plays by women authors was published by an American university press, was alone in overtly disregarding performance. She advises translating for the love of the process, not for the goal of having the plays staged. Her position is, of course, diametrically opposed to that of theatre people, such as retired theatre professor H. Rick Hite, who affirms that a 'translation of a theatre piece should always be thought of as something to be performed for an audience.' American playwright and translator Caridad Svitch feels a spiritual kinship with the plays and poetry of García Lorca. She speaks of 'the joy of collaborating with a master playwright such as Lorca' and provides this complete definition of the author–translator relationship in the context of drama:

> Translation is above all an active, imagined conversation between artists that occurs in the mind, on the page, and is made witness by actors who embody the text and an audience who experiences it.

Because of the interactive nature of performance, many of the respondents have participated in rehearsals and have found the process to be not only beneficial but essential. Several of the academic translators have never had this experience, and a few people mention directors who appropriate the text, making unwarranted changes to work of author and translator alike, but most would agree with Cabal, who says that the more collaboration, the better. Through rehearsals the translator may function as a dramaturg, who clarifies aspects of the play for the actors while at the same time learning from the actors how to improve the phrasing of the text. Through rehearsals Meidrun Adler learned that no matter how good a translation might be, 'it will never work if the actors can't move with the text.' Carnicke treats the play 'not as a finished work of literature, but rather as a score for performance that maintains areas of ambiguity for which the actors can make interpretive choices.' Nahum reports that he always attends rehearsals, whether the play is his own or a translation: 'It's the most fascinating part of the process; I don't open my mouth, but I love to experience these unique moments.'

I solicited advice for aspiring theatrical translators because, as editor of ESTRENO Plays, I frequently receive such requests myself. All too often, the person posing the question has no theatrical background, has not considered the suitability of the text for his or her target audience, and does not realize the difficulty of getting a play translation staged or published.[7] Even some people with amateur acting or directing experience who are excited about a particular play have not researched the availability of existing translations or have not explored the matter of author's rights. Occasionally neophyte translators have prefaced their inquiry by asking me how much they should expect to ask in fees or earn in royalties. Most experienced translators would find the question laughable. With slight variations, many of my respondents agree with John London. Despite London's own high level of success as a theatrical translator from six Romance languages, German and Hebrew, and his regular collaboration with London's Royal Court Theatre, he succinctly urges: 'Get a proper job.' Speaking from other countries and diversified experiences, Almuth Fricke, Susanne Hartwig, Miguel Sáenz, and Nicole Thévenin likewise specifically warn that theatrical translation pays badly: one cannot earn a living this way. Paugam suggests that most theatrical translators are primarily professors, actors, directors, or other kinds of theatre professionals.

Among his insightful published comments on the pitfalls of translating drama, Boehm mentions low pay, 'with royalties usually derived from the original author's share of the take'; moreover, 'the take, generally speaking, is pretty meager, at least in the United States, where most theatre is produced by nonprofit organizations struggling to make ends meet' (Boehm, 2001: 28). For contracts issued by France's Société des Auteurs et Compositeurs Dramatiques (SACD) and Spain's Sociedad General de Autores y Editores (SGAE), the standard split on royalties is 60% for the author and 40% for the translator. According to Geneviève Ulmann, the division in Germany drops to 20% for the translator, a policy she believes contributes to the proliferation of bookish translations (Ulmann, personal interview, 2003). Societies like SACD and SGAE make a concerted effort to collect royalties for their members, but there is no counterpart watchdog for American playwrights and translators. Kirsten Nigro, an American translator of Latin American plays, recalls the surprise of a French translator of Shakespeare when she mentioned that she has never thought about royalties at all (Nigro, 2000: 120). Short runs in small college and community theatres or off-off Broadway showcase performances – the case with most productions of contemporary translated plays in the United States – are unlikely to generate meaningful income.

In contrast, an established translator of classic authors in France or elsewhere, particularly one who is commissioned by major theatres, may well earn real money. American playwright Paul Schmidt, who holds a PhD in Russian from Harvard, recalls spending several years translating Chekhov instead of creating his own plays. Writing in *Dramatists Guild Quarterly*, with a touch of humour he explains why: 'I make more money translating other people's plays than I do writing my own. I keep hoping that will change, but so far most theatres prefer to stage Chekhov rather than me' (Schmidt, 1997: 18).[8]

It must be noted that when theatres commission a new translation of a play by Chekhov, an author whose works are now in public·domain, all other translators of Chekhov are pushed aside. Sharon Carnicke, who won a translation award for *The Seagull* at the American College Theatre Festival in 1997, wonders 'why theatres need such an extraordinary proliferation of contemporary translations of the same plays by writers who do not read the original language' (Carnicke, 2002). She points out that a list of those who have 'translated' Chekhov reads like a who's who of playwrights: Clifford Odets, Tennessee Williams, Lanford Wilson, and David Mamet, from the United States; Pam Gems, Tom Stoppard, and Michael Frayn, from the United Kingdom. Among these, only Frayn knows Russian. Boehm thinks it would be great if theatres would 'commission new translations of unknown works as opposed to retranslations of known plays' (Boehm, 2001: 28).

In any country, a play that enjoys a long run in an important theatre or that is produced by a large number of small theatres, amateur ones included, can provide significant income to the playwright and to the translator – if the latter's rights are properly protected. André Camp and Claude Demarigny, who co-translated José Sanchis Sinisterra's *¡Ay, Carmela!* from Spanish to French for director Pierre Chabert, had no complaints about those royalties; the production ran for over 700 performances. When I first met Camp, in 1987, he explained that if SACD has recorded a contract acknowledging an official translation for a particular play, that translator receives the royalties for subsequent productions even if the director decides to commission a new translation or create one of his or her own.[9]

If a translator-friendly policy, like the ideal one that Camp describes, existed in Spain, Raquel Merino Álvarez might not have uncovered a tradition of plagiarism on the Spanish stage. In her analysis of 40 years of 'new translations' of English-language plays in her country, Merino Álvarez convincingly establishes that many of them are, purely and simply, plagiarized versions of earlier translations (Merino Álvarez, 1995: 75). To arrive at this conclusion, she studied 'chains of translations' from Argentina as well as Spain, and meticulously compared the British or American source against a series of Spanish-language translations, speech by speech. Directors, including some of the stature of José Luis Alonso, figured prominently among the culprits she identified.

For a model of what directors should do, we can look at the programme for Pirandello's *Enrico IV* from the Shakespeare Theatre of New Jersey in September 2002. Bonnie J. Monte, the theatre's artistic director and director of this particular production, identifies the Italian play as her own new version, 'based on the 1922 translation by Edward Storer'. Monte, by the way, does know Italian.

The problem of not giving appropriate, open credit like this to the original translator unfortunately is not limited to Spain and may occur in France, despite SACD. In response to my question, 'In general terms, what factors hinder theatrical translators from having play translations performed?', French translator Jörn Cambreleng cites plagiarism and quasi plagiarism: 'Directors who do not speak the language of the play, combine four existing translations and sign it as their own.' Alonso's productions were usually in major theatres where royalties for the translator would not have been a budgetary concern, but it is likely that directors in theatres that are struggling financially are tempted to save money by leaving the real translator out and keeping the translator's share of royalties for their production.

In the United States, too, both translator and playwright may be by-passed, as evidenced in two recent productions of contemporary Spanish plays in New York City. In the fall of 2000, when ESTRENO Plays published *Packing up the Past*, Ana Mengual's authorized translation of Sebastián Junyent's *Hay que deshacer la casa*, the author sent copies of the translation to a number of theatres, including Miriam Colón's bilingual, off-Broadway Teatro Rodante Puertorriqueño. Colón responded that she would read the play, and Junyent patiently awaited her reaction. While he waited, she scheduled an 18 April 2001 premiere of an unauthorized, presumably different translation, with the literal and hence meaningless title, *The House Must Be Dismantled*. She did so not only without Junyent's approval but without his knowledge; his first news of the pending production came on 14 April via the advisory board of ESTRENO Plays (Junyent, personal communication, 2001). Junyent lodged a protest through SGAE but the production was not dismantled.

It is possible that SGAE's New York office, if they knew about the pending production at all, accepted the staging without question, as they did David Gaard's adaptation of Paloma Pedrero's *Wolf Kisses*, which ran briefly in September 2002 in an off-off Broadway theatre. Gaard, who moved the play's action from Spain to the Caribbean and hence replaced Pedrero's metaphorical train with a bus, never asked the playwright for her approval of these significant changes. He did submit the English-language script to SGAE, but Pedrero does not read English and, because of time constraints, signed the SGAE contract before having someone else read and evaluate Gaard's version. In conversation with an ESTRENO Plays collaborator after a performance, Gaard said that he had based his adaptation on the published British translation by Roxana Silbert of Royal Court Theatre (Lamartina-Lens, personal communication, 2002); the programme did not recognize his source.

The SGAE in Madrid makes an effort to protect its members, including translators, but the New York office does not always function well. The November 2002 revival of Buero-Vallejo's *The Foundation* at an off-off Broadway theatre almost did not take place because of the local representative's rigidity. Holt, as translator, reports that the final contract 'was complicated unnecessarily by NY SGAE's apparent unfamiliarity with the basics of New York production'.

For theatrical translators, how helpful is membership in SACD, SGAE and their counterparts in the United Kingdom, the Society of Authors or the Scottish Society of Playwrights?[10] In France, all but one respondent belongs to SACD. The late André Camp was a member for over

40 years, from 1962 until his death, in March 2004. The translators generally see SACD's function as restricted to collecting their royalties. Thévenin adds that they provide help in case of legal disputes. Guido Nahum, who resides in Italy, belongs to SACD; the society sends him his royalties but, he notes, with considerable delay. American translator and theatre professor Felicia Londré also complains that SACD is slow, in her case in responding to inquiries about obtaining rights to translate a work. In that SGAE referred me to translators in Spain, all of my respondents from that country belong to the Sociedad. Like SACD, SGAE's principal function, from the translator's point of view, is collecting royalties. Sáenz affirms that SGAE functions well; once a translation is staged and hence on the records, royalties are forwarded periodically. On the other hand, Jaume Melendres raises concerns not unrelated to Holt's. Melendres finds that SGAE employees 'tend to be incompetent people who don't even know, for example, that Strindberg is an author in public domain'.

Among my respondents from Great Britain, only David Bradby acknowledged membership in the Society of Authors. John Clifford, a professor of Theatre and Creative Writing in Edinburgh, however, expressed strong satisfaction with the Scottish Society of Playwrights. He states that the Society not only provides moral support and stands ready 'as back up in cases of dispute', but has also negotiated a basic rate for playwrights that is better than that offered to playwrights in England. For Clifford, who is both a playwright and translator, membership has a double aspect.

In the United States, of ten respondents for whom I have information relative to The Dramatists Guild, four belong. Playwright and translator Caridad Svich has been a regular contributor to the Guild's monthly magazine, *The Dramatist*. Londré belongs precisely because of the stimulus of that journal. Carnicke was invited to join in 1979 because of the successful professional production of her translation of Chekhov's *Three Sisters*. The Dramatists Guild, unlike SACD or SGAE, does not collect royalties for its members, but Holt provides a number of reasons why serious translators would wish to join:

> If a play is optioned for Broadway (known as First Class production), then the contract is reviewed and approved by the Guild's attorneys. And, this actually happened in my case for López Rubio's *The Blindfold*, which never reached production because of lack of funding. The Guild specified certain documents from SGAE in Madrid confirming that the play was free of legal entanglements. The Guild will also provide advice on contracts at other levels – that is, off-Broadway, off-off Broadway, LORT (League of Resident Theatres) . . . Their publication provides

useful information on copyright, obtaining rights, etc. There are two
levels of Guild membership. Basic membership can be obtained on
application by a translator who has completed a couple of full-length
scripts. Active membership is available only after an off-Broadway or
major LORT regional production of a play or translation. Although I
technically was eligible for active membership after the Baltimore
Center Stage production of Buero's *Sleep of Reason* in 1985, I did not
apply until the Atlanta Alliance production of [Skármeta's] *Burning
Patience* in 1999.

Some neophyte translators have also asked me about getting an agent
to handle their work. Again, most of my respondents would find the
question laughable. Agents, after all, are in it for the money, and, as
Boehm observes, the theatrical translator's take is 'pretty meager'. One
translator believes that agents in his country play a marginal role,
unlike those in England and the United States. That observation, too,
may raise a chuckle. In the United Kingdom, Bradby reports that he
used to have an agent 'but a couple of years ago he decided he could
no longer keep me on his books (presumably because I was not a good
commercial proposition for him).' Tushingham's experience is similar: 'I
don't generate sufficient revenue for them and they don't get me any
more work than I get by myself.' Among my British respondents, only
Maria Delgado has an agent, and hers negotiates publications, not productions. In the United States, only Holt has an agent. In fact, he has
two: one who represents the Chilean playwright Antonio Skármeta and
thus has secured some 20 stagings of Holt's translation *Burning Patience*,
and one who handles his translations of Spanish playwrights. The latter
agent has never achieved a production directly but rather has made
arrangements based on Holt's contacts or inquiries he has received
about his published translations. Indeed, his agent's listing with The
Dramatists Guild stipulates 'no translations'.
    In February 1991, at the urging of Cuban-French playwright Eduardo
Manet, I wrote to Esther Sherman at William Morris, a major agency in
New York City. Manet's *The Nuns* (trans. Robert Baldick) had just been
revived, off-off Broadway. That particular play, which premiered in
Paris in 1969, had been translated to 21 languages and staged around
the world. With the encouragement of Manet and Bill Hunt, the director
of the New York production of *The Nuns*, I was about to translate
Manet's *Lady Strass*, and I had recently translated several Spanish plays
that I thought would be successful in the United States, including
José Luis Alonso de Santos's big hit, *Bajarse al moro (Going Down to*

Marrakesh). The latter had run for two years in Madrid, had been aired on television and made into a movie in Spain. I naively thought that the agency might be interested in handling established playwrights like Manet and Alonso de Santos if not myself, as their American translator. In April 1991, I followed up the unanswered letter with a phone call. Esther Sherman emphasized the word 'commercial' in our conversation. She explained that the William Morris agency deals solely with play-wrights, not translators, and that for theatre often there is 'not enough financial reward in limited territory'. Agents are interested in plays for which there might be 'movies or other pay off'. The fact that *Going Down to Marrakesh* had already been made into a movie therefore made it less attractive to an agency. She advised me to continue being my own agent.[11]

Several of my respondents indicate that they are essentially their own agents or that publishers sometimes serve as quasi agents. For example, Tushingham notes that Nick Hern Books in Great Britain handles amateur rights for plays they have published. Paugam alone speaks in glowing terms of her agent, Geneviève Ulmann. Ulmann, who is motivated by her deep knowledge and love of theatre, is such a catalyst for networking that she is included in the next chapter, where we deal with that subject.

Not all financial problems for translators are limited to matters of meagre pay or of having their work usurped by 'adapters'. Hence I raised the question, 'Have you ever had problems getting rights to trans-late a play, or problems getting rights to have a play translation published or performed?' Boehm, who translates both into and out of Polish, had a unique response; he reports that agents for American playwrights during a certain period refused permission for stagings in Poland 'for royalties paid in zlotys, when the zloty was non-transferable'. More typically, complaints relate to unreasonable demands from heirs. Carnicke tells the story of how an American publisher was sued over copyright from Europe by 'a long lost relative' of a Russian author whose translated plays they had published, 'even though the translator had written per-mission from the author, who had died prematurely'. The press had tried unsuccessfully to locate family but 'could find none until after the book came out'. In 1979 Cabal's version of Brecht's *La ópera de dos centavos* was not staged because of 'economic disagreement with the heirs'.

Clifford, Holt, and Thorau also report difficulties with heirs. For Clifford's translation of *The House of Bernarda Alba*, the Lorca estate wanted him 'to sign a clause which would extend their copyright over the translation beyond its normal expiry, indefinitely, "throughout the

universe"'. Clifford, who refused to sign but did eventually get permission, was told that this clause was normal practice for Lorca translations; he suggests that the practice 'explains why most of them are so
bad'. Holt says that the heirs of Alejandro Casona almost prevented
publication in 1970 of *The Modern Spanish Stage: Four Plays* because they
tried to impose a time limit on how long Hill and Wang could have the
book in print. Holt sought help from another playwright who was
included in the volume: 'Only through the persistent personal intervention of José López Rubio was this [matter] resolved.' While Thévenin
may reflect a general case when she says that 'playwrights are very happy
to become known abroad', Thorau is no doubt equally on target when he
affirms that widows and other heirs want 'more money and give rights
only for a fixed period (one that is usually very short)'.

Miguel Sáenz emphasizes that there are three factors that prevent
having a translation staged: 'money, money, and money'. Money may
not be the root of all cancelled productions or all failures of translators
to get directors interested in foreign theatre, but it is certainly an important factor. For this reason, many well-known translators limit themselves
to invited, commissioned translations. Tushingham says, 'I made it a rule
for myself only to translate a play if I was being paid to do so.' But that
cautious approach does not guarantee that the work will be staged.
Heidrun Adler in Germany and Bradby in the United Kingdom report
invited projects involving plays by famous authors that fell through for
lack of funds (Carlos Fuentes and Koltès, respectively). In France,
Barlind and Demarigny allude to expected financial support not materia-
lizing. Several respondents pointed out that funding, or the lack of it,
often explains the difficulty that translators have in getting theatres to
consider their scripts. Carnicke mentions that in recent years it has
become increasingly difficult to raise money for the arts in the United
States. Lorenzo Mans, literary manager/dramaturg for INTAR Hispanic
American Arts Center in New York City, states that 'the current funding
climate limits our choices considerably. The few grants that are still out
there to fund a specific play, make it very clear that it has to be a new
American play' (Mans, personal letter, 1998). Both Londré and Boehm
speak of economic risk. As Boehm clarifies: 'Most theatres consider
themselves strapped for funds. The current climate does not favor new
work, especially "foreign" plays, which are perceived as risky.'

Anthony Meech expresses this same opinion in an article about East
German drama. He asks what must be done to make GDR theatre acceptable for the West End or Broadway and concludes that the cultural and
logistical problems are enormous because both British and American

mainstream theatre is a commercial institution. 'These companies feel themselves compelled by financial exigency to rely on productions of the tried and tested classics and musicals with high production values, rather than attempt to introduce their audiences to the unfamiliar' (Meech, 2000: 135).

Cabal observes that Spain is different: there is no problem there in staging translations because neither Spanish audiences nor producers reject foreign plays. On the other hand, respondents from Great Britain, the United States, France, and Germany find enormous resistance.

Clifford refers to the insularity of British culture and the British theatre's fear of the new. Sasha Dugdale laments the 'tame tastes of the UK public.' In the United States, according to Holt, one enduring obstacle is 'a general suspicion of "foreign" plays'. He urges aspiring translators 'to focus on one or two plays' and never talk about 'Spanish theatre': 'It's the play and the playwright that matter. Avoid placing your work in a niche.' The difficulty in the United States is compounded by the fact that audiences that are open to Latin American theatre may still reject plays from Spain, as Mans discovered when his co-adaptation of Benavente's *The Art of Swindling* played in Atlanta: some members of the community were reportedly dismayed that the author was Spanish and that Benavente's satire of human foibles failed to give a positive image of Latinos (Mans, telephone interview, 1997). Boehm, too, refers to niches when he alerts us to stereotypes about certain cultures, such as 'German plays are too philosphical and therefore boring.' Patricia O'Connor suggests that American audiences may not be geared to foreign plays culturally, and directors need to satisfy their audience. H. Rick Hite compares the difficulties faced by translated plays with those of beginning playwrights: 'Theatres prefer to do plays that are popular and by well known writers. Plays by unknown playwrights don't draw audiences.'

In France, playwright and translator Hugo Paviot echoes Hite. He finds general 'indifference and scorn' for contemporary theatre: 'The problem in France is that living authors are seldom performed and Spanish authors, except for the Catalans, are little known.' Laurence Sendrowicz, who translates from Hebrew to French, finds special problems for unknown authors who write in minority languages. In Germany, Hartwig believes that the theatrical market for translations favours English-language and French works but that there is little interest in plays from Spanish-speaking countries beyond theatre festivals. Fricke likewise finds that translation is a marginal activity and that German spectators know even less about the culture of certain Latin American countries, like Paraguay and Bolivia, than they do of Argentina and Chile.[12] Adler notes, however, that from time to time there are stagings of foreign plays for political reasons, of Cuban theatre, for example.

Not only audiences but also theatre professionals may lack knowledge of and interest in foreign cultures. With reference to the United States, Boehm states, 'The number of dramaturgs, literary managers and artistic directors who do not read in other languages is regrettable; those who are truly committed to exploring other cultures and advancing international projects are few and far between and often at smaller-sized theatres.' How the translators I have cited would envy Irina Prokhorova, a Russian translator who resides in Paris. When she finds a play in France that she believes will work well in Russia, she translates it, sends it to her theatre contacts there, and the play invariably is staged (Prokhorova, telephone interview, 2003).

Some of the responses to my question, 'What factors hinder theatrical translators from having play translations performed?', overlap the advice already noted for aspiring theatrical translators. A translation is doomed if it is bookish, if it or the source text is mediocre, or if the translator does not understand the theatrical culture of his or her national stage. As David George says, 'Translating an author in whom there is unlikely to be interest in the country of the target language is unlikely to bear fruit.'

Tushingham helpfully spells out in detail what may contribute to failure or success as a theatrical translator. Items he places on the negative side of the ledger are these:

> Inexperience in terms of how theatre is made, what the concerns of theatre producers may be. Misunderstanding the text, having a very limited or literal grasp of the possibilities of the theatrical medium. Being interested in plays because they are in the right language for you to translate them rather than because they have something new or original to contribute.

On the positive side, Tushingham says that the translator must write well, must understand how plays function in performance, and must translate the right plays, 'ones that people who are creating theatre are going to be inspired by'. With respect to Tushingham's latter comment, it is imperative that the translator be familiar with world theatre for a variety of reasons, including the quick recognition of plays that have obviously been influenced by works from other countries and hence may not be seen as contributing something new or original.

Beyond the merit of the chosen text and the translator's work, there is always an element of luck and, to paraphrase London, Thorau, and others, the need for contacts, contacts, and contacts. For translators who choose their own texts and then serve as their own agents, Delgado's advice is apropos: 'Have a passion for the play...It could be a long haul before it's staged or published.'

Aspiring theatrical translators should not let themselves be completely discouraged by these various comments. Among our respondents, particularly those in Europe, there are some who have achieved stagings of their translations at major theatres, and there are successes even for translators in the United States, the country that most resists foreign plays. As John London says, in addition to luck and contacts, one needs patience.

What about publication? Is it easier or harder to have a translated play appear in a book or magazine than on the stage? The answer varies considerably, depending upon the country of the translator, the importance of the authors translated, and previous published translations of the same plays. In some cases there are publishers or journals specificially dedicated to theatre; in others, there are theatre collections created by the authors or translators themselves. In general, it is easier to publish a play after it has had a visible production, but whether the staged play leads to publication or the published play leads to staging also seems to be a matter of circumstance.

Of the 36 respondents to my questionnaire, only four have not yet seen any of their play translations in print. Two of these translators are from the United States, where publishing theatre is especially difficult.[13] David Ball is a retired professor of French and Comparative Literature who has had a distinguished career as translator of poetry and prose, has been the recipient of the Modern Language Association's prestigious Scagilione Prize for Outstanding Translation of a Literary Work, and currently serves as president of the American Literary Translators Association. He has translated only two plays – from French, one each by Picasso and Jarry – both of which have been staged. He conjectures that the 'existence of previous translations, no matter how bad' may hinder publication. Carnicke found just that situation when in the 1980s she tried unsuccessfully to publish her Chekhov translations:

> Not only does every publisher have their own set of translations, but whenever a publisher decided to consider one of mine, either one of two things would happen. The editor would ask me to 'novelize' my translation and make it more appropriate for reading (alas, I thought that my translations were unique specifically because they were stage worthy), or a non-Russian speaking but famous playwright would submit his version, and that would bump mine from consideration.

Our seven theatrical translators from the United Kingdom report a high level of success, in large part because of two publishing houses: Methuen, which has a particular interest in foreign plays in translation, and Nick Hern, which routinely considers play texts that have been performed at an established theatre. Bradby, Delgado, George, and London have published play translations at Methuen; Clifford, Dugdale, London, and Tushingham have published with Nick Hern, sometimes because of their association with Royal Court Theatre. Among other publishers that appear more than once in Clifford's list are New Theatre Publications and the now defunct American journal *Modern International Drama*.

All four translators in Germany have likewise been able to publish their plays. Theater- und Mediengesellschaft Lateinamerika, the society for promoting Latin American theatre to which Adler and Fricke belong, cooperates with the Vervuert publishing house in Frankfurt. They have prepared a series of anthologies, with introductions, by country (Mexico, Brazil, Argentina, Cuba, Chile), as well as a volume of women authors and one of Latin American authors in exile. In summary, Adler comments that his group has translated and published many plays in anthologies and will continue to do so although they almost never see these works staged in Germany.[14] Adler also has translations that have appeared in Rowohlt and Henschel, publishers that, like Nick Hern in the United Kingdom, specialize in dramatic works. Hartwig, a relative newcomer to translation who concentrates on Spain, successfully proposed a play by Rodrigo García to Henschel. In the past 20 years, Thorau has translated 15 Brazilian plays, all of which have been published. He is part of a group of authors and translators that owns a publishing company, Verlag der Autoren, in Frankfurt, where ten of his translations appear. Thorau has also published in Henschel, among other places.

In Spain, where our four translators have all succeeded in having works published, theatre journals are an important outlet. Of Fernando Gómez Grande's 27 published translations of French plays, three appear in *Escena* (Barcelona), five in *Art Teatral* (Valencia), a journal edited by playwright Eduardo Quiles and dedicated to the short play, and five in *ADE Teatro* (Madrid), the journal of the Spanish association of theatre directors or in the association's related play series. Jaume Melendres has had three translations in *ADE Teatro* and one in an edition of *Escena*. Gómez Grande lives in Valencia; the majority of his other published translations have been issued by presses there, such as the University of Valencia's important collection 'Teatro Siglo XX'.

Melendres, who resides in Barcelona and is associated with that city's Institut del Teatre, lists seven plays in the institute's theatre collection. Miguel Sáenz is an eminent translator from German whose many awards include an honorary doctorate in Translation and Interpretation from the University of Salamanca and a National Translation Prize in 1992 for his collective work. In that Sáenz often translates narrative and concentrates on major dramatists, it is not surprising that his translations have been published by presses not restricted to theatre; he has published in Alianza Editorial (almost all of the plays of Bertolt Brecht), Hiru (several plays by Thomas Bernard), and the Goethe Institute in Spain (various authors). Cabal, whose original plays are readily published and who has had some 15 productions of translations and adaptations, had nevertheless seen only four of his translations published. These were, however, in important presses, including two that specialize in theatre: MK Ediciones and Fundamentos.

According to Thévenin, 'In France, many spectators like to read or reread the text. If the play is staged by a well-known director or performed in an important theatre, it will be published by specialized presses like *L'Avant-Scène Théâtre*, Éditions Théâtrales, Éditions du Laquet, etc.' French theatre-goers are often given the opportunity to buy the play at the performance. Eight of the nine respondents in France identify translations that have appeared in print. Thévenin has had multiple publications in both the journal *L'Avant-Scène* and in Laquet of her translations from Italian, done jointly or alone. Paugam and Paviot have both published translations of plays from Spain in Laquet. Sendrowicz has two volumes of plays by Hanokh Levin, translated from Hebrew, in Éditions Théâtrales, a press where Cambreleng has published translations from German. Camp, whose close association with *L'Avant-Scène* extended back for several decades, to the founding of the journal, not only published many of his own translations from Spanish there but was instrumental in opening the pages of that prestigious journal to news of and texts from the Hispanic theatre world; Camp also has multiple translations in the series Libraire Théâtrale. Demarigny has published translations in *L'Avant-Scène*, as well as in Actes Sud Papier, another press that frequently publishes staged plays, and in anthologies of Latin American theatre published by UNESCO. Barlind's translations appear in Éditions Très-Tôt Théâtre and l'École des Loisirs.

American translators have a harder time publishing their work than do translators in Spain, the United Kingdom, or other countries. In the United States, Samuel French and the Dramatists Play Service function on a par with Nick Hern but are less receptive to foreign works. Holt reports that his agent's inquiry to Dramatists Play Service about his staged translations met with a negative response. Even though Holt's translation of Buero-Vallejo's *The Sleep of Reason* has been performed by important professional theatres in Baltimore, Philadelphia, London, and Chicago and his translation of Buero's *The Foundation* has been showcased in New York City, the agent was told that Buero and other authors Holt has translated lack name recognition (Holt, telephone interview, 1999).[15]

At times, translators who reside in the United States publish elsewhere or, in the case of Boehm, in languages other than English. Sharon Feldman has two translations in print: both appeared in an anthology of Catalan plays published by Methuen, in the United Kingdom. Of O'Connor's 19 play translations that are in print or press, 15 appear in English-language or bilingual anthologies published in Spain. One of Hite's translations also appears in an anthology published in Spain. Director and playwright Boehm's translation of Sam Shephard's *Buried Child* was published in Polish.

Even translators with theatre connections do not easily see their work in print. Londré, a distinguished dramaturg and staged playwright, has translated ll plays (six French, two Spanish, and three Russian), six of which have been produced; the only one in print appeared in an anthology by Ubu Repertory, a New York City theatre dedicated to French and Francophone plays that routinely published what they staged. Caridad Svitch is a well-known playwright in her own right and has translated from Spanish a dozen plays, most of which have been performed at INTAR in New York City and/or other professional theatres; her published translations to date are limited to five experimental plays by García Lorca that appear in a Smith and Kraus anthology. Dramaturg and playwright Mans has had three translations of major Spanish playwrights in highly visible productions at INTAR in New York City or at Alliance Theatre in Atlanta; only a text by Arrabal is published, in ESTRENO Plays. Hite, whose theatre background includes acting and directing, has translated 15 plays from Spanish; the only published ones in the United States appear in three volumes in the ESTRENO Plays series.

ESTRENO Plays, founded by Martha T. Halsey in 1992 at Penn State University, is a major outlet for translations of contemporary Spanish plays. Among our respondents, O'Connor and Holt have also published there.[16] Additionally two of O'Connor's translations appeared in *Modern International Drama* and one in an anthology of contemporary Spanish plays that she edited for University Press of America (1992). Holt's other published translations include the anthology he edited for Hill and Wang (1970), anthologies of drama from Spain and from Latin America that he edited or co-edited for Performing Arts Journal Publications (1985, 1986), and an anthology of three plays by Buero-Vallejo as well as an edition of an additional Buero play (1985, 1987) for an important series of Spanish plays, both Golden Age and contemporary, at Trinity University Press – a series that was subsequently discontinued. There are two bright notes after this decade or more of silence on the US publishing front. Two of O'Connor's translations were chosen for reprinting in the anthology *Modern Women Playwrights of Europe* (Barr, 2001) and the University Press of Colorado in 2004 published an anthology of plays by Jaime Salom (Racz, 2004). That volume has the potential of initiating a new series in translated theatre.

The pattern noted in the United Kingdom for Nick Hern or in France for *L'Avant-Scène Théâtre* is clearly one of successful staging first, publication second. Does it work the other way? Sometimes, yes. Two of the seven co-translated plays in Margarita Vargas's anthology of Latin American women authors have been staged: interested directors contacted Vargas. At least two of the six plays in O'Connor's anthology *Plays of the New Democratic Spain (1975–1990)* were subsequently staged because some interested person (author, translator, or friend) passed a particular text along to a theatre. Rare is the director who goes to the library seeking a translated play. Atlee Sproul at Colgate University did just that, however; when he realized that during his long career he had never directed a Spanish play, he determined to do so. From the anthology *Masterpieces of the Modern Spanish Theatre* (Corrigan, 1967), he chose Leonard C. Pronko's translation of Alfono Sastre's *Death Trust* and staged it in November 1989.

But Sproul's initiative was exceptional. Holt is doubtless right when he recommends that translators approach directors to 'sell' one or two special plays, not a national theatre. Holt also believes that heavy, expensive anthologies are not an effective vehicle for selling plays to potential directors. Editions that have facilitated multiple stagings of particular plays – like those published by Dramatists Play Service, Nick Hern, and Librairie Théâtrale – are small enough for a potential director to tuck into a jacket pocket or purse and read on the subway. Under Holt's influence, ESTRENO Plays was designed to be that kind of lightweight, inexpensive text.

The story of publication of theatrical translations in the United States has two repeated themes: self-promotion and networking. An extreme case of the former is Charles Philip Thomas, who has translated 49

Latin American plays, published them in four volumes, and identifies himself as both translator and literary agent. When he could not find a publisher for his initial, general anthology, he financed the project himself; he appears to be a one-man equivalent to the collective efforts of Theater- und Mediengesellschaft Lateinamerika in Germany.[17] Holt acquired the contract from Hill & Wang after talking to that publisher's representative during an MLA convention. His first contract from Trinity University Press came 'through the recommendation of a friend (Phyllis Zatlin)'. The recent project at University Press of Colorado, which includes translations by Holt, Racz and Zatlin, came through Racz's contacting the director of that press.[18] The subject of translators helping translators is included in the next chapter, which deals with various kinds of networking.

Notes

1. The subject of Logan's recent piece is not new. In her examination of 'translation' as plagiarism, Merino Álvarez cites three earlier articles in the United Kingdom that deal with appropriation of someone else's translation and hence the need for a code of conduct: 'The War of the Words,' *The Sunday Times*, 27 January 1980; 'A Code for Theatre Translations and Adaptations,' *Language Monthly*, 11 May 1985; 'Gained in the Translation,' *The Independent*, 9 August 1990 (Merino, 1995: 82).
2. As we shall note in the next chapter, Le Moine's project, Channels, was conceived as a way of developing cultural exchanges between French and British playwrights, not as a means of trampling translators. I am grateful to Le Moine for sending me a package of informational materials on his work.
3. I have not been in contact with Pam Gems and therefore have not verified her quotation in Logan's article.
4. In designing the original questionnaire, I benefitted from the guidance of Sharon Carnicke, Associate Dean of the School of Theatre at University of Southern California. The English questionnaire was translated to Spanish and French, the latter with assistance from French translator and playwright Hugo Paviot. The distribution outside the United States was facilitated in Germany by Wilfried Floeck, who forwarded my request to Heidrun Adler, founding member of the Theater- und Mediengesellshaft Lateinamerika; in Spain by Alfredo Carrión of the Sociedad General de Autores y Editores; in the United Kingdom by Maria Delgado and by Ramin Gray of the Royal Court Theatre; in Montpellier, France by the Maison Antoine Vitez-Centre International de la Traduction Théâtrale, and, in Paris, by Geneviève Ulmann, who provided names of translators working into or out of French from several languages.
5. I wish to express my appreciation to the following translators who responded to my request by completing the questionnaire or sending their curriculum vitae or, in most cases, both: Heidrun Adler (Germany), David Ball (USA), Anne Alice Barlind (France), Philip Boehm (USA), David Bradby (UK), Fermín Cabal (Spain), Jörn Cambreleng (France), André Camp (France),

Sharon Carnicke (USA), John Clifford (UK), Maria Delgado (UK), Claude Demarigny (France), Sasha Dugdale (UK), Sharon Feldman (USA), Almuth Fricke (Germany), David George (UK), Fernando Gómez Grande (Spain; vita only), Susanne Hartwig (Germany), H. Rick Hite (USA), Marion Peter Holt (USA), John London (UK), Felicia Londré (USA), Lorenzo Mans (USA; Mans did not respond specifically to this questionnaire but has previously provided me with much of the same information), Elishéva Marciano (France), Jaume Melendres (Spain), Guido Nahum (Italy), Patricia O'Connor (USA), Pascale Paugam (France), Hugo Paviot (France), Miguel Sáenz (Spain), Laurence Sendrowicz (France), Caridad Svich (USA), Nicole Thévenin (France), Henry Thorau (Germany), David Tushingham (UK), and Margarita Vargas (USA). Unless otherwise indicated, references to experience and opinions of translators are drawn from these responses; all translations of their answers are my own.

6. Paviot kindly read over a draft of this chapter and offered a further clarification on his comment about maintaining Spanish songs in his French translations. With reference to Alonso de Santos's *L'Album de famille*, a play that was performed in November 2003 at the Théâtre du Rond-Point in Paris, Paviot affirms that his audience, without actually knowing the songs, can distinguish between love songs and military ones. In the latter case, spectators will know if the song is Republican or Francoist from context and by who sings it (Paviot, personal communication, 2004). Although I apparently misunderstood Paviot's point in our earlier discussion, my conclusion may still be valid: a French audience will have greater familiarity with modern Spanish history than do most American spectators and hence will grasp the context more easily whether or not specific songs have crossed the Pyrenees.

7. Aspiring playwrights can also be naively enthusiastic. Thévenin indicates that young Italian playwrights have contacted her and her colleague, thinking that once their plays are translated, the translators can easily get them staged in France. I have received requests of this nature from Spanish and Spanish-American playwrights, who similarly seem to believe that the mere existence of a translation will lead to fame and fortune on the American stage.

8. Schmidt has also translated plays by various other Russian and classic French authors, as well as Brecht.

9. The one contract I have received through SACD specifically identified my translation of Eduardo Manet's *Lady Strass* for a proposed West End production. Before plans fell through, the British directors attempted to generate a 'new' translation – that is, someone of their choosing changed a word here or there in my translation and put his name on the manuscript – in violation of the contract. Manet sent the 'new' first act to me as soon as he received it from the directors. I subsequently met with the directors in London, discussed the text with them with respect to their potential British audience, and revised it myself, with the help of Carys Evans-Corrales, a translator friend in the United States who is a native of Great Britain. I would suggest that this kind of compromise is a useful model for protecting the translator and yet meeting the director's concerns.

The issue of contracts that protect the translator should also be considered from the author's perspective. Ulmann has told me of contracts, signed in Germany, that unwisely give exclusive rights to a particular translation ad perpetuum; if the translation is inadequate, the playwright's work may never be performed in that country. While I believe that Camp was describing a special kind of contract between the playwright or his/her heirs and a translator with a relatively long period, production contracts normally have specified geographical and time limits. The SACD contract for *Lady Strass* was an option that gave the directors exclusivity for a West End production during a period of a year.

10. My initial survey in English referred to the Dramatists Guild without specifically citing the British equivalent, the Society of Authors; an early respondent supplied the correct name, which I later added to the survey, but not all negatives to the question accurately indicate nonmembership. For Germany, where I circulated a questionnaire written in Spanish with a reference to SGAE or equivalent, no one claimed membership in such a society. Most mentioned other kinds of associations.

11. Being one's own agent is not easy. Many American theatres that are listed in The Dramatists Guild directory or other sourcebooks specify that they only consider plays submitted by agents. In 1991, I sent my translation of Manet's *Lady Strass* to Françoise Kourilsky, artistic director of Ubu Repertory Theater in New York City. I then spoke to her assistant on the phone and learned that they were not interested in the project. Several years later, Kourilsky met Manet in Paris and decided to stage one of his plays. She requested my translation of *Lady Strass* from SACD and surprised me with a phone call in 1996 to announce a production, which took place that October, under the direction of André Ernotte.

12. Adler, Fricke, and Hartwig report great difficulty in having their translations of Spanish-language plays staged in Germany. Other sources of information suggest relative success in Germany for certain Spanish playwrights, particularly those who have agents. For the 1996–1997 season Marvin Carlson identified three German productions of plays by Catalan author Sergi Belbel: *Liebkosungen* at Staatstheater Kassel (February); and *Nach dem Regen* at the Dresden Staatschauspiel (September) and Stadttheater Konstanz (June). The productions of the latter comedy preceded Belbel's 1999 Molière prize in Paris for that same play (*Après la pluie*). In Madrid in March 2003, I confirmed positive information on German stagings for several authors. José María Rodríguez Méndez showed me a contract from agent Felix Bloch Erben for a forthcoming production of *Flor de Otoño*. Jaime Salom reconfirmed that a number of his plays have been staged in Germany. José Luis Alonso de Santos told me that he has an agent in Germany and receives an annual report and payment for his works staged there. The staff person for SGAE who handles accounts from Germany told me that Belbel and J. M. Benet i Jornet have agents there who actively and successfully promote their work. She added that the Spanish playwright for whom SGAE receives the most royalties from Germany continues to be Alfonso Paso (1921–1978), a prolific writer of light comedies.

13. The others are the Italian playwright Guido Nahum and Marciano Elishéva, who began translating plays only four years ago and anticipates help from the Maison Antoine Vitez in making contact with publishers.

14. Although the German translators of Latin American theatre seldom see their plays performed on stage, Adler reports success with the airing of radio

adaptations. Radio is also an important outlet for foreign theatre in France and Great Britain.

15. Samuel French handled plays by several Spanish authors in the early decades of the 20th century but has not done so recently (Zatlin, 2001).

16. In the distribution of my questionnaire, I limited the input from ESTRENO Plays translators. Of 15 translators represented in the 26 volumes published 1992–2004, I chose four who have a diversified background in theatre or have a number of translations published elsewhere as well. I assumed editorship of the series in late 1998.

17. I spoke briefly to Thomas during a Latin American Theatre conference at the University of Kansas, 2–5 April 2003, but he did not answer my questionnaire. Data on his publications is drawn from Heather McKay's website www.intranslation.com.ar.

18. Not only this Salom anthology but also my other published theatrical translations follow paths related to those of some of my respondents. Three appear in ESTRENO Plays, one in the anthology edited by O'Connor, and two, both translated from French, in *Modern International Drama*; one of the latter, in a revised version, also appeared in a volume edited by Ubu Repertory.

References

Alonso de Santos, J. L. Personal interview, 12 March 2003.

Barr, A. *Modern Women Playwrights*. Oxford University Press, 2001.

Boehm, P. Some pitfalls of translating drama. *Translation Review* 62 (2001): 27–29.

Buero-Vallejo, A. Telephone interview, 24 May 1986.

Camp, A. Personal interview, 12 May 1987.

Carlson, M. The upcoming season in selected German theatres. *Western European Stages* 8.3 (1996): 49–52.

Carnicke, S. The Nasty Habit of Adapting Chekhov's Plays. Talk delivered at the American Literary Translators Association convention, Chicago, 17 October 2002.

Corrigan, R. *Masterpieces of the Modern Spanish Theatre*. Collier Books, 1967.

Demarigny, C. Personal interview, 6 May 2003.

Enrico IV, by Luigi Pirandello. Dir. Bonnie J. Monte. Programme for production, 3–29 September 2002. New Jersey Shakespeare Festival, Madison, NJ, USA.

Espasa, E. Performability in translation: Speakability? Playability? Or just Saleability? In C.-A. Upton, ed., *Moving Target. Theatre Translation and Cultural Relocation*, 2000, 49–62.

Farrell, J. Participant in 'Round Table on Translation' (Gate Theatre, London, December 1994). In D. Johnston, ed., *Stages of Translation*. London: Absolute Classics, 1996, 281–94.

Formosa, F. Teatro y traducción. *Quimera* 213 (March 2002): 41–50.

Holt, M. P. Telephone interview, 7 February 1999.

Holt, M. P. E-mail to Megan French Fuller, 7 September 2002.

Junyent, S. E-mail, 14 April 2001.

Lamartina-Lens, I. E-mail, 27 September 2002.

Lima, R. Homenaje a José Martín Recuerda y memorias de una colaboración a distancia. *Estreno* 26.2 (2000): 5–7.

Logan, B. Whose play is it anyway? *The Guardian*, 11 March 2003. Downloaded from the Internet by Caridad Svich and forwarded by e-mail, 13 March 2003.
Mans, L. Telephone interview, 29 January 1997.
Mans, L. Personal letter, 18 June 1998.
Mans, L. The New York Staging of Arrabal's *The Body-Builder's Book of Love. Estreno* 27.2 (2001): 45–46.
Meech, A. The irrepressible in pursuit of the impossible: Translating the theatre of the GDR. In C.-A. Upton, ed., *Moving Target. Theatre Translation and Cultural Relocation*. Manchester, UK & Northampton, MA: St. Jerome Publishing, 2000, 127–37.
Merino Álvarez, R. La traducción del teatro inglés en España: cuarenta años de plagios. In *Perspectivas de la traducción inglés/español*. 3er Curso Superior de Traducción, coord. Purificación Fernández Nistal and José Mª Bravo Gozalo. Valladolid: Universidad de Valladolid, 1995, 75–89.
Nigro, K. Getting the word out: Issues in the translation of Latin American theatre for U.S. Audiences. In C.-A. Upton, ed., *Moving Target. Theatre Translation and Cultural Relocation*. Manchester, UK & Northampton, MA: St. Jerome Publishing, 2000, 115–25.
Paviot, H. Personal interview, 5 June 2002.
Paviot, H. E-mail, 2 January 2004.
Prokhorova, I. Telephone interview, 16 May 2003.
Racz, Gregory J., ed. *Three Comedies by Jaime Salom*. Boulder: University Press of Colorado, 2004.
Rodríguez Méndez, J. M. Personal interview, 6 March 2003.
Salom, J. Telephone interview, 11 March 2003.
Schmidt, P. Translating Chekhov all over again. *Dramatists Guild Quarterly* 33.4 (1997): 18–23.
Sherman, E. Telephone interview, 11 April 1991.
Sociedad General de Autores y Editores. Telephone Inquiry to Office of International Royalties, 6 March 2003.
Thomas, C. P. Personal interview, 4 April 2003.
Ulmann, G. and Ulmann, P. 18 May 1992.
Ulmann, G. and Ulmann, P. Personal interview, 5 May 2003.
Upton, C.-A., ed. *Moving Target. Theatre Translation and Cultural Relocation*. Manchester, UK & Northampton, MA: St. Jerome Publishing, 2000.
Webster, D. J. Rendering modern English-language drama into living Japanese: An interview with Koshi Odashima. *Translation Review* 64 (2002): 3–10.
Wellwarth, G. E. Special Considerations in Drama Translation. In M. G. Rose, ed., *Translation Spectrum. Essays in Theory and Practice*. Albany: State University of New York Press, 1981.
www.intranslation.com.ar (website, maintained by Heather McKay, includes extensive list of theatrical translators working from Spanish to English).
Zatlin, P. Brecht in Spain. *Theatre History Studies* 10 (1990): 56–66.
Zatlin, P. Twentieth-century Spanish theatre on the American stage. *Theatre Survey* 42.1 (2001): 69–84.

Chapter 3
Networking: Collaborative Ventures

Pascale Paugam considers herself lucky to have Geneviève Ulmann as an agent. And well she should, for few theatrical translators anywhere have agents, and few agents serve as effectively as a catalyst for international bridge building as Ulmann. Paugam states that her association with her Parisian agent over time has become a relationship based on both trust and friendship: 'She reads my work, suggests corrections and modifications, asks questions about certain choices.'[1] Ulmann has led Paugam to explore new directions and new authors, particularly young Spanish playwrights. She has also led Paugam to establish numerous contacts: 'She weaves a complete, professional network among authors, adapters, directors, actors, producers, publishers, etc.'

On the basis of my experience, I can confirm the accuracy of Paugam's comments. Ever since playwright Jaime Salom referred me to her a decade ago, I consider myself part of Ulmann's network. It is not coincidence that Paugam and I have translated some of the same Spanish plays, she to French and I to English, or that a number of translators I cite in this book are people whom Ulmann knows. These translators work in a variety of language combinations, just as Ulmann herself maintains ties with a number of European countries. From her I have learned much about the theatre worlds of Germany, Italy, the Scandinavian countries, and Great Britain, as well as France. Her advice on what makes a play stageworthy often comes to mind when I recommend a text to translate or evaluate a translation.

For other reasons, too, it is fitting that a chapter on networking for theatrical translation should begin in France. Not only do several key projects reside there, but they tend to be unique ventures in fostering theatrical translation far beyond anything I know of in the United States, the United Kingdom, or elsewhere. Mentioning these projects here, however briefly, may allow some interested translators to connect with them and inspire others to use them as models for new activities in their own countries.

In the late 1980s, when I began research on cross-cultural connections between the Spanish and French stages, I skimmed through years of *L'Avant-Scène Théâtre*, an excellent source of information on foreign theatre performed in France. It was impossible to review those pages without becoming aware of the deep involvement in promoting Spanish theatre of critic and translator André Camp, who had been associated with *L'Avant-Scène* since 1950 and whose father, Jean Camp, was also an influential translator of Spanish playwrights. André Camp kindly responded to my letter of inquiry and: invited me to see him when I was in Paris. There he introduced me to Claude Demarigny and these two translators told me about Ibéral, a group they had recently formed for the purpose of promoting Hispanic theatre in France.

Among the founding members of Ibéral were the actress Maria Casarès, a Spaniard who achieved great fame on the French stage and who was named honorary president; Spanish-born playwrights José Martín Elizondo and Carlos Semprun-Maura; Jorge Lavelli, a renowned director of the French stage who was born in Argentina; and José Valverde, the son of Spanish émigrés and director of the Théâtre Essaïon in Paris where some early Ibéral events were held. Also included in the founding group were other distinguished writers, scholars, translators, and people connected with the culture and communication worlds. The organization proposed to select significant Hispanic texts, arrange for their translation, and promote their publication and staging. To see that Hispanic plays reached French audiences, they would create a special database for Théâtrothèque to list translations of Ibero-American works. They would also sponsor Hispanic theatre festivals in Paris and visits to France by Hispanic playwrights.

Ibéral's first major endeavour took place in March–April 1989, in Paris; it featured staged readings of seven plays from three countries (Argentina, Chile and Spain), a full production of one Spanish play, round table discussions with invited authors, and the publication in *L'Avant-Scène Théâtre* of two of the texts from Spain. Most of the translations were done by Camp or Demarigny or the two in collaboration. On 3 October 2003 Ibéral, in cooperation with Celcit (Centro Latinoamericano de Creación e Investigación Teatral), sponsored its 9th Fair of Latin American and Iberian Theatre in the French capital (Demarigny, personal communication, 2003). The preliminary programme for this marathon event listed 16 plays or performance pieces, representing seven countries (Argentina, Brazil, Chile, Colombia, Mexico, Uruguay and Venezuela) and identified ten different translators. Jacques Jay, who translated two plays by Colombian author Pedro Pablo Naranjo, is the only translator to be listed twice. For 11 February 2004, Ibéral and Celcit announced another event: readings of fragments from nine plays, this time including France (a work of Latin American theme by Demarigny) and Spain, as well as Latin America (Demarigny, personal communication, 2004).

Ibéral continues to be an active group and is spreading its net wider to involve more and more people. Demarigny, who is the French representative to Celcit, mentions with satisfaction that the Celcit website www. celcit.org.ar is now publishing Latin American and Spanish plays on line (Demarigny, personal interview, 2003).[2] The accessibility of texts facilitates the work of Ibéral although the Celcit site remains silent on available translations.

Les Anachroniques is also dedicated to promoting Hispanic theatre in France. Founded at the University of Toulouse–Le Mirail in 1988 by Monique Martinez Thomas and Antonio Fernández Pérez, the project began as a university theatrical group that put on an occasional Spanish play, in Spanish, but has since expanded to encompass a cooperative venture with Théâtre de la Digue and the Cervantes Institute. Since 1998, the group has also undertaken the performance of French translations of Spanish plays, the creation of a translation workshop, and, starting in 1999, the publication of a series of bilingual (French-Spanish) play editions. In 2000, the group spearheaded its first annual theatre festival and symposium (Rencontres du théâtre hispanique contemporain). Part of the celebration of its 15th anniversary year was the world premiere in March 2004 of José Sanchis Sinisterra's *Sangre lunar*, performed in Spanish but subtitled in French.

Martinez not only co-directs some productions with Matthieu Pouget, is president of Les Anachroniques and chair of the related research group at the university in Toulouse, but is actively involved in Roswita, a national research group dedicated to contemporary Hispanic theatre. Information on these various activities may be found at www. espana31.com.

The range of interest of Les Anachroniques also now extends to Spanish America, not just Spain, and has inspired the formation in Toulouse of a counterpart company, La Vieille Dame, which promotes German theatre in France.[3] During the long Franco regime in Spain, Toulouse was the unofficial capital for Spanish exiles. It is not surprising that a number of bilingual, bicultural faculty and students in Toulouse are interested in making contemporary Spanish theatre better known in France, where plays from Germany and English-speaking countries are more likely to reach the stage. Nevertheless, Hilda Inderwildi and Catherine Grünbeck of La Vieille Dame note that French knowledge of

German theatre ends with Heiner Müller (1929–1996) and that younger playwrights are not being translated and staged as they should. In response to this situation, their venture focuses on living authors.

The outstanding feature of Les Anachroniques is its unique level of collaboration across sponsoring organizations. Since 1998 the group has had a formal, contractual relationship with the University of Toulouse–Le Mirail, the Cervantes Institute in Toulouse, and the Theatre Association of Midi Pyrenées (housed at Théâtre de la Digue). Not only can Les Anachroniques count on the Théâtre de la Digue as a venue for productions, but they also hold workshops and meetings there, in a building that is also home to an important theatre library. While initially productions were limited to a short run in Toulouse, more recently their plays have been taken on tour to other cities in France and to Spain.

Les Anachroniques added French translations to their repertoire somewhat by accident in 1998. The group was working on *Notas de cocina I*, by Rodrigo García; when Marcelo Lobera realized that some of the actors did not fully understand the difficult Spanish text, he did a French translation so they would not lose the more subtle meanings. The Spanish play was staged, as planned, that February at the Théâtre de la Digue, but the French translation was performed at a theatre festival in Paris the following November and ultimately became the first volume in the series of bilingual editions (Collection Hespérides Théâtre, later renamed Nouvelles Scènes Hispaniques). The series is published at the rate of two volumes a year and is distributed by the university's Presses Universitaires du Mirail.

There are three divisions of Les Anachroniques: administrative (*gestifs*), artistic (*créatifs*) and translation (*traductifs*). The translators find that their colleagues in the artistic area, who will be creating the production, often contribute significantly to the quality of the final translation. As directors, Pouget and Martinez emphasize the importance of rhythm in dialogue. Some scripts for the group are prepared by individual translators, while others are done by two-person teams or, as was the case of José Sanchis Sinisterra's *Pervertimiento* in 2003, as a collective, workshop project. Translators are considered professionals and are paid, however modestly. Theatrical translators working in Toulouse are fortunate in having the opportunity not only to interact with other translators but also to participate in a production from selection of text through staging and publication.

The groups in Toulouse concentrate on bringing foreign theatre to France. The Société des Auteurs et Compositeurs Dramatiques follows the opposite path: promoting French-language theatre abroad. The website associated with SACD specifically stresses the existence of translations of plays from French to other languages. In announcing SACD's new bilingual (French-English) website, Sabine Bossan highlights both the database of authors ('La moisson des auteurs') and that of translations ('La moisson des traductions'). The latter harvest is a rich one: for the update of 1 December 2003, the site referred to 9000 translations of contemporary plays originally written in French. Bossan observes that the database, which was initiated in 1997, 'is not yet accessible on the website due to the complex legal and technical issues involved' (Bossan, 2003: 5). At least temporarily, for further information one needs to contact SACD directly.

In France, theatrical translators from various languages may benefit from the Maison Antoine Vitez–Centre International de la Traduction Théâtrale, located in Montpellier. According to Dorothée Suarez, the association's secretary general, the centre includes numerous professional translators, working from 'more than 20 languages and exploring contemporary foreign repertoire with the goal of eventually securing translation grants' (Suarez, personal communication, 2003).[4] Members among the respondents to my questionnaire speak of this translation centre in positive terms. Jörn Cambreleng, who translates from German, secured his early contracts with publishers through the intervention of the Maison Antoine Vitez; he also mentions receiving a translation grant in 2000 from SACD's Beaumarchais Foundation in the context of his association with the centre. Elishéva Marciano, who translates from English, counts on the centre to function in lieu of an agent and advises aspiring theatrical translators, working into French, to become members. Laurence Sendrowicz credits the Maison Antoine Vitez with arranging for the publication of her two volumes of plays by Hanokh Levin, translated from Hebrew.

The dual focus of Jacques le Ny's enterprise at Scène Nationale d'Orléans is both playwright and translator, despite the name: Atelier Européen de la Traduction (European Translation Workshop). The AET, created in 1997–1998, is truly international in scope. The workshop is funded half by the European Union and half by cooperating theatres in various countries. It has contacts with Italian, Greek, French, Spanish, Portuguese, Irish, Slovak and Romanian institutions and by early 2003 had fostered some 50 translation projects dealing with selected contemporary plays. From the outset, each play was translated, simultaneously, into at least three of four target languages: French, Greek, Italian and Spanish. According to the AET's website www.atelier-traduction.com, for the 2003/2004 season the list of target languages has been expanded to include English, Portuguese and Romanian. Despite being primarily a European project, the workshop has included an English-language text by American playwright José Rivera and has disseminated Spanish translations to Latin America as well as to Spain. A unique aspect of the workshop is bringing the several translators together with the author in order to discuss the text collectively; this networking process proves illuminating for all concerned.

Spanish playwright Juan Mayorga's *El traductor de Blumemberg* was one of the chosen texts, and it was he who first alerted me to the existence of le Ny's translation workshop. Mayorga's play, which we shall discuss in some detail in the chapter on bilingual theatre, poses special difficulties in that it is written in Spanish and German, with some limited use of French. Mayorga's meeting in Madrid with his translators to French, Italian and Greek lasted almost four days and generated revisions at several levels. The translators spotted minor mistakes in Mayorga's use of German, but other matters were more significant. In the original text, the German-speaking fascist writer Blumemberg is traveling on a train with Calderón, his Spanish-speaking translator, but initially the disguised Blumemberg pretends to be French. With his translators, Mayorga determined that the translator-character should be from the country of the spectators and that the surname should be changed appropriately. When the Calderón character is French, then in the opening scene, Blumemberg should pretend to be English. French translator Demarigny pointed out that language is the protagonist of this complex play.[5] The observation led the group to discuss the need to clarify Calderón's motivation along with the causes for the particular characteristics of Blumemberg's speech in both native and second languages. (Why is Calderón reluctant to speak German? Is Blumemberg's rusty German difficult to understand?) Mayorga found the workshop beneficial and believes that an author should be flexible about the need for changes to his text, provided that he is consulted as was true in this case (Mayorga, personal interview, 2003).

Jacques le Ny, AET's coordinator, observes that spectators may see a bad film and yet keep going to the movies but that a bad play can turn them off theatre. Plays for AET are thus chosen with considerable care. Le Ny believes that France, with its long tradition of theatrical translation and the presence of cultural centres across the country, is a natural location for this international workshop. Although there is some friction between theatre people and academics in France, as elsewhere, the AET has sought to include university contacts in workshop projects. There is no guarantee that productions will result for every project, but efforts are made to have all translations performed, at least at the level of a staged reading, and to have them published in good editions (le Ny, personal interview, 2003).

In Germany, the purpose of Theater- und Mediengesellschaft Lateina-merika/Sociedad de Teatro y Medios de Latinoamérica is similar to that of Ibéral in France. Initiated at about the same time, it was founded in Stuttgart in 1988. As previously noted in comments by Heidrun Adler and Almuth Fricke, the group promotes Latin American theatre through translation, publication, and cooperation with theatre festivals. Theater- und Mediengesellschaft Lateinamerika revised its website, www.tmg-online.org, in November 2003. Its new catalogue of German translations of Latin American plays includes 180 titles, listed by country of origin and then alphabetically by author within country. The list, which will be updated monthly, is not limited to the group's own anthologies and cites both published and unpublished texts. The group excludes Spain but includes texts from Brazil that have been translated to German from Portuguese.

There is a comparable on-line catalogue for published and unpublished translations to English of plays written in Spanish, from the Americas and Spain. Coordinated by Heather McKay, www.intranslation.com.ar cites translated plays by author but also includes an extensive list of translators that gives information on the plays they have translated, where those plays have been published or staged, and what special interests the translators have. Several translated plays are now available on-line and more will be added in the future. The site was created as an outgrowth of a theatre translation conference at the Casa de América in Madrid in October 2002 and is intended to foster intercultural communication by providing a nexus for translators, playwrights, theatre people, agents and others interested in drama. The links to relevant organizations and theatres clearly indicate that this is a place where translators may make connections with one another. Besides periodic updating of translator information, McKay plans to expand the site to include synopses, character breakdowns, and sample pages of translated plays (McKay, personal communication, 2004). The intranslation website is much more inclusive than that of ESTRENO Plays, which is limited to Spain and to contemporary plays that have been staged. The website www.rci.rutgers.edu/~estrplay/webpage.html highlights translations published by ESTRENO Plays but also includes listings of other translations.

In a fashion somewhat related to McKay's website, Caridad Svich is developing the US Theatrical Translators Database, a project she initiated while serving as TCG/Pew Resident Artist at INTAR Hispanic American

Arts Center in New York City. Through this ongoing project, she has recruited translators for an on-line translation workshop. Building on her previous experience with writing collaborations conducted over the Internet, in August 2003 Svich proposed that workshop members create a collective piece, tentatively titled 'Living in Translation', that would address the act of translation as theme. With a total of nine participants and Svich in the role of moderator/curator/editor and contributing writer, the piece, definitively renamed 'Wandering Tongues', was built line by line, phrase by phrase, through a series of weekly exercises.

In late spring 2004, Royston Coppenger at Hofstra University announced the American Theater Translation Project www.drmrpc@ hofstra.edu. The project will be a searchable database of information, including synopses, on unpublished and out-of-print theatrical trans-lations available in English.

In the United Kingdom, the Channels project has adopted a different approach but shares some goals and methods with le Ny's AET. Initiated in 2000 at the Royal National Theatre Studio with special funding from the British Council, the French Embassy and the Institut Français in London, Channels is directed by Philippe Le Moine, International Projects Manager for the Studio. The Studio has existed since 1984 as a centre for developing young British playwrights. When Le Moine, who is French, discovered that British theatre people knew nothing about French playwrights more recent than Jean Paul Sartre (1905–1980) and Jean Genet (1910–1986), he became distressed at this 'huge lack of knowledge of foreign theatre' and determined to do something about it (National Theatre, 2002). The result is an ambitious exchange programme that pairs playwrights from the Studio with counterparts from another country for the purpose of promoting performable translations.

In its first cycle, Channels produced English translations of five French plays and French translations of three British ones. The plays from France were presented in staged readings as part of the National's Transform-ation season in 2002 and, quite exceptionally considering that they had not yet been given full stage productions, were published by Oberon Books. Channels then launched exchange programmes in Argentina and the Balkans. The 2003 project in Argentina involved three languages: the translation to Spanish of two British and two French plays and the translation of two Argentine plays into English and two into French. During an interview in Argentina, Le Moine mentioned his previous connection in London with the Gate, a small theatre that is dedicated to staging foreign plays. His last production there before assuming his present position at the Studio was an Argentine play (Le Moine, 2003b: 3).

From the translator's point of view, the controversial aspect of Le Moine's project is the use as translators of playwrights whose limited language skills require the aid of literal translations. Le Moine maintains that Great Britain has 'an illustrious line of playwright–translators including Tom Stoppard, Martin Crimp and Christopher Hampton...' (Le Moine, 2003a: 135). Once Le Moine selected the French plays, the Studio commissioned annotated literal translations for a dual purpose: so that Jack Bradley, Head of Scripts, and Sue Higginson, Director of the National Theatre Studio, could become familiar with the texts, and in order to guide the playwright–translators. Le Moine emphasizes that in Great Britain, 'translating has traditionally been a domain for playwrights', unlike France, where there is a centre for theatrical translation and 'this kind of "work for four hands" is very rare and frowned upon by translators' (Le Moine, 2003a: 135, 139). In the translation of British plays to French, the Maison Antoine Vitez has collaborated with Channels. Despite that collaboration, Le Moine echoes comments found in Brian Logan's March 2003 article in the _Guardian_ by expressing a certain disdain for translaters: 'The quality of the translation is always the weakest aspect of a play in another language' (Le Moine, 2003b: 2).

A key element of Channels is the use of residencies to bring the paired playwrights together for intensive work on the translated script. Through direct contact, the translator can acquire a thorough understanding of the author's attitude and culture. According to Le Moine, 'matching translator and writer is like a marriage; it can easily go wrong' (National Theatre, 2002). Of the four original pairings of British playwright–translators with French authors, three turned out well. Le Moine considers the success rate commendable: 'That's only one failed marriage out of four, so we're still below the national average!' (Le Moine, 2003a: 137).

In practice, these marriages are, in fact, ménages à trois, for the authors of the literal translations are included in the residencies. In writing about the project, Le Moine mentions the translators by name, identifying such threesomes as Philippe Minyana (French playwright), Steve Waters (playwright–translator) and Christopher Campbell (translator); Marie NDiaye (French playwright), Sarah Woods (playwright–translator) and Rachael McGill (translator) (Le Moine, 2003a: 137). This open recognition of the translators' contribution is significant; on the other hand, Campbell and McGill's names do not appear on the announcement for the 12 June 2002 meeting and book launch with playwrights, translators and directors. It appears that their work becomes invisible once the residencies are over.

During the residencies, the three-person teams had to make decisions on such specific matters as how to handle the many references to provincial French cities in Minyana's *Habitations* or whether to transpose the action of Jean-Paul Wenzel's *Faire Bleu* to the north of England, but they also dealt with general differences between the language of the two theatres. Le Moine affirms:

> French allows neutral writing, while English is obsessed with regional and class-related accents that force you to 'situate' the language right away within a certain context or voice. Then there is the influence on the writing itself caused by a difference in the relationship between playwright and director down to the very essence of the latter's role, which is hegemonic in France and text-oriented in Britain. There is a marked contrast in the use of and need for scene indications. (Le Moine, 2003a: 137)

Le Moine observes that, despite language barriers, the playwright and playwright–translator pairs managed to understand each other. One assumes that the authors of the literal translations also served as liaison interpreters to facilitate these dialogues. By contrast, in the AET project, communication between playwright and translator is direct in that the translator knows the playwright's language well.

At least one of the first translations generated by Channels quickly reached the London stage in a full production. In December 2002, six months after the National Theatre's staged readings, Philippe Minyana's *Habitats* (trans. Steve Waters), was produced at the Gate Theatre. It is not surprising that the Gate would receive a French play by a living author, for this theatre is exclusively international in its focus. Moreover, as the theatre's artistic director Erica Whyman notes, the Gate likes to 'explore work of imagination, theatricality and ideas' (Whyman, personal interview, 2003). She describes Minyana's text, which interweaves three stories, as a magical collage. Rather than play to conservative British tastes, the Gate challenges its spectators – and theatre critics – with new experiences. When Stephen Daldry was associated with the Gate, he directed a series of Spanish Golden Age plays there.[6]

Located at Notting Hill Gate, the Gate Theatre is a tiny, flexible space with only 70 seats. Despite its small size, it is categorized as Off West End because it is a producing house. To encourage theatrical translation, the Gate now offers a translation award on alternate years. The most recent cycle for submissions was October 2003–February 2004. Translated plays are welcome from all sources provided they have no performance history in England. Texts are reviewed by a panel of prestigious judges. Outstanding submissions that may not be appropriate for the Gate may nevertheless be placed on a short list of finalists; a series of Gate translations have been published by Methuen or Oberon.

Winner of the Gate's Translation Award in 2002 was Cecilia Parkert's *Witness*, translated by Kevin Halliwell. Parkert's monologue, which focuses on chilling stories of torture from survivors of the war in the former Yugoslavia, is one of the most acclaimed Swedish plays of the late 1990s. Halliwell is a professional translator who works for the European Union.

The philosophy of the Gate Theatre differs not only from Channels by inviting the participation of translators per se but also from that of Royal Court by being open to all kinds of plays. The Gate's Whyman characterizes plays produced at Royal Court, British or foreign, as 'naturalistic'. In a similar vein, theatre professor and translator Maria Delgado suggests that Royal Court has a 'colonizing attitude' toward foreign theatre (Delgado, personal interview, 2003). If this kind of assessment by theatre people in London is accurate, Royal Court would be less responsive to a 'magical collage' like Minyana's text than were Channels and the Gate.

Delgado's position is not contradicted by Ramin Gray, an International Associate at Royal Court, when he speaks of the London theatre's play development projects in Brazil, Cuba, India, Palestine, Russia, Uganda and a dozen other countries. Gray laments that most of the unsolicited manuscripts received by the theatre are not the right kind of plays. He clarifies that authors participating in Royal Court's residencies in London and workshops abroad are informed about what Royal Court values. They are told to avoid historical and biographical subjects; instead, they should 'describe the world we live in now' (Gray, personal interview, 2003).

In Argentina, Le Moine stated that Channels had not gone to South America to tell authors how they should write: 'This isn't a workshop, but an exchange of experiences' (Le Moine, 2003b: 4). Royal Court's position is quite the opposite in part because it does not seek out established playwrights. Elyse Dodgson, Royal Court's International Director, made this point clearly in a 2002 interview. To a question about what project in her career as producer has given her the most satisfaction, she responded: 'I have always loved the play development work best – working with emerging playwrights in many different countries on a long-term collaboration and watching them mature and develop over a number of years' (Dodgson, 2002: 2). The *Guardian* labels her a 'tireless champion of international collaborations' (Dodgson, 2002: 1).

The international aspect of Royal Court can be traced to 1956. The theatre's website points out that during Royal Court's early years, its repertoire included new plays by such German-language authors as Brecht and Frisch and such French-language ones as Genet and Ionesco. In 1989 the theatre inaugurated a four-week residency in London for emerging writers and directors; by early 1996, the current international department had been created, and within the past few years, Royal Court has begun conducting play development programmes abroad. Their international projects are funded by the British Council as well as various private foundations and sponsors.

Plays submitted to the international department are first read in the original language, but participants in the workshops conducted in London are expected to have a good command of English in that interpreters are not provided. Unlike Channels, Royal Court supports translations as opposed to free versions by playwright–translators. To be commissioned to do a translation for Royal Court, one must be fluent in the source language (Gray). That does not necessarily mean that Royal Court recruits known translators for their projects. The theatre has 'pioneered' the recruitment of actors and directors as translators, and translators become an integral part of the play development and rehearsal process (www.royalcourttheatre.com/rc_international: 3).

Located at Sloane Square and classified as part of London's commercial West End theatre, Royal Court has two playing spaces: a 400-seat auditorium downstairs and a smaller space, upstairs, that may seat 80–90. It is in the latter theatre that translated plays are more likely to be performed. While there is no guarantee that translations commissioned by Royal Court or plays developed abroad will receive a full performance, many of the translations are published.

As we have seen, in London a cluster of important theatres are actively promoting the development and translation of foreign plays for the British stage. In France, several organizations exist to create connections among translators and playwrights. In Germany and internationally, special projects exist to encourage networking among translators of Hispanic theatre and to promote stagings of translated plays. Most of these initiatives began relatively recently, since the last decade of the 20th century. No doubt I speak for many theatrical translators when I express the hope that these projects will not only flourish but will inspire other efforts at increasing communication among groups of translators, playwrights, and other theatre practitioners.

Notes

1. Opinions attributed to translators are drawn from their responses to my questionnaire, unless otherwise indicated.
2. As of 14 December 2003, the Celcit list of available Latin American and Spanish play texts numbered 140.
3. I am grateful to Monique Martinez Thomas for welcoming me to Toulouse on 13–15 May 2003 and finding time in her busy schedule on all three days to meet with me and answer my many questions. On 15 May she arranged a session for me at Théâtre de la Digue with the translation workshop, where I had an excellent opportunity to interact with several members of Les Anachroniques as well as two representatives of the German group. My thanks to all for sharing their experience and insights.
4. To my knowledge, the Maison Antoine Vitez does not maintain a website. For information, contact their e-mail address: maison antoine-vitez@easy connect.fr. I am aware of two other associations in France that may be of interest to translators. They are Écrivains Associés du Théâtre, located at the Théâtre du Rond-Pont in Paris (eatinfo@wanadoo.fr) and the Résidence de Traducteurs, La Lettre de la Chartreuse (Avignon Cedex 04 90 15 24 24). Inderwildi and Grünbeck mentioned on 15 May 2003 that their residence at Chartreuse was instrumental in honing their skills as translators, specifically in helping them 'put the text in the mouths' of the actors.
5. Readers will quickly realize that this chapter on networking includes examples of networking in action. Because Mayorga identified his French translator by name, in France I was able to contact my longtime friend Demarigny and ask his help in contacting le Ny, who had not yet responded to my e-mail inquiry.
6. As noted in the chapter on screen adaptation, Daldry is the director of *The Hours.*

References

Anachroniques, Les. Special meeting with group, 15 May 2003.
Atelier Européen de la Traduction. Program. Commission Éducation et Culture de l'Union Européenne. Scène Nationale d'Orléans. Temporada 2002/2003– janvier/février/mars.
Bossan, S., ed. Editorial. In *Entr/Actes. Actes du théâtre.* Bilingual publication 17. SACD (May–November 2003), 4–7.
celcit.org.ar (website includes on-line Latin American/Spanish play texts).
Delgado, M. Telephone interview, 2 May 2003.
Demarigny, C. Personal interview, 6 May 2003.
Demarigny, C. E-mail, 17 September 2003.
Demarigny, C. E-mail, 19 January 2004.
Dodgson, E. Interview. 'Special report: Who's who in new British theatre.' 6 July 2002. www.guardian.co.uk/arts/britishtheatre/story/0,12195,748697,00. html, 5pp.
Gray, R. Personal interview, 30 April 2003.
http://entractes.sacd.fr (website for the Société des Auteurs et Compositeurs Dramatiques; has reference to database of translations).
Le Moine, P. Channels (France). In *Entr/Actes. Actes du théâtre.* Bilingual publication 16. SACD (November 2002–April 2003a), 135–39.

Le Moine, P. Interview with Andrew Graham-Yooll. www/pagina12.com.ar, 23 April 2003b, 4pp.

le Ny, J. Personal interview, 5 May 2003.

Logan, B. Whose play is it anyway? *The Guardian*, 11 March 2003. Downloaded from the Internet by Caridad Svich and forwarded by e-mail, 13 March 2003.

Mayorga, J. Personal interview, 3 March 2003.

McKay, H. L. E-mail, 12 January 2004.

McKay, H. L. E-mail, 5 February 2004.

National Theatre. *News04*. Summer 2002.

Suarez, D. Secrétaire générale de la Maison Antoine Vitez. Personal letter, 4 February 2003.

Svitch, C. E-mail to translation workshop participants, 13 August 2003.

Whyman, E. Personal interview, 25 April 2003.

www.atelier-traduction.com (website for the Atelier Européen de la Traduction, Scène Nationale d'Orléans).

www.espana31.com (website for Groupe de recherche toulousain sur l'Espagne contemporain de l'université Toulouse II; has information on Les Anachroniques and Roswita).

www.intranslation.com.ar (website lists translators of Spanish-language plays working into English and provides information on where the texts have been published and staged; includes several complete scripts).

www.mynottinghill.co.uk/nottinghilltv/theatre.htm.

www.rci.rutgers.edu/~estrplay/webpage.html (website for ESTRENO Plays includes descriptions of English translations of plays from Spain published by ESTRENO and elsewhere. Also has links to other translation and theatre sites).

www.royalcourttheatre.com/rc_international.

www.tmg-online.org (website of the Theater- und Mediengesellschaft Lateinamerika/Sociedad de Teatro y Medios de Latinoamérica; has list of German translations of Latin American plays).

Chapter 4

Practical Approaches to Translating Theatre

Investigating copyright and acquiring permission before deciding to translate a play heads the list of practical concerns (see Chapter 2). In addition to securing rights to translate, it is important to identify the appropriate version of the text. Those of us who work with contemporary playwrights sometimes learn that the author is still in the process of creating the play; if we translate the first manuscript we receive, we will end up retranslating to keep pace with the author's rewriting. After going through four versions of Jaime Salom's *The Other William*, I have vowed not to repeat that experience and recommend that others avoid it as well.[1]

The problem of identifying the appropriate version does not disappear after plays have already been staged successfully. Ortrun Zuber recounts the complications that arose when she tried to establish which text Berthold Viertel had used for the first German translation of Williams' *A Streetcar Named Desire*. She discovered published pre-production (1947), revised (1950), and post-production (1953) editions. The latter, which included detailed stage directions, might be considered an acting edition, as opposed to the earlier reading edition, which contained helpful information on characterizations.

Theatrical translators should be aware that format varies in preparing an acting versus a reading version of a play. If they intend to send the manuscript to potential directors, they should rigorously follow playscript format, with characters' names centred on the page. (See David Spencer's helpful 2003 article in the *The Dramatist*.) In reading editions for publication, characters' names are generally placed flush left with second and subsequent lines of dialogue indented. (Never use the tab key for this purpose. An indent command will save hours of frustration in any revision process.)

Translators need to familiarize themselves with terminology and style for stage directions in the target language. They should recognize the

terms for upstage and downstage and use those English words, not a
through translation of source language expressions, like foreground and
background. The French *côté cour* (literally, courtyard side) and *côté
jardin* (garden side) are really stage left and right, respectively. Spanish
uses the words for left and right, but that does not necessarily eliminate
problems. The convention in American theatre is to designate stage left
and right from the perspective of the actor. Spanish plays, as Antonio
Buero-Vallejo usually stipulated clearly in his stage directions, view left
and right from the perspective of the spectator. Part of the task of the
translator in cases like this is to turn right into left and left into right –
without comment. Buero's explanation should be omitted, not translated,
in that it will raise a red flag to American directors if included, as inexperi-
enced translators tend to do.

Brigitte Schultze laments that translating for the theatre 'may lead to
translating only for the use of theatres, at the cost of that portion of
drama which can only be taken in by readers' (Schultze, 1998: 180). As
an editor who would like to sell books, I share her desire to have more
people read plays, but her viewpoint is an academic one that should be
ignored if the goal is, in fact, getting the play staged. For that purpose,
the ideal readers are literary managers, directors, actors and stage managers. Marion P. Holt, whose translation of Buero-Vallejo's *The Sleep of
Reason* was first staged in 1983, remembered years later how an agent
had advised him to prepare scripts for theatres: 'He sat me down and
insisted that I start using playscript format for my translations if I
wanted to avoid the negative impression the form I was using would
get from readers at theatres' (Holt, personal communication, 1995). Holt
had his initial translation of *The Sleep of Reason* retyped. Translators
today, using macro commands in their word processors, should be able
to convert a script from one format to the other within an hour or two.

Format can be readily changed. Choosing one is therefore not as crucial
as answering this key question: Will the action of the play remain in its
original setting or will it be moved closer to the target audience? Although
we will focus primarily on matters related to geographical setting, distance may also refer to time period and style. The practice of modernizing
classic texts, common to both intralingual and interlingual translation,
often requires a concomitant decision on whether to convert a play to
prose or retain the original's verse form. There is no single correct
response except to recognize that poetic talent is absolutely essential for
someone to translate verse drama to verse drama successfully. Michael
McGaha wisely asserts that the translator of Spanish Golden Age
drama has to be a poet (McGaha, 1989: 80). David Gitlitz, who translates

classic Spanish texts to English verse, confesses that he is addicted to the 'labor of weaving intricate webs of rhyme and meter' (Gitlitz, 1989: 45). Louis Nowra, an Australian translator from German, has a firm rule against translating verse plays into verse: 'Unless one has a poetical genius similar to Kleist's, then all one will end up with is bad poetry' (Nowra, 1984: 18).

In commenting on English translations of Molière, some in verse and some in prose, David Edney observes that in 17th-century France, rhymed verse was the convention for theatrical dialogue while today it is not: 'In English, rhyming verse removes the play from real life and emphasizes its elegance, wit and humour at the expense of its realism' (Edney, 1998: 64). For Edney, updating a text is an 'attempt to set up a dialogue between our world and the playwright's' (Edney, 1998: 68). Yet he believes that some spectators may be disappointed by modernizations that bring classic plays closer to their own experience because the 'pleasure of being transported to a different time and place is indeed one of the great attractions of theatre' (Edney, 1998: 67).

Whether directors and audiences welcome or reject foreign, distant settings on the contemporary stage is open to question. Gerson Shaked contends that we are suspicious of those who are different from us and hence we translate 'alien worlds and cultures into the language of our own world' in the hopes that the foreign culture will turn out to be the same as ours (Shaked, 1989: 14). But we can certainly document occasions when the opposite phenomenon has occurred: settings that would seem familiar enough are deliberately turned into something exotic. It is Paul Schmidt's dictum that a 'translation must never incorporate strangeness, even accidentally, unless it exists in the original' (Schmidt, 1997: 23).

Directors often ignore this principle. Notable is the desire, both in France and in the United States, to make Spanish theatre fit the image of Andalusia. The practice works well with García Lorca, whose plays are rooted in his native region of Southern Spain, but does not fit Valle-Inclán, whose plays take place either on the Northwest coast of Spain or in Madrid. When Valle-Inclán's _Divine Words_ was first staged in Paris in 1946, the cool mists of his native Galicia – a region not unlike the comparable Northwest coast of France – were converted into the blinding sun and overwhelming heat of Southern Spain. When Paloma Pedrero's _Parting Gestures_ was staged at Pace University in New York City in 1991, the theatre department produced a lovely poster with a typical Andalusian building as the background; the problem is that Pedrero is from Madrid, where such architecture is not found.

Plays by Chekhov are open to whimsical interpretations of his world. Schmidt recalls a production of Chekhov's *Three Sisters* with the military characters dressed up 'like doormen at the Russian Tea Room'; they even performed a Cossack dance. Schmidt offers the fanciful analogy of a Russian production of O'Neill's *Long Day's Journey into Night* with male characters dressed in Western garb (Schmidt, 1997: 21–23). Roger Pulvers finds a similar curiosity in the reluctance in Australia to stage Japanese plays. One director told Pulvers, 'We would have to squint our eyes, bow all the time, and speak with funny Japanese accents'; but when the same director stages Ibsen, Pulvers doubts 'that he asks the actors to speak their lines with Norwegian accents' (Pulvers, 1984: 23).

Excesses in setting, costumes, and acting arise in performance. A translator who is not involved in the production cannot prevent them but perhaps can forestall them by avoiding imposed strangeness in the written text. For plays that do not emphasize location, the translator can decide whether to under-translate (generalize) passing references to the setting. *A Streetcar Named Desire* has to take place in New Orleans; *The Sleep of Reason*, a historical drama dealing with the painter Goya, has to take place in early 19th-century Madrid. But through modest changes, the action of some plays might take place anywhere.

That was the stance I took, after consultation with the authors, in translating Jean-Paul Daumas's *The Elephant Graveyard* and José Luis Alonso de Santos's *Hostages in the Barrio*.[2] Daumas lives in Nice and had that city in mind when he wrote his play. I made no attempt to shift the action somewhere else, but I downplayed references to France or French culture. I felt that the story of lonely and frightened elderly people seeking a sunny, seaside resort could take place in any number of cities and countries. Alonso de Santos lives in Madrid. The original title of his play, *La estanquera de Vallecas*, calls attention to a working-class neighbourhood on the outskirts of the capital. When the play has been staged elsewhere in the Spanish-speaking world, local neighbourhoods have routinely been substituted for Vallecas. The characters, in my view, could be Hispanics who had emigrated to the city from any warmer or friendlier place. Rather than coming to Madrid from Andalusia, they might have come to the Bronx from Puerto Rico or – as we discovered through staged readings at the Bridge Theater in Miami – to Hialeah from Cuba. My revised title, *Hostages in the Barrio*, eliminated geographic specificity and instead emphasized the human situation.

If the action of the play obviously takes place in the country of the source text and the translator decides to leave it there, some over- or under-translation may still be advisable.[3] Franz H. Link reminds us that the farther removed the audience is from particular historical events, the less informed it is about the details relating to them. The author does not tell the audience what it already knows, but 'the text is supposed to supply all the information necessary to understand the action and its motiviation' (Link, 1980: 31). Link further observes that allusions can be eliminated when they are not important (Link, 1980: 32). José López Rubio put that concept into practice when he rendered *Death of a Salesman*; his *La muerte de un viajante* (1952), continues to be the classic translation in Spain of Arthur Miller's great tragedy. Willy Loman's passing reference to a particular New York hotel and the American business lunch disappears completely from López Rubio's version:

> The whole wealth of Alaska passes over the lunch table at the Commodore Hotel, and that's the wonder, the wonder of this country, that a man can end with diamonds here on the basis of being liked! (Miller, 1976: 86)

> Toda la riqueza de Alaska puede venir a sus pies. Eso es lo maravilloso de este país, el que un hombre pueda llegar a donde quiera ... (Miller, 1983: 66)

Link's advice on history is equally applicable to geographic and other cultural references. As Rick Hite observes, 'A careful balance needs to be found so that cultural matters aren't completely lost in too much homogenizing or universalizing and yet not present material that is meaningless for an American audience.'[4]

Giving meaning to references by including a glossary in the programme – a suggestion I have found sporadically in my reading of articles on theatrical translation – is not a viable solution. Spectators go to the theatre to see a play, not to read at length about it, and directors will quickly discard a script that requires footnotes. Ute Venneberg discusses a staging in Mainz in 1970 of Sean O'Casey's *Juno and the Paycock* that provided a visual, cinematic solution. To prepare the German audience for the Irish play, the performance began with a projection of events from 1922 to 1970 (Venneberg, 1980: 126). The remedy may work well for the audience, but first the potential director has to be convinced that it is worth the effort.

Hite recently faced the problem of *Tejas Verdes*, the title of a play by Fermín Cabal. The name refers to a specific place in Santiago, Chile, and the action takes place there during Pinochet's reign of terror. Hite was not at liberty to change the proper noun; on the other hand, he could and did choose a different play title: *If Anything Is Sacred*.

Susanne Hartwig says that spectators in Germany could not be expected to recognize El Corte Inglés as the name of a major department store chain in Spain; she had to adapt the reference for her translation.

When I translated Alonso de Santos's *Bajarse al moro* (*Going Down to Marrakesh*), I left the action in Madrid. The title is a slang expression that alludes to getting drugs from North Africa, and the play revolves around changes taking place in democratic Spain. Moving the play elsewhere would require rewriting the text in its entirety. I rejected such major revision and then reached varying conclusions for minor problems that remained.

The name Simago appears in the text only once: 'Trabajaba ella en Simago, allí en la Avenida de la Albufera' (Alonso de Santos, 1985: 62). I opted for a combination of under-translation and deletion because the allusion, to the store and its location, was not important: 'She worked at a discount store' (Alonso de Santos, 1992: 342). Conversely, I felt that a reference to Atocha could not be ignored. The name is repeated seven times in a segment of dialogue between Chusa, an experienced drug smuggler, and Elena, a new recruit, and is mentioned again in later scenes. The use of repetition should have a comic effect. I used the gloss 'station' and slightly over-translated the first reference. Although I assumed that few American actors or spectators would know Atocha, the name is easily pronounced and easily enough remembered that the early repetition would get a laugh and the subsequent reference would be clear. Of course, historical context for any play may change; after the terrorist attack in Madrid on 11 March 2004, the name Atocha is known throughout the world, with tragic rather than comic connotations.

I consider the French translation of this same comedy to be an academic rather than theatrical project. The Simago reference is carried over literally with an added footnote: 'Elle, elle travaillait à Simago, là-bas, avenue de l'Albufera' (Alonso de Santos, 1997b: 58). Naturally the repeated allusions to Atocha are also maintained, with an explanatory note.

Whichever route one chooses, the Simago and Atocha problems are simple compared to the reference within Valle-Inclán's *Luces de Bohemia* to Callejón del Gato, the popular name for Calle Álvarez Gato. The author's ideal spectator in Madrid in the 1920s would quickly associate the little street in the old part of the city with windows there that functioned like concave mirrors. From several published translations of the play, David Johnston praises that of John Lyon, who eliminated the specific street and went instead for the association: 'a hall of distorting mirrors' (Johnston, 1998: 34–35).

The translator must also confront the matter of character names. If the setting will be changed, should the names be translated? If the translation keeps the original setting, can all of the characters' names stay as they are or must some be changed for ease of pronunciation or understanding?

With respect to the first of these questions, again there is no single correct answer. Edney reports that American translators of Molière have tended to use the original French names while British translators have Anglicized some of them (Edney, 1998: 66). If foreign names are unpronounceable or have unwanted connotations in the target language, change is clearly required. López Rubio kept Miller's original names in his translation of *Death of a Salesman*, but in performance in Spain Uncle Ben is replaced by Tío Fred, no doubt to avoid confusion between 'Ben' and a word that is pronounced identically, *ven*, meaning 'come', as a command.

I confronted several basic problems with names in translating *The Elephant Graveyard*. Daumas has an actress-character whose stage name is Ludivine Desforets. When correctly pronounced, Ludivine Desforets is a bit exaggerated but has a nice sound. Pronounced incorrectly, it could be more ludicrous than poetic. I changed it, with the author's approval, to Madeline Delaforet. The new name should pose no troubles even for people who have never studied French and prove less distracting than a mispronounced version of the original name. A somewhat different problem was posed by the name of a cross-dresser. Originally Fernand, he began calling himself Fernande after he began wearing his late wife's clothes. My assumption was that American actors might not know that the final consonants in Fernand are silent; the masculine and feminine names might turn out identical, thus losing their significance. My solution was the pairing Paul/Paula.

For historical drama, there is less flexibility. In preparation for the Quincentennial in 1992, director Manuel Duque at Penn State invited me to translate *Bonfire at Dawn*, Salom's play about Bartolomé de las Casas. The text was subsequently rejected by the theatre department, in part because three of the characters – all of them historical figures – were named Pedro. The translator should consult history books to find the accepted translation of names where they exist but should not rewrite history when the original author chose not to do so. One might observe that a drama about the American Revolution could easily involve three characters named George.

Of concern are names with unwanted connotations in the target language. In *Going Down to Marrakesh*, one character is named Jaimito, the diminutive of Jaime. If properly pronounced, Jaime sounds very similar to Hymie, a name with Jewish connotations. The author clarified that he chose the original name because there are stock Jaimito jokes in Spain. There are also stock Pepito jokes, so we agreed to go with the latter name instead; I was sure that Pepito would sound funny to spectators with or without knowledge of the related jokes. When Ana Mengual translated Sebastián Junyent's *Hay que deshacer la casa* (*Packing up the Past*) for ESTRENO Plays, she thought that references to an off-stage character, Jorge (Hor-hay), might evoke unwanted laughter; with Junyent's approval, she changed the name to Carlos.

Courtesy titles, as well as proper names, may cause problems. Susan Bassnett quotes a flippant remark from Robert Adams about how Paris must be Paris and 'our hero must be Pierre, not Peter', but that it would be silly to have him say, 'I am enchanted, Madame' (quoted in Bassnett-McGuire, 1980: 119). With that sound advice in mind, I eliminated the use of 'Madame' in the polite interchanges among the women in Daumas's play; in English, unlike French, we are not used to this kind of polite address. Edney says to avoid the use of *madame* and *monsieur* because they are hard to pronounce. If the dialogue calls for it, he recommends the use of 'madam' and 'sir'. For dialogue between intimate friends, he recommends dropping titles altogether and switching to first names (Edney, 1998: 66). In American English, in a modern setting, the equivalent polite expression for 'Oui, madame' or 'Sí, señora' would more likely be 'Yes, ma'am' than 'Yes, madam'.

Absent problems of modernization and poetic form, there are still many questions besides setting and names that must be answered before and during the process of translation. Are the translated lines of dialogue not only speakable but do they also reflect the same rhythm as the original so that they will fit properly with the actors' gestures and movements? Do all of the characters speak in standard language or are there dialects or slang that will pose special challenges? Even if there is no use of dialect, is there a differentiation in register between characters of different ages or social groups that must be recreated in the translation? Are there other cultural or historical references that will be inaccessible to the audience and, if so, how will these gaps be bridged? Are there references in the stage directions to specific music, or do the characters sing or recite poetry? If so, how will these intertexts be handled? What is the general tone of the play and how will it be preserved? Are there specific problems caused by word play and can they be adequately handled through the strategy of compensation? And finally, will a through translation of the title yield a good result in the target language or is there a need for a new title?

A play must be translated as a whole. The elements cited above are like pieces in a jigsaw puzzle. They must all fall into place to form the total dramatic picture. The quality of the theatrical language can be compared to the edge pieces that outline the puzzle and thus facilitate its completion. At some point in the revision process, after the accuracy of the translation has been established, the translated play should be revised without the source text at hand, just to listen. An effective play translation must sound like an original text. Every line has to be tested aloud, paying careful attention to all aspects of its impact. George Wellwarth advises us to avoid an 'excess of sibilants in a sentence, or awkward consonantal clusters' (Wellwarth, 1981: 141). The translator either must assemble a group of actors to read the text or, working alone, has to learn to 'hear' the various voices – in conjunction with the action taking place as the lines are spoken.

To recreate dialogue that flows well and that actors can handle with ease requires a linguistic sensitivity akin to the translation of poetry but is yet more demanding because of the need to maintain the desired rhythm for performance. As Heidrun Adler indicates, a translation does not work 'if the actors cannot move with the text'. Ron Christ relates that he successfully recreated the rhythm of the lines in a play by Manuel Puig because he and the Argentine author together walked through the translated text several times. Angel-Luis Pujante gives examples from his 1988 translation of Shakespeare's _The Merchant of Venice_ to show how rhythm can be maintained even when translating Elizabethan verse to Spanish (Pujante, 1989: 145–46).

In comparing the rhythm of the original and translated texts, there are two factors that need to be taken into account. Is there a significant difference in speed of delivery between actors of the source and target cultures? Does one of the languages tend to be wordier than the other? Robert W. Corrigan properly tells us 'that duration _per se_ in stage speech is a part of its meaning, and stage time is based upon the breath' but also recommends that the translator keep 'the same number of words in each sentence' (Corrigan, 1961: 106). This last advice overlooks the complexity of the matter, at least for some language combinations.

With respect to my first point, Spanish actors speak much more rapidly than American ones, particularly in comedies. Indeed part of Spanish comic acting style is directly related to speed. Spanish is known to produce sentences, on average, that are about 25% longer than their counterparts in English. This is true because Spanish has fewer monosyllabic words and often uses prepositional phrases where a single adjective will serve in English. (Example: 'my son's dog' = three syllables; *'el perro de mi hijo'* = six syllables, when *mi* is correctly elided with the following *hi-*.) The automatic reduction in word or syllable count that takes place in translation from Spanish to English is generally not sufficient to offset the slower delivery of American actors.

Pruning is also called for in drama because acting styles in the Mediterranean countries (Spain, Italy, Greece) – like the corresponding languages – are more passionate than in Northern Europe or the United States. For this reason, Wellwarth suggests that translators into English tone down the natural emotion of the Romance languages to keep the dialogue from seeming too florid (Wellwarth, 1981: 144).

Beyond these factors is the tendency in the contemporary theatre of Spain, the United States and various other countries to reduce the length of plays. Older texts that once ran for three acts are now played with just one intermission. In parallel with movie showings, many plays are staged without an intermission at all. Philip Boehm states that 'whole lines, scenes, and characters are often cut and dialogues reshaped to fit the production' (Boehm, 2001: 27). Schultze is again speaking from an academic rather than a practical viewpoint when she expresses dismay that plays are being reduced to two or two and a half hours to meet current preferences of the German and Austrian stages (Schultze, 1998: 186). Both for modernizations within the same language and for translations, plays are being cut back almost everywhere.

I have elaborated on the comparison between Spanish and English because that is the theatrical language pair that I know best, but translators may confront similar problems in other language combinations. Thinking specifically of German, Venneberg alerts us that 'the translation as a whole should not become longer than the original version' (Venneberg, 1980: 123). She further recognizes the need to 'consider the various and carefully worked-out relationships between symbols, dialogue and action in the play' (1980: 125). Zuber reaches the same conclusion in her analysis of *A Streetcar Named Desire* in German. If a speech in the target language is longer than in the original play, those involved in staging it will have to decide whether to slow down the corresponding action, incorporate additional gestures or motion, or shorten the text (Zuber, 1980: 96). These comments by Venneberg and Zuber have broad implications.

The bilingual plays editions published by Presses Universitaires du Mirail–Théâtre de la Digue in Toulouse in a side-by-side format give us the opportunity to see the comparative length of each page of the two texts. Many pages are essentially the same in the French and Spanish.

Where they differ, French is always longer.[5] That visual difference on the printed page might not matter in performance given the number of silent letters in spoken French except that Spanish acting style tends to be more rapid than French; in cases where the French lines come out longer, some abbreviation may nonetheless prove advisable.

The case of English and German is more obvious. If we assume that delivery of lines in English and German will be at a similar speed – in part because neither of the languages typically elides syllables as does Spanish – a translation from English to German must be carefully edited to fit the actors' movements. German lines will routinely be longer than the English ones. The impact may also be affected by the introduction of the verb right after the subject in English and at the end of the sentence in German. As Reba Gostand says, 'the position that a word occupies in a sentence, for example in a language like German, may subtly influence the meaning of the original passage or may be vital to the characterization, communicating something additional to the mere surface meaning of the word by itself' (Gostand, 1980: 2). Ilse Winter suggests that the grammatically correct position of the verb at the end of the German sentence could 'weaken the impact of a dramatic statement' if the translator does not find a way to compensate. She provides this example of lines from *Hamlet*:

> There are more things in heaven and earth, Horatio,
> Than are dreamt of in your philosophy.

'I tend to think that "philosophy" at the end of the line really drives home Hamlet's message. In German, some kind of verb form of *träumen* would have to go to the end – not nearly as effective as the English' (Winter, personal communication, 2004).

My previous reference to 'the various voices' of the text is deliberate. Some plays may require that several characters sound alike, but most do not. Good playwrights give each character his or her own voice. Good translations maintain that differentiation; and inspired translators may enhance the differentiation if the playwright has failed to do so effectively, thereby turning a good source play into a yet more stage-worthy translated text. Pulvers believes that a translator must have a clear idea of how the work will be directed: 'When translating plays, one has to direct them in the mind as one translates. The language must be acceptable, and the characters must have distinct verbal personalities' (Pulvers, 1984: 24).

When I translated Jean Bouchaud's *C'était comment déjà* (*Is That How It Was?*) I had to deal with three women characters of different generations.

For the elderly woman, the idiolect I sought was my mother's remembered voice; the voice of the middle-aged woman was mine; for the young woman, I mentally heard my daughter speak the lines. I suspect that all practising theatrical translators similarly cast the parts they are translating to hear the several voices clearly. The voices might be those of family and friends, or of people we hear speaking in the street or on television, or they might be those of actors who would be suitable for the roles and whose performance style comes to mind.

This necessary differentiation between characters explains why conscientious translators are easily irritated by monotone editors. Ian Reid has wisely said that translators and producers 'need to be responsibly aware that tinkering with the surface of a text – however well-intentioned the alterations may be – can have profound consequences' (Reid, 1980: 82). The same advice holds for editors.

In translating Alonso de Santos's *Going Down to Marrakesh*, I realized that Elena, a middle-class university student, would speak in a more refined language than Chusa, who lives on the fringes of society. A copy-edited version of my translation, which I rejected, censored Chusa's language and hence made the two women sound alike. When Enrique Yepes translated Lanford Wilson's *Eukiah* for a special issue of the Valencian journal *Art Teatral*, he carefully avoided any specific regional dialect when recreating the substandard speech of the title character, a mentally retarded stableboy in Kentucky. As a co-guest editor of that issue, I successfully fought off the Spanish copy editor's misguided efforts to correct the boy's grammar.

Catalan translator Feliu Formosa makes the excellent point that sometimes the translator should use incorrect language to capture the character's speech, particularly when comparable errors added colour to the original text (Formosa, 2002: 50). Jörn Cambreleng cites the specific example of the prostitutes' supposedly 'popular' speech in Fassbinder's *Der Müll die Stadt und der Tod*. In his French translation, *Les Ordures la ville et la mort*, Cambreleng resisted the temptation to polish the characters' lines so that they would 'sound better', like 'good French'. He concludes that sometimes the translator has to attack 'good French'.

It is relevant to our discussion that the action of *Eukiah* was kept in Kentucky and that the issue of *Art Teatral* consisted of 12 translations – not adaptations – of ten-minute plays from Actors Theatre of Louisville. At times it may be appropriate to shift the setting of a particular play to one more familiar to the target audience. Eukiah's name might have been changed and he might have been portrayed specifically as an uneducated rural labourer in Spain. The underlying story would have been the same. But the purpose of this special issue was to familiarize the readers of *Art Teatral* with a selection of recent short plays from the United States, so the American settings and characters were consistently retained.[6]

What is the difference between a translation and an adaptation? In a detailed typology, J. C. Santoyo has developed a wide range that includes definitions of 'translation' as a faithful, literary rendering into another language (Santoyo, 1989: 97), 'version' as a translation that takes performance requirements into account (1989: 102), and 'adaptation' as a term that has been used 'to disguise all manner of unacceptable textual and staging manipulations' (1989: 103).

Adaptations, even ones that involve few textual changes, may radically alter the underlying meaning of a play. Reid has compared Lewis Galantière's two translations from French to English of Jean Anouilh's *Antigone*. The first, staged in New York in 1946, establishes the premise 'And now Creon is King. A reign of terror has begun'; the revised version, staged in London in 1949, affirms 'Now Thebes is at peace and Creon is King' (Reid, 1980: 86). Reid concludes that the later translation is faithful to the original and that American viewers had seen a different play (Reid, 1980: 90).

Santoyo states that adaptation may propose to naturalize or domesticate the text in order to achieve an equivalent impact on the target audience (Santoyo, 1989: 104). According to Terry Hale and Carole-Anne Upton, 'the dilemma over foreignization or domestication of the text is one shared by all literary translators, although the decision to relocate is arguably more consequential with a text for performance than with a text intended to be read privately' (Hale & Upton, 2000: 7).

Illustrations from the United Kingdom of the two extremes described in Santoyo's scale are the approaches that Gwynne Edwards and David Johnston have taken to Federico García Lorca (1898–1936) and Ramón del Valle-Inclán (1866–1936), respectively.

In a discussion of works by García Lorca on the English stage, Edwards reveals his preference for relatively literal translation and uses his rendering of *Blood Wedding* for staging in Manchester in 1987 as a model. Edwards wished to convey as accurately as possible 'the essential Spanishness of the play' (Edwards, 1988: 344). He sought the 'exact translation of references to food, dress, houses, climate, flowers, plants, landscape, customs, and other things which create' Lorca's special world (1988: 345). He therefore says that his literal reference to a 'good crop of esparto', despite the low frequency of the word 'esparto', is superior to 'hemp harvest', the expression that was used by James Graham-Luján and Richard L. O'Connell in their 1945 translation of the same tragedy (Edwards, 1988: 355).

When I tested these phrases in spring 2004 in my advanced translation class, students laughed at 'hemp harvest' because for them 'hemp' is a reference to marijuana. Anyone staging this 1945 translation today would have to take into account the prevalent contemporary meaning of the word. The students had no idea what 'esparto' might mean. As Alan Thomas points out, 'an actually attempted literal translation would produce opacity not transparency' (Thomas, 1988: 4). Exact words for flora and fauna may fail totally at creating for a theatre audience the special world of a particular playwright who is at a distance from them.

The opposite stance to that of Edwards is taken by Johnston in adapting several of Valle-Inclán's plays. Johnston shifts the action and the characters to Ireland. He explains:

> I felt Irish voices would not only serve to provide a viable cultural equivalent for Valle's rural Galicia obsessed with sex, sin, guilt and redemption, but would also recreate the same experience of language that a Madrid audience would have watching the original plays.[7] (Johnston, 1998: 41)

Johnston made the shift in his adaptation for broadcast by BBC Radio 4 of *Divine Words* and in *Bohemian Lights*, where the action takes place in Madrid. He moved the latter play to Dublin in 1915, introduced Irish names for the characters – Don Latino becomes Sweeney and Pica Lagartos is Mulligan – and resolved the problem of clarifying Valle-Inclán's key concept, *esperpento*, not merely by glossing or over-translating to stress the word's allusion to a grotesque, deforming aesthetic, but by using a word of Gaelic Irish, 'ainriochtan'. Sweeney thus says: 'Ainriochtan, Mr Mulligan. Ainriochtan. A groteskery, that's what it is' (Johnston, 1998: 44). Gone totally is the 'Spanishness' that Edwards would seek.

Adaptation is a frequent strategy that takes many forms. Franz H. Link mentions altering stage directions so that a play may be performed in a different kind of theatre; for example, staging a Greek tragedy in a modern playhouse is a kind of adaptation (Link, 1980: 34).[8] Reid considers adaptation to include any play with substantial excisions or additions (Reid, 1980: 82). Pascale Paugam reports that for her French translation in the 1990s of Paloma Pedrero's *La llamada de Lauren*, written a decade earlier, she changed the husband's refusal to let his wife work outside the home to his desire to have her finish college first; her adaptation reflected new social patterns in democratic Spain. Miguel Sáenz recounts seeing in Madrid a thoroughly Mexican adaptation of Heinrich von Kleist's early 19th-century play, _Der zerbrochene Krug_; the adaptation worked amazingly well because of the 'quality of the text, the actors, and the direction'.

Sometimes adaptation may be the only route by which a particular play can travel. The Mexican version of the German play was unexpected, but adaptation has been the norm for Eve Ensler's _The Vagina Monologues_ because the dialogue is filled with slang and local references. An international hit, by 2002 it was in its second season in both Madrid and Paris. The Spanish version by Victor Cremer includes numerous examples of clever rewriting. Great Neck, Westchester, and New Jersey, with the identification of their supposed corresponding colloquialisms for vagina, are transformed into the various regions of Spain. In that 'coño', the principal slang word for vagina in Spanish, has become a common and relatively mild expletive, used by women as well as men, it offers a wider range of comic uses than the English word 'cunt'. Cremer's text takes full advantage of those possibilities, and the actors involve the audience in chanting the two-syllable 'coño' rhythmically in one of the Spanish performance's funniest moments. In French, as Luise Von Flotow points out, 'con' has lost its original meaning and now designates a weak man; French feminists have wanted to reclaim the term as a reference to the female anatomy (Von Flotow, 1997: 18–19). _The Vagina Monologues_ provides a vehicle for doing so.

Recent discussions of translation versus adaptation, inspired by postcolonial theory, have focused on how Western artists have appropriated myths from other nations and on how artists in those countries have assimilated Western canons. Some of this cross-cultural activity may be a deliberate response to specific needs, as is often true in women's theatre. Julie Holledge and Joanne Tompkins examine how European texts 'have served women's political struggles in Japan, China, Iran, and Argentina. These texts are translated, adapted, or completely rewritten by non-western artists for explicitly socio-political as well as aesthetic reasons' (Holledge & Tompkins, 2000: 19).

Although on occasion there may be justification for relative fidelity to the source on the one hand or for relatively free adaptation on the other, most of the concrete recommendations in this chapter are aimed at a performable version that would fall in the centre of Santoyo's spectrum. More than a half century ago in France – before the term 'adaptation' came to be associated with the playwright–translator syndrome discussed in Chapter 2 – Edmond Cary astutely noted how successful theatrical translations tend to belong to a middle ground. Taking into account the way a play may resonate over the centuries and at great distance, Cary asserts:

> Theatrical translation ... is conceived for performance before a flesh and blood audience at a given time and in a given space. It is a living work, or it simply isn't. That's why theatrical translation often prefers the label of adaptation, even when one discovers that it approaches the original in an honest and thoroughly respectful manner. Instinctively, the translator adopts the opposite attitude of the academic translator of classic texts. (Cary, 1986: 53)

Despite the translator's desire to be as faithful as possible to the original, there are numerous linguistic factors that may require creative adaptation. As several translators wrote in their responses to my questionnaire, high on the list of challenges is dialect.[9] Dialect was also a matter of concern for the *Art Teatral* project. Among the dozen American short plays to be translated to Spanish were four in particular that posed major problems of dialect (at the level of language) or idiolect (at the level of individual speech).

We have already referred to Wilson's *Eukiah*, with its use of substandard, regional American English that Yepes conscientiously rendered in geographically neutral Spanish. Margot Revera chose a similar tactic in recreating the dialect of the two black women characters in Lynn Nottage's *Poof!* Jane Anderson's *Lynette at 3 AM* led translator Francisco Olivero to adopt a somewhat different approach. One of three characters in Anderson's play is Puerto Rican; he interjects an occasional word of Spanish or Spanish name in his speech, and his English sentence structure is not standard. As a Puerto Rican, Olivero found the language patterns of the supposedly Latino character in the source text to be false; he decided not only to correct the spelling of the name *Estaban, but also to make Esteban's Spanish a more authentic reflection of his ethnicity. He compensated for Anderson's bilingual word play by having Esteban occasionally code switch into English. (We will deal at length with variations of bilingual plays in Chapter 5.)

The action of Richard Dresser's *Bed & Breakfast* takes place in England; it juxtaposes the proper speech of the British owner of the establishment with the more colloquial language of two American couples. Translator Carmen Ferrero's solution to the problem of different accents was to count on the collaboration of future actors by merely pointing out accent and tone in the stage directions.

Starting from an analysis of translations to German and Italian of plays by Edward Bond and George Bernard Shaw, Manuela Perteghella has developed useful definitions of five possible strategies for transposing dialect and slang in practice: dialect compilation, pseudo-dialect translation, parallel dialect translation, dialect localization, and standardization (Perteghella, 2002: 50–51).

In Perteghella's classification, dialect compilation retains the original setting and milieu of the play but incorporates a mixture of target dialects or idioms; her caveat is that the resulting translation may be so strongly regional that it will be hard to reach a wide audience. In pseudo-dialect translation, names and cultural references are retained and the translator creates a fictitious, non-specific dialect that will be widely accessible; in performance, the actors may use regional accents. Among our previous examples, the translations of *Eukiah* and *Poof!* belong to this second category.

Parallel dialect translation also keeps the names and cultural references from the original but the translation deliberately uses a specific target dialect, normally one with similar connotations to that of the source text, and the actors will speak in their regional accents. Perteghella observes that potentially such a translated play will be incorrectly perceived as belonging to the audience's culture. Link has parallel dialect translation in mind when he advises that 'the play must always be translated into the dialect which is recognized by the audience as being used by the corresponding social group in their part of the country' (Link, 1980: 29). Local references in the translation may require corresponding changes.

Olivero's rendering of *Lynette at 3 AM* might be seen as a special case of parallel dialect translation: the bilingual Puerto Rican character can function equally well in English- and Spanish-speaking worlds. With the influx of immigrants from the Caribbean to Spain, he can reside in Madrid as easily as in New York. More typical examples of Perteghella's classification of parallel dialect translation are the experiments that Bill Findlay has described in translating Canadian French texts into dialect for Scottish audiences. Findlay argues persuasively that Scotland offers a more hospitable climate than does England for translation into dialect (Findlay, 1996: 202) and that, unlike homogenized English, the many dialects of Scots provide equivalents for the various accents of Canadian French (1996: 206).

Perteghella's fourth strategy, dialect localization, involves domesticating or acculturating. It changes the names and setting to that of the target culture, as was true with Johnston's adaptation of Valle-Inclán's *Bohemian*

Lights. At the opposite pole from this kind of adaptation is standardiz-ation. While standardization may keep occasional colloquialisms, it essentially eliminates the use of dialect completely. Perteghella suggests that this strategy may be of some use for scholarly editions but warns that in performance 'the characterization will lose its strength and the dialogues some of the musicality and colorfulness of the source dialogue' (Perteghella, 2002: 51).

Ferrero's translation of *Bed & Breakfast* might be viewed as standardiz-ation. She resists the temptation to replace British and American English with Castilian and some variant of Latin American Spanish. Rather she counts on the actors to convey the difference in national origin of the char-acters. Her solution is similar to that of Maria Delgado for Valle-Inclán's *Divine Words*; Delgado writes in standard English but recommends in her translation that the parts be played by Irish actors (quoted in Johnston, 1996: 40).

Although Findlay believes that Scotland is more hospitable than England for translation into dialect, Boehm points out that regionalisms work better in England than in the United States precisely 'because Britain has so many true dialects' (Boehm, 2001: 28). Boehm also explains that because British English is class-coded it offers advantages over American English when translating a playwright like Chekhov: 'On this side of the Atlantic, theater companies frequently attempt to convey class by using faux aristocratic accents based on a generic stage British, a ploy more likely to backfire than hit the mark' (2001: 28).

In deciding which strategy to follow for solving problems of dialect, translators should normally keep in mind Patrice Pavis' more general comments with respect to intercultural translation. They should evalu-ate the distance between source and target cultures and realize that 'trying too hard to maintain the source culture' can make their text unreadable but that normalizing it too much can make its origin incom-prehensible (Pavis, 1989: 37). Pavis once again recommends a middle road, cautioning us that 'total adaptation to the target culture can betray a condescending attitude to the source text and culture' (1989: 38). Sirkku Aaltonen affirms that translation represents a struggle against the foreign: 'For this reason, a complete translation will always be a reflection of the receiving culture rather than that of its source text' (Aaltonen, 2000: 114).

Strategies for dealing with extensive passages in slang are so closely related to those for dialect that Perteghella combines these two linguistic challenges in her study. Both kinds of language are identified with spe-cific geographical locations, but slang may pose the greater difficulty.

Holt offers these useful remarks, which apply equally to other language combinations:

> Slang can be tricky since converting a Spanish expression to English runs the risk of creating a regional slanginess that sounds out of place in a play set outside that region. That is, using New York borough slang can be jarring, if the play is still set in Spain or elsewhere. Also, since slang is eternally evolving, it can be the part of a translation that dates most quickly.

I have already alluded to these issues in Chapter 1, where I acknowledged that the slang I used in _Going Down to Marrakesh_ works better in the New York City area than it will in other regions of the United States.

When a character speaks street language or slang throughout the play, the translator quickly sees the problem and sets about solving it. More dangerous is the occasional slang expression that may slip by unnoticed. The required strategy is the same as that for other idiomatic and colloquial expressions: the text must be examined with extreme care in order to identify correctly the intended meaning. Sharon Carnicke gives this example from Buravsky's _The Russian Teacher_: 'The main character pulls "a white ticket" (a literal translation) meaning that he was classified as unfit for the army and so "4 F" '. Carnicke has correctly sought the equivalent colloquial expression in the target language. The following line is spoken by the groom to his bride in the opening scene of Yolanda Pallín's _Luna de miel_ (_Honeymoon_) – moments after carrying her over the threshhold: '¿Te quieres quedar conmigo?' The literal rendering, 'Do you want to stay with me?' makes no sense under the circumstances. What he really says, in response to her previous comment, is 'Are you kidding?'[10]

Whenever an expression translated literally is meaningless in context, it probably does not mean what it says on the surface. The lexical unit will comprise the idiom in its entirety; the words cannot be translated one by one.[11] Translators are well advised to invest in slang dictionaries and to consult native speakers of their source language who keep abreast of colloquial language.

The possibility of misinterpreting isolated colloquial expressions is true in all translation and is one reason why it is always wise to have someone with appropriate expertise read over one's work. Better yet is being able to do that reading with the author present, to clarify any doubts. In 1991 I had such an opportunity with Paloma Pedrero and a bilingual friend of hers when I was in the process of translating three of her one-act plays for staging at Pace University. Paloma read a line in

Spanish and I then read my translation of the same line. If the friend laughed at both, we continued. If he laughed at one and not the other, we stopped to find out what had gone wrong. It was in that helpful encounter that I first learned the colloquial, Spanish meaning of 'quedarse con alguien'.

Lives there a translator who has never misread an idiom and thereby created a howler? I doubt it. While translation mistakes are as lamentable as they are inevitable, the chances that they will be truly noticeable and embarrassing are greater in theatre than in narrative. The individual reader may glide over an error or quickly forget it, but a bad gaff on stage will be viewed simultaneously by the whole audience. Such was the case in September 2003 at the municipal theatre in Giessen for *Aufgefahren*, the German premiere of Ernesto Caballero's *Auto*. The production coincided with a conference on contemporary Spanish theatre sponsored by the university in that city, and the author was present.

The Spanish work is a modern *auto sacramental* (eucharistic play); its four characters have just been killed in an auto accident but do not yet realize they are dead. Near the end, there is a long silence followed by five lines of dialogue that play on the idiom 'ha pasado un ángel' (Caballero, 1994: 32). Literally the words say that an angel passed by, but any fluent native speaker of Spanish or good bilingual dictionary will define the expression as signifying a break in the conversation. Moreover, the character who introduces the expression immediately clarifies for her husband that it is 'una frase hecha', an idiom. Within the context of *Auto*, 'ha pasado un ángel', like the play title itself, functions on more than one level. Unfortunately, the translator failed to recognize the challenge. The literal rendering in German, like English, misses the basic meaning and seems to refer only to an actual presence of an angel. Taking it that way, the director brought the word to life by adding a fifth character to the cast: an angel-waiter who walked across the stage carrying a tray and then joined the others for curtain calls. Aside from losing the original meaning of the idiom, the appearance of the angel made more specific than the source text what awaited the characters in the afterlife. The author and other audience members who knew the original play were bewildered.

Literary references within the text, like colloquial expressions, may slip by the translator unnoticed; as a result, the translator may fail to render the allusion appropriately. Unless the author of the source play is deliberately misquoting an intertext, the translator should identify the quoted passage and use the original wording or, if one exists, its recognized translation to the target language. If at all possible, one should not translate a translation. (If the quoted passage is long and still under copyright, the theatre staging the play or the editor publishing it will have to confirm authorization for use.) In translating _The Other William_, Salom's comedy dealing with the real author of the plays signed by William Shakespeare, I was guided by the principle that the title character would get his famous lines right.[12] Salom facilitated my work by providing me with a list that identified all of his Shakespearean quotations and references; tracking down the original lines was easy. On the contrary, Holt has found the translation of Sanchis Sinisterra's _El lector por horas_ (_The Hired Reader_) to be the most difficult he has tackled:

> [It] contains passages from American and British literatures (Faulkner, Conrad), from French (Flaubert) and Italian (Lapedusa). Locating those passages in the original works has been time-consuming and is still incomplete, as is the translation. Quoting the passages from the original English texts is relatively easy but what about the Italian, which appears in the plays in Spanish? Translate from Spanish or from original Italian?

Apparent literary references that are not really quotations are perhaps harder yet. Boehm, whose translation of Brecht's _In the Jungle of the City_ was staged in Atlanta in 1998, says that rendering the colloquial speech of a playwright like Lanford Wilson is easier 'than a Brecht character paraphrasing Rimbaud'. The challenge would be to recreate in English Brecht's efforts in German to recreate the French poet's tone.

Whether American audiences will recognize Rimbaud is perhaps irrelevant. Lee Blessing's _Cold Water_ contains a long reference to Alexander Pope. Joan Torres-Pou, the Spanish translator of the text for the _Art Teatral_ project, retained the reference, even though he was quite sure that audiences in Spain would know nothing about Pope. He explained that he was following the concept of 'dynamic equivalence': Blessing's protagonist complains that his literature students know nothing about Pope and have no interest in the subject. Their ignorance of an important British poet of the 18th century will doubtless be mirrored by audiences in Spain, the same as in the United States.

Daumas's _Le Cimetière des éléphants_ (_The Elephant Graveyard_) includes three extended literary references, each of which requires a different solution. One of the elderly women reads aloud to another whose eyesight is failing. The comically dreadful novel she reads is of Daumas's own creation; as would be true with an original metaphor, the translator should render it faithfully.[13] Another character has been a great actress. Each of her entrances is dramatic: with theatrical tone and gestures, she recites poetic passages that relate to the dialogue. Her first recitation is two lines from Paul Valéry's poem 'Le Cimetière marin'. The connection between one graveyard and another is obvious enough even if spectators in both languages may fail to recognize the source. I used C. Day Lewis's published translation of Valéry, weaving his rendering into the text consistent with the pattern of the original play. The real problem here was the character's repeated use of lines from Racine's *Phèdre*, the tragic role that had made her famous.

French audiences would know both Racine's style and the specific play. American audiences could not be expected to have a comparable knowledge of the play-within-the-play. James Magruder, who has achieved widespread acclaim for his translation of Marivaux's *The Triumph of Love* has stated that Racine is untranslatable. Louis Nowra affirms that good Racine translations are 'as rare as a good leg spinner in cricket' (1984: 15). Whether or not their statements are true, there is, to my knowledge, no widely acclaimed English translation of *Phèdre*. Something essential in Daumas' play would be lost in the English-speaking world were Racine to be preserved at the cost of the audience's ability to relate the intertext to the frame story. I decided to hunt for a different but yet related text. Racine is the great classic French writer of tragedies; his counterpart in the English-speaking world is Shakespeare.

Daumas incorporates lines from *Phèdre* at three points in his play. The intertext emphasizes the protagonist's anguish resulting from unrequited love and her wish to die. The aspect of dying alludes as well to the general situation of the elderly characters in the frame story. With the author's approval, I substituted *Anthony and Cleopatra* for Racine's *Phèdre*. Like Phèdre, Cleopatra suffers from an unhappy love affair and commits suicide. The parallel lines from Shakespeare contained similar connotations and were easily woven into Daumas's dialogue.

Roger Pulvers explains why he chose a radical solution and wove titles of numerous English-language works into dialogue from Inoue Hisashi's *The Adventures of Dogen*.

> Kanehira addresses Dogen in a speech that is riddled with classical and other literary references. The effect is highly comic. The Japanese audience recognizes these. We would not. So, the effect must be maintained by shifting the context. If someone objects that the 'Japaneseness' is lost, then either he doesn't know what that quality, in essence, is; or he misses the point of drama. (Pulvers, 1984: 25)

Theatrical translation demands talent for finding creative answers to difficult problems. As Clifford Landers states: 'The essential requirement is to retain the humor, suspense, satire, or any other preponderant effect of the play, however much it may entail textual modifications' (Landers, 2001: 105). Pulvers has followed that concept in substituting titles that will be equally familiar, and hence comic, to his target audience as the ones used by Hisashi were to the original audience.

Just as translators need to distinguish between real literary quotations and made-up ones, they must identify stock metaphors, sayings, and proverbs in contrast with original ones. The translator owes loyalty to the source author when the expression is the author's own invention. The standard advice on translating a fixed expression is to look for the equivalent in the target language. The text may say *entre la espada y la pared* (literally, between the sword and the wall), but we will write 'between the devil and the deep blue sea' or 'between a rock and a hard place'. Usually that approach works well. (Indeed, as we saw with the German version of *Auto*, failing to find the underlying meaning may lead to angels suddenly emerging from the wings.) The Spanish title for Shakespeare's *All's Well That Ends Well* thus rejects a literal rendering and instead adopts a proverb: *A buen fin no hay mal principio.*

Sometimes the proverb for proverb approach may miss a key element in the theatrical text. In a study of play titles as signs, Sandra Messinger Cypess has pointed out that a fixed expression may have implications that transcend its equivalent meaning. She uses the example of Elena Garro's *Andarse por las ramas*, a title that has been translated in scholarly commentaries as *To Beat About the Bush*. In Garro's play, a character literally walks along the branches of a tree (Cypess, 1985: 100–102); 'to beat about the bush' in no way captures that visual image. The translator must examine the text as a whole to discover whether the author has given an expression both its figurative and its literal meaning. When the equivalent figurative expression in the target language does not serve the double function, it may be necessary to invent a new one that does.

Authors, too, may invent 'proverbs'. David George recalls that translating a play by the Catalan author Joan Brossa proved problematic precisely because of its use of expressions that 'sounded like sayings or proverbs but which actually were invented. The blend between banal dialogue and striking imagery was disconcerting.'

Translators who feel they lack poetic talent and hence studiously avoid verse plays may still find poetic passages interspersed in otherwise normal dialogue.[14] In Buero-Vallejo's *Las Meninas*, Holt confronted this little satirical rhyme:

> Ya el pueblo doliente
> llega a sospechar
> no le echen gabelas
> por el respirar. (Buero-Vallejo, 1997: 182)

He created this jingle, somewhat altered – not a tax on breathing but on dying – but of equivalent impact:

> A tax to see, a tax to buy,
> And soon we'll pay a tax to die. (Buero-Vallejo, 1987: 65)

Song lyrics potentially represent a greater puzzle than scattered passages of poetry. Henry Thorau, who translates Brazilian plays to German, cites Augusto Boal's *Arena contra Zumbi* as the most difficult text he has faced in large part because of the songs. On the other hand, Hugo Paviot does not translate songs to French when the words have no impact on the play's action; background music is not a problem if the audience can guess its symbolic value. The challenge lies with songs that are woven into the dialogue.

When the lyrics are significant, the translator must decide whether to keep the original song or substitute another one. The substitute might be from the source culture but better known to the target audience. Or it might be from the target culture and contain similar values: a lullaby for a lullaby, for example. I generally have three ways of seeking substitute songs: my own collection of songbooks, songbooks in the local library, and, indirectly, fakebooks belonging to my sister Helen June, who has had a long career as a professional singer and piano player. If the original song is maintained, should the lyrics be left in the original language or translated? Will the music be accessible to potential directors in the target country? Will the potential actors be able to sing it? If the song has already been translated, do these lyrics in the target language serve the same function as the original lyrics? Is the song still under copyright? How about the translated version? Quoting a few lines in a published text may not violate the law, but singing those same lines in a theatre, without permission, might.

In the case of Alonso de Santos's *La estanquera de Vallecas*, songs are carefully integrated into the performance text. The lyrics refer intertextually to the action and, at times, are woven into the dialogue. But the original songs, in my opinion, will not work for American audiences. In the 'birthday party' scene, the author specifies records with the 'His

Master's Voice' label and the song 'Suspiros de España'. Because this particular song would be unknown to most Americans, for my translation, *Hostages in the Barrio*, I substituted another Spanish paso doble that was popularized decades ago in the United States on the Victor label: 'Valencia'. The song could be understood as a nostalgic reference to the warmer climate left behind by workers seeking employment in the city, rather than an ironic comment on Spanish historical and political reality. The second song, near the end of the play, in the original was the popular flamenco-style 'Los campanilleros'; popular in Spain, that is, but unknown in the United States. I substituted the more familiar 'Granada'; while maintaining the reference to Andalusian culture, the substitute song alludes historically to the surrender of the Moors and hence to the situation of our would-be-thieves who are about to admit defeat. Moreover, the song, in Dorothy Dodd's English lyrics set to Augustin Lara's music, even emphasizes the early morning hour when this action takes place: 'The dawn in the sky greets the day with a sigh for Granada.' The already translated lyrics of 'Valencia' and 'Granada' could readily be worked into the text; these familiar songs are old enough that they could have been favourites of the elderly grandmother, thus removing a potential obstacle in performance.

Far greater complications are faced by translators of musical comedies, for the songs generally must be maintained and lyrics made to fit both sense and music. In 2002–2003 *My Fair Lady*, Lerner and Loewe's classic 1956 musical adaptation of Shaw's *Pygmalion*, finally reached the Madrid stage and became the hit of the season. Ignacio Artime and Jaime Azpilicueta passed the test of 'The rain in Spain stays mainly in the plain' by keeping the rain but cleverly changing Eliza's pronunciation puzzle from a vowel sound to b/v, consonants that cause spelling, if not pronunciation, problems for uneducated speakers of Spanish: 'La lluvia en España bellos valles baña'. Because h is silent in Spanish, for the aspirated h of 'Hartford, Havershire and Hampshire' they substituted the Spanish j: 'jardín japonés, jaula'. The solution works well even though the Spanish j is not equivalent to Eliza's struggle with the English h. In the dubbed French version of the 1964 film adaptation of *My Fair Lady* (dir. George Cukor), lyrics are made to fit the music by changing the rain to a cloudless sky: 'Le ciel serein d'Espagne est sans une brume' but the Hartford, Havershire and Hampshire challenge was left with geographic names from England. In French, like Spanish, h is silent and there is no counterpart to the Spanish j.

Sharon Feldman emphasizes that the main aspect of successful theatrical translation is 'capturing the same linguistic registers in English that are transmitted by the original text'. Her position is impeccable. The translator must pay close attention to the tone or tones of the source text. When playwrights have deviated from standard language to achieve certain effects, the translator must do so as well. If the audience for the original play would laugh at something someone says, or gasp in dismay, the audience for the translation should too.

In theory at least, an obscenity should be translated by an equivalent obscenity – taking into consideration the actual shock effect of the expression in one language before choosing the equivalent in the target language. In practice, as we noted in Chapter 1, censorship may intervene because of the anticipated response of the target audience.

To translate comedy – or occasional word play within a serious text – the translator needs a sense of humour. The goal should be a pun for a pun and a joke for a joke, although it is not always possible to handle double meanings and laugh lines on a one-for-one basis. The translator thus resorts to a strategy of compensation: inventing a new pun somewhere close by to make up for the one that was lost.[15] André Lefevere explains the process:

> Translators frequently insert puns of their own to make up for puns they found themselves unable to translate. Since the pun turns out to be an important stylistic feature of the source text, it is probably advisable to keep the number of puns in source text and translation roughly the same. Since, moreover, a pun that is not translated as a pun still yields its information content and since a pun that is translated where there was no pun in the original only heightens the illocutionary power of the passage without notably changing the information content, no real harm is done by the insertion of 'new' puns. (Lefevere, 1992: 52).

Puns and other word play pose an enormous challenge in all literary translation, but are especially difficult in theatre: the spectator has to catch the double meaning on the fly. If any particular example of word play recurs in the text, the translator must exert special care so that the spectator can grasp it quickly the first time and call it up mentally for subsequent use.

Special attention is relevant when characters' names or nicknames have a double meaning. A classic example is Oscar Wilde's *The Importance of Being Earnest*, a comedy about artifice that treats the name 'Earnest' ironically. The standard Spanish translation of the title, *La importancia de llamarse Ernesto*, misses the point in that Ernesto is not a word. Jaume Melendres's 1983 translation to Catalan, *La importància de ser Frank*, hits the mark by playing on *franc*, meaning sincere. In Paloma Pedrero's one-act play, *A Night Divided*, an actress-character uses the professional name 'Luna Aláez'. Near the end of the play, the other character looks up at the sky, sees the moon, and says 'La Luna'; the woman, thinking he is speaking to her, responds, and the audience laughs. The name calls for transformation. Not only is Aláez difficult to pronounce but the meaning Luna-Moon would not be clear. Neither Luna nor Moon will work in English as a first name. I settled on Venus Vega. Audiences at the Pace University premiere and recently at New Jersey Repertory (9–10 May 2004) laughed heartily when the man identified the planet and the woman responded, 'What?'

For his translation of Alfred Jarry's *Ubu roi* (*Ubu the King*), David Ball had to begin the process of recreation with the first word: *Merdre!* Jarry stunned Paris spectators in 1896 by using on stage a term that, while not identical, was shockingly close to *merde* (shit). Ball points out that 'the word-ending -re runs though the play from one end to the other, sometimes on real words, sometimes on invented ones.' Ball wanted to find a suitable equivalent for the -re suffix that could be used through-out the text. Previous translators had used such variants for the opening word as 'Shee-yit' and 'Shite' but those solutions were not applicable elsewhere in the dialogue. Once Ball settled on 'Shitsky!' for the opening '*Merdre!*', he had found a workable and funny -sky suffix for the whole text (Ball, 2002).

In translating Enrique Jardiel Poncela's *Eloísa está debajo de un almendro* (*Eloise Is Under an Almond Tree*), Steven Capsuto had to consider through-out the play what he would do with the final word: the insulting *pelagatos*. Ezequiel has been using stray cats in biological experiments; when Clotilde learns this at play's end, she calls him, literally, a 'cat skinner'. But *pelagatos* is a standard pejorative, referring to a poor wretch, someone of limited resources. The humour of the last word stems from the term being applied, unexpectedly, with its literal meaning. Capsuto creatively invented a non-existent insult based on an existing term:

CLOTILDE: (*Eyeing him with contempt.*) You … you … kitty slitter! (Jardiel Poncela, 1992: 102)[16]

In order to invent an equivalent in the target language, the translator needs to examine the text carefully to determine precisely how the word play functions. In Michael Frayn's *Benefactors*, Colin has started editing a women's encyclopaedia; other characters rattle off words he will have to define that start with F: fornication, fetishism, frigidity, foreplay, feminin-ity, fallopian tubes, father-figure, fun, foot fetishists (Frayn, 1994: 18–19).

Most likely some but not all of the corresponding terms will begin with the same letter in the target language; translating all of them literally will not work. The translator should choose the dominant letter, which may or may not be F, and then skim through the dictionary to find other, equivalent words, that share that initial and have related connotations.

Similar in challenge but more complicated are the word games Cuban-American playwright Matías Montes-Huidobro introduced in the final scene of his 1961 one-act play *El tiro por la culata* (*Backfire*). A clever young girl turns the tables on the lecherous landowner when he takes her to his house to teach her the ABCs. For each letter, he suggests words with positive or amorous connotations: A is for *'amigo, amistad, adoración ... y amor'*; B is for *'bueno, bondad, bello, bonito ... y beso y besito'*; C is for *'cama y cariño'* (Montes-Huidobro, 1991: 146–47). For starters, friend, friendship and love do not begin with A; kiss does not begin with B and bed does not begin with C. The translator is advised to use transposition as a strategy and the dictionary as a tool. The landowner might end up saying that A is for 'agreeable, affectionate, adoring ... and amorous'; B is for 'bright, beautiful, beneficial, bosom, and ... bed'; C is for 'covers and caress'. For each letter the girl provides numerous, alternate examples that emphasize the peasants' struggle against the upper class. Some of these – like abuse, agriculture, burro, and campesino – can be carried over virtually without change; others require transformations similar to those in the landowner's speeches.

Repetition is not usually included in the variations on word play discussed in translation manuals but it plays an important role in theatre, particularly in comedy. Repetition – of a simple gesture or an extended action, of a short expression or a passage of dialogue – has functioned for centuries as a stock comic device. Repetition of a word may also serve as a rhythmic device. In the passage from Pallín's *Luna de miel*, the author chose the particular expression 'quedarse conmigo' because it continues a repetitive pattern of the syllable 'que', meaning 'what':

ELLA.   ¿Qué?
ÉL.   ¿Qué de qué?
ELLA.   ¿Cómo que de qué?
ÉL.   ¿Te quieres quedar conmigo?

The challenge to the translator is to work in as many uses of 'what' as possible:

SHE: What?
HE: What about what?

SHE: What do you mean, about what?
HE: You kidding me or what?

Although we have already looked at some problematic play titles, in my list of questions for theatrical translators, I put title in last place. I did so both because the title may be the last matter to be resolved and because it is the most important item for marketing the play. Playwrights often have a series of working titles for a script in progress, so it is not surprising if theatrical translators do not immediately settle on a final answer. Would _Death of a Salesman_ have been a hit if Miller had stuck with his original title, _The Inside of His Head?_ If we envision a play title on a marquee, we can see why the title is more critical for a play than for a novel. If the play title is not attractive, our intended reader will never get to the opening pages of the script or, even if we find a willing director despite an unexciting, lengthy or awkward title, our potential spectator may decide against buying a ticket and entering the theatre.

Peter Newmark distinguishes between descriptive and allusive titles. The former 'describe the topic of the text' while the latter 'have some kind of referential or figurative relationship to the topic' (Newmark, 1988: 57). He recommends keeping descriptive titles of literary works, including ones that give the protagonist's name, and reworking allusive ones only if necessary.

Many titles carry over easily. Strindberg's _Fröken Julie_ is readily translated from Swedish to other languages: _Miss Julie, Fräulein Julie_ (Room, 1986: 171). Shaw's _Man and Superman_ transfers without problem: _Homme et surhomme, Uomo e superuomo_ (Room, 1986: 159). But titles in this form are sometimes deceptive. At first glance, Alonso de Santos's _La estanquera de Vallecas_ appears to be descriptive, but in fact the tragicomedy does not have a main character and, even if it did, there is no simple translation for the original title. I therefore dropped all reference to a female owner of a tobacco shop in a working-class neighbourhood on the outskirts of Madrid and created a new title, _Hostages in the Barrio. La posada del Arenal_, a pastiche of Golden Age farce by Eduardo Galán and Javier Garcimartín, has a nice ring to it in Spanish but 'The Inn on Arenal Street' would be pedestrian in English; translator Leonardo Mazzara creatively came up with _Inn Discretions._ The complete title of Salom's _El señor de las patrañas_ – a rollicking play about a Renaissance dramatist – would similarly be plodding in English; Gary Racz honed in on _patrañas_ and opted for _Rigmaroles._

When I translated Eduardo Manet's _Lady Strass_ from French to English, I left unchanged the original title, referring to a British character. I foolishly did not test it on anyone and therefore did not realize that

English speakers would not understand the allusion to the character's being a fraud. The word 'strass', meaning imitation gemstones, is found in English, French, and bilingual French-English dictionaries but, as a potential director in London alerted me, is low frequency in English. For the British staging, which never took place, he offered an allusive alternative: *The House of Dreams*. When *Lady Strass* was done in New York at Ubu Repertory, the theatre director and the director of the particular production, both native speakers of French, did not question the use of 'strass'. To aid the audience in catching the allusion, I added lines of dialogue that defined the word as meaning fake jewelry.

As a rule, a play title should not be left in a foreign language. Potential spectators will probably not understand what it means and may not realize that the production is in English. Holt, however, fought to keep *Las Meninas* as the title when his translation of Buero-Vallejo's play about Velázquez was published in 1987. The famous painting is known internationally as 'Las Meninas' not as 'the ladies in waiting' or 'the maids of honor' (quoted in Boyd, 1987: 6). The title thus points to the artist-protagonist and other characters; and it foreshadows the recreation on stage of the painting as a *tableau vivant*. When Michael Martorano gave the play its American premiere in New York City in 2000, he changed the title to *Velázquez*, obviously assuming that the painter had greater name recognition than his masterwork.

Titles that contain cultural references are particularly problematic. A noteworthy example is López Rubio's *Celos del aire*. The title refers inter-textually to Calderonian honour plays and, secondarily, to a popular song in the period preceding the comedy's 1950 premiere. On a Spanish marquee, it might correctly suggest to spectators that they were about to see a bourgeois comedy related to marital infidelity. For American audiences, 'Jealousy of the air' would suggest nothing. For his translation, Holt came up with the ingenious solution, *In August We Play the Pyrenees*, an allusion to a common summer stock expression, 'In August we play the Catskills'. The American title hints at the comedy's strong metathea-trical current and geographically places the action. The comedy has received multiple stagings, in various parts of the United States.

Comic titles also require major adaptation. Landers cites the adroit sol-utions that Norman R. Shapiro has created for farces by Georges Feydeau (Landers, 2001: 105). Adept at word play, Shapiro transforms Feydeau's *Un Fil à la patte* into *Not by Bed Alone* and *Dormez, je le veux!* into *Caught with His Trance Down*. He performs his magic as well on farces by Eugène Labiche: *La Main leste* becomes *A Slap in the Farce* and *La Lettre chargée, A Matter of Wife and Death*. Indeed Shapiro's titles are more likely to get a laugh than the originals.

The American stage leans heavily towards realism/naturalism. For that reason, allusive titles that are long and poetic require special thought, although there is no fixed rule against them. Playwright and translator Caridad Svich has had multiple stagings of her original plays with titles like these: *Alchemy of Desire/Dead-Man's Blues, Iphigenia Crash Land Falls on the Neon Shell That Was Once Her Heart*. Nevertheless, translator Bethany Korp was doubtless wise to negotiate a new title, *Killing Time*, for Beth Escudé i Gallès's *El color del gos quan fuig* – rather than using the literal translation of the Catalan expression: 'The colour of the fleeing dog'.

Adaptation is sometimes recommended for titles and often useful for handling such matters as dialect. It is almost always necessary for dealing with bilingual plays. Bilingualism on stage is such a complex matter that we devote the next chapter to its analysis.

Notes

1. I first translated Salom's *El otro William* in 1995; my revised, fourth translation was published in 2004. Salom's play initially called for one actress to double in three roles. In his second version, Salom expanded the cast; he gave me a copy and I carefully rewrote the translation. When the play premiered in 1998, the cast included three actresses and one of the female roles was expanded significantly because of the stature of the actress cast in the part. Salom marked for me the affected passages in the new version, which was published in the theatre journal *Primer Acto*. But he forgot to warn me that a later edition contained further revisions. An alert reader for University Press of Colorado noticed discrepancies between that 1998 Fundamentos edition and my translation. Salom confirmed that Fundamentos superseded *Primer Acto*.
2. For further discussion on translating the Daumas and Alonso de Santos plays, see my articles in *Translation Review* (Zatlin, 1998, 2002).
3. Peter Newmark defines over-translation as one 'that gives more detail' (1988: 284) and under-translation as one that 'gives less detail and is more general than the original' (1988: 285).
4. Unless otherwise indicated, opinions attributed to translators are drawn from their responses to my questionnaires.
5. I have at hand four volumes in this bilingual series. They contain a total of six plays and represent the work of seven translators, some of them working in pairs: Christilla Vasserot, Rosine Gars, Agnès Surbezy and Marcelo Lobera, Antoine Rodriguez, Patrice Pavis and Isabel Martin.
6. Some of these plays have been performed in Spain and in Mexico. For information on *Vale, cuéntamelo pero rapidito* (Okay, Tell Me About It, But Make it Quick . . .), a Madrid production directed by Jesús García Salgado in 2002 that clustered five of the plays, see my review in *Western European Stages* (Zatlin, 2002).
7. In his 1998 article, Johnston refers to his versions of plays by Valle-Inclán as translations. He later clarifies that his 'radical relocation of an Irish milieu' might best be labeled a 'transubstantiation' (2000: 85).
8. For a discussion of a modern staging of a Greek tragedy, see Michael Ewans, who contends that translators have a duty to help 'potential actors and

directors in their task of preparing to re-create the Greek experience in a modern production' (Evans, 1989: 122).

9. Maria Delgado relates that when she confronted a 'very colloquial Argentine dialect' she resorted to a 'kind of cockney idiom' in her English translation. Henry Thorau cites the difficulties presented by the dialect of black characters in Brazilian plays. David Tushingham gives a range of problems to be confronted: 'wordplay, puns, invented language, combinations of different dialects, juxtapositions of contrasting social and ethnic groups'.

10. I have used the first page of Pallín's play in my translation class at Rutgers and in translation workshops at conferences of the American Translators Association (November 2003) and Florida International University (February 2004). The expression *quedarse con* is invariably translated incorrectly by all native speakers of Spanish – except Spaniards. By the same token, 'to take the mickey out of somebody', the British translation provided in the Collins Spanish-English dictionary, would be incomprehensible to Americans.

11. In his groundbreaking *Introducción a la traductología*, Gerardo Vázquez-Ayora (1977: 8–16) devotes several pages to the analysis of lexical units as a preliminary step to dividing sentences for translation. Peter Newmark (1988: 285) believes that the unit of translation should be 'as small as is possible and as large as is necessary'.

12. Two potential gaffs with quotations from Shakespeare come to mind. An anonymous reader for University Press of Colorado apparently did not recognize a passage from *Othello* and carefully rewrote my quotation from the Bard to make it closer to Salom's Spanish wording. In the draft of her translation of a Cuban play, one of our Rutgers masters candidates failed to recognize the Spanish version of the 'Life's but a walking shadow' speech from *Macbeth* and initially put it in her own words.

13. For a helpful commentary on varieties of metaphor and how to approach them, see Newmark (1988: 104–13).

14. Children's plays, even modern ones, are often written in verse and therefore require special skills, like those of Carys Evans-Corrales who rendered two volumes of plays for young audiences for the ESTRENO Plays collection.

15. Hervey, Higgins and Haywood provide a detailed explanation of various compensation strategies in *Thinking Spanish Translation:* compensation in kind, in place, by merging, by splitting (Hervey *et al.*, 1995: 27–32). Hervey and Higgins are also authors of a parallel text on French translation.

16. I chose Capsuto's ingenious 'kitty slitter' for a 1994 article in *Translation Review* (Zatlin, 1994). A literal-minded proofreader for the journal thought she had found a typo and, without consulting me, changed the quoted expression to 'kitty litter'. I hope that some of readers of that article find the clarification here for their bewilderment then.

References

Aaltonen, S. *Time-Sharing on Stage. Drama Translation in Theatre and Society.* Clevedon: Multilingual Matters, Topics in Translation 17, 2000.

Alonso de Santos, J. L. *La estanquera de Vallecas.* Madrid: La Avispa, 1982.

Alonso de Santos, J. L. *Bajarse al moro.* Madrid: Instituto de Cooperación Iberoamericana, 1985.

Alonso de Santos, J. L. *Going Down to Marrakesh* (trans. P. Zatlin). In P. W. O'Connor, ed., *Plays of the New Democratic Spain (1975–1990)*, 1992, 313–79.

Alonso de Santos, J. L. *Hostages in the Barrio* (trans. P. Zatlin). University Park PA: ESTRENO, 1997a.

Alonso de Santos, J. L. *Descente au Maroc* (trans. F. Bonfils and C. Lepage). Tours: Presses de la Sorbonne Nouvelle, 1997b.

Alonso de Santos, J. L. *L'Album de famille* (trans. H. Paviot). Martel: Les Éditions du Laquet, 2003.

Art Teatral (Valencia, Spain). 8 (1996). Special issue featuring twelve plays from Actors Theatre of Louisville. Guest editors: R. Cornish, M. Bigelow Dixon, and P. Zatlin.

Aufgefahren, by Ernesto Caballero. Stadttheater Giessen. Dir. Henri Hohenemser, 21 September 2003. German translator's name not listed on programme.

Ball, D. 'Translating Wild and Crazy Texts: Jarry and Picasso.' In session 'From the Classics to the Tango: Theatrical Translation in Action.' Conference of American Literary Translators Association, Chicago, 19 October 2002.

Bassnett-McGuire, S. *Translation Studies*. London and New York: Methuen, 1980.

Boehm, P. Some pitfalls of translating drama. *Translation Review* 62 (2001): 27–29.

Boyd, L. A. and Boyd, G. N. The translator's voice: An interview with Marion Peter Holt. *Translation Review* 23 (1987): 3–7.

Buero-Vallejo, A. *Historia de una escalera. Las Meninas*, 26th ed. Madrid: Espasa Calpe, Colección Austral, 1997.

Buero-Vallejo, A. *Las Meninas. A Fantasia in Two Parts* (trans. M. P. Holt). San Antonio: Trinity University Press, 1987.

Caballero, E. *Auto. Rehen.* Madrid: Sociedad General de Autores de España, 1994.

Cary, E. (adopted name of Cyrille Znosko-Borovski, died 1966). *Comment faut-il traduire?* Introduction Michel Ballard. Presses Universitaires de Lille, 1986.

Christ, R. Videotaped presentation as guest speaker in Theory and Practice of Translation class. Rutgers, The State University of New Jersey, 29 November 1990.

Corrigan, R. W. Translating for actors. In W. Arrowsmith and R. Shattuck, eds, *The Craft & Context of Translation*. Austin: University of Texas Press (for Humanities Research Center), 1961, 95–106.

Cypess, S. M. Titles as signs in the translation of dramatic texts. In M. G. Rose, ed., *Translation Perspectives II. Selected Papers, 1984–85*. Binghamton, NY: National Resource Center for Translation and Interpretation, 1985, 95–104.

Daumas, J.-P. *The Elephant Graveyard* (trans. P. Zatlin). *Modern International Drama* 28.1 (1994): 5–48.

Edney, D. Molière in North America: Problems of translation and adaptation. *Modern Drama* 41.1 (Spring 1998): 60–76.

Edwards, G. Lorca on the English stage: Problems of production and translation. *New Theatre Quarterly* 4.16 (November 1988): 344–55.

Ewans, M. Aischylos: For actors, in the round. In R. Warren, ed., *The Art of Translation. Voices from the Field*. Boston: Northeastern University Press, 1989, 120–39.

Findlay, B. Translating into dialect. In D. Johnston, ed., *Stages of Translation*, 1996, 199–217.

Formosa, F. Teatro y traducción. *Quimera* 213 (March 2002): 41–50.

Frayn, M. *Plays: Two. Benefactors. Balmoral. Wild Honey,* 2nd ed. London: Methuen, 1994.

García Lorenzo, L., ed. *Traducir a los clásicos.* Cuadernos de Teatro Clasico 4. Madrid: Ministerio de Cultura, Instituto Nacional de los Artes Escénicos y de la Música, 1989.

Gitlitz, D. Confesiones de un traductor. In L. García Lorenzo, ed., *Traducir a los clásicos,* 1989, 45–52.

Gostand, R. Verbal and non-verbal communication: Drama as translation. In O. Zuber, ed., *The Languages of Theatre. Problems in the Translation and Transposition of Drama,* 1980, 1–9.

Granada. English lyrics by Dorothy Dodd. Music by Augustin Lara. Copyright 1932, renewed 1959 by Peer International Corporation.

Hale, T. and Upton, C.-A. Introduction to Carole-Anne Upton, ed., *Moving Target. Theatre Translation and Cultural Relocation,* 2000, 1–13.

Hervey, S., Higgins, I. and Haywood, L. M. *Thinking Spanish Translation. A Course in Translation Method: Spanish to English.* London and New York: Routledge, 1995.

Holledge, J. and Tompkins, J. *Women's Intercultural Performance.* London and New York: Routledge, 2000.

Holt, M. P. Personal letter, 4 December 1995.

Jardiel Poncela, E. *Eloise Is Under an Almond Tree* (trans. S. M. Capsuto). In P. W. O'Connor, ed., *Plays of the New Democratic Spain (1975–1990),* 1992, 1–102.

Johnston, D. ed. *Stages of Translation.* Bath, England: Absolute Classics, 1996.

Johnston, D. Valle-Inclán: The Mirroring of Esperpento. *Modern Drama* 41.1 (Spring 1998): 30–48.

Johnston, D. Valle-Inclán: The Meaning of Form. In C.-A. Upton, ed., *Moving Target. Theatre Translation and Cultural Relocation,* 2000, 85–99.

Landers, C. E. *Literary Translation. A Practical Guide.* Clevedon, Buffalo, Toronto and Sydney: Multilingual Matters, Topics in Translation 22, 2001.

Lefevere, A. *Translating Literature. Practice and Theory in a Comparative Literature Context.* New York: The Modern Language Association, 1992.

Link, F. H. Translation, adaptation and interpretation of dramatic texts. In O. Zuber, ed., *The Languages of Theatre. Problems in the Translation and Transposition of Drama,* 1980, 24–50.

Magruder, J. Panel discussion on translating for the theater. 22nd Annual Conference of the American Literary Translators Association, 22 October 1999. New York City.

McGaha, M. Hacia la traducción representable. In L. García Lorenzo, ed., *Traducir a los clásicos,* 1989, 79–86.

Miller, A. *Death of a Salesman.* New York: Penguin Books, 1976.

Miller, A. *La muerte de un viajante* (trans. J. López Rubio). Madrid: Ediciones MK, 1983.

monólogos de la vagina, Los. By Eve Ensler. Adapted by Victor Cremer. Arlequín Theatre, Madrid, 29 May 2002. Dir. Antonia García.

Montes-Huidobro, M. *El tiro por la culata. Obras en un acto.* Honolulu: Editorial Persona, 1991, 131–48.

My Fair Lady. Dir. George Cukor. 1964. 1998 Warner Home Video. Soundtracks in English and French.

My Fair Lady. By Alan Jay Lerner and Frederick Loewe. Adapted by Ignacio Artime and Jaime Azpilicueta. Dir. Jaime Azpilicueta. Coliseum, Madrid, 20 March 2003.

Newmark, P. *A Textbook of Translation.* New York and London: Prentice Hall, 1988.

Nowra, L. Translating for the Australian stage (a personal viewpoint). In O. Zuber-Skerritt, ed., *Page to Stage. Theatre as Translation,* 1984, 13–21.

O'Connor, P. W., ed. *Plays of the New Democratic Spain (1975–1990).* Lanham, Maryland, and London: University Press of America, 1992.

Pallín, Y. *Luna de miel. Estreno* 26.1 (2000): 25–32.

Pavis, P. Problems of translation for the stage: interculturalism and post-modern theatre (trans. L. Kruger). In H. Scolnicov and P. Holland, eds, *The Play Out of Context. Transferring Plays from Culture to Culture,* 1989, 25–44.

Perteghella, M. Language and politics on stage: Strategies for translating dialect and slang with references to Shaw's *Pygmalion* and Bond's *Saved. Translation Review* 64 (2002): 45–53.

Pujante, A.-L. Traducir al teatro isabelino, especialmente Shakespeare. In L. García Lorenzo, ed., *Traducir a los clásicos,* 1989, 133–57.

Pulvers, R. Moving others: The translation of drama. In O. Zuber-Skerritt, ed., *Page to Stage. Theatre as Translation,* 1984, 23–28.

Reid, I. Hazards of adaptation: Anouilh's *Antigone* in English. In O. Zuber, ed., *The Languages of Theatre. Problems in the Translation and Transposition of Drama,* 1980, 82–91.

Room, A. *Dictionary of Translated Names and Titles.* London, Boston and Henley: Routledge & Kegan Paul, 1986.

Santoyo, J. C. Traducciones y adaptaciones teatrales: ensayo de tipología. In L. García Lorenzo, ed., *Traducir a los clásicos,* 1989, 95–112.

Schmidt, P. Translating Chekhov all over again. *Dramatists Guild Quarterly* 33.4 (Winter 1997): 18–23.

Schultze, B. Highways, byways, and blind alleys in translating drama: Historical and systematic aspects of a cultural technique. In K. Mueller-Vollmer and M. Irmscher, eds, *Translating Literatures. Translating Cultures. New Vistas and Approaches in Literary Studies.* Berlin: Erich Schmidt Verlag, 1998, 177–96.

Scolnicov, H. and Holland, P. eds. *The Play Out of Context. Transferring Plays from Culture to Culture.* Cambridge and New York: Cambridge University Press, 1989.

Shaked, G. The play: gateway to cultural dialogue. (trans. J. Green). In H. Scolnicov and P. Holland, eds, *The Play Out of Context. Transferring Plays from Culture to Culture,* 1989, 7–24.

Spencer, D. You are what you submit. Script formatting for competitions and other professional considerations. *The Dramatist* 6.4 (March/April 2003): 20–25.

Thomas, A. Introduction. In special issue on translation. *Modern Drama* 41.1 (1998): 1–6.

Upton, C.-A., ed. *Moving Target. Theatre Translation and Cultural Relocation.* Manchester, UK & Northampton, MA: St. Jerome Publishing, 2000.

Vázquez-Ayora, G. *Introducción a la traductología.* Washington, DC: Georgetown University Press, 1977.

Venneberg, U. Problems in translating Sean O'Casey's drama *Juno and the Paycock* into German. In O. Zuber, ed., *The Languages of Theatre. Problems in the Translation and Transposition of Drama,* 1980, 121–31.

Von Flotow, L. *Translation and Gender. Translating in the 'Era of Feminism'.* Manchester: St. Jerome Publishing & Ottawa: University of Ottawa Press, 1997.

Wellwarth, G. E. Special considerations in drama translation. In M. G. Rose, ed., *Translation Spectrum. Essays in Theory and Practice.* Albany: State University of New York Press, 1981. 140–46.

Winter, I. E-mail, 5 April 2004.

Zatlin, P. Observations on theatrical translation. *Translation Review* 46 (1994): 14–18.

Zatlin, P. From Vallecas to Hialeah: Translating Alonso de Santos's Spaniards into Cubans. *Translation Review* 56 (1998): 32–35.

Zatlin, P. From Louisville to Madrid: An anthology of five ten-minute plays. *Western European Stages* 14.3 (Fall 2002a): 123–24.

Zatlin, P. On translating *Le Cimetière des éléphants* by Jean-Paul Daumas. *Translation Review* 64 (2002b): 31–35.

Zuber, O., ed. *The Languages of Theatre. Problems in the Translation and Transposition of Drama.* Oxford and New York: Pergamon Press, 1980.

Zuber-Skerritt, O., ed. *Page to Stage. Theatre as Translation.* Amsterdam: Rodopi, 1984.

Chapter 5
Variations on the Bilingual Play Text

Theatrical translation poses special difficulties because of the desire to make the oral text readily accessible to the target audience. These difficulties may be compounded when the source text is bilingual or multilingual. Spectators of the original production may have competency in a second language that is not understood by the target audience; or if that second language is English, the bilingual component will disappear in an English translation that does not compensate. There is a wide range of possibilities in the creation of bilingual plays that in turn require varying translation strategies. At one end of the spectrum are scripts with characters who ostensibly speak different languages although the texts are written entirely in the language of the spectators. At the opposite end are works written in two languages without any expectation that spectators will understand both. Between these two extremes, which may require relatively little modification on the translator's part, there are numerous levels of linguistic games that the potential translator needs to address with imagination.

Two illustrations of monolingual plays with bilingual characters are José Rivera's *The House of Ramón Iglesias* (1982) and Ignacio del Moral's *La mirada del hombre oscuro* (1991). The family in Rivera's play are Puerto Ricans living near New York City. The protagonist, Javier, has rejected Puerto Rican cultural values – including bilingualism – as inferior.[1] The action in Del Moral's work takes place on an isolated beach in Spain where a comically racist Spanish family discovers two Africans, one dead and one alive, who have washed ashore. Ombasi knows only a few words of Spanish and his dead friend, who also has a speaking role, apparently knows none.

Rivera, writing for a mainstream American audience, deliberately avoids the use of Spanish on stage. Javier's mother speaks only Spanish *'although we hear her words in English. Characters who do not speak Spanish cannot understand her'* (Rivera, 1987: 197). Other characters, whether they understand her or not, speak English. The stage direction,

'*It should be clear that Dolores is speaking in Spanish throughout the play*' (Rivera, 1987: 197) places the responsibility on the actors, through the use of such signs as gestures and facial expressions, to convey the sense of bilingualism without actually using two languages. Neither translator nor spectators need make special efforts. In a situation like this, Susan Bassnett's advice to theatrical translators is apropos:

> Once we accept that the written text is not fundamental to performance but is merely one element in an eventual performance, then this means that the translator, like the writer, need not be concerned with how that written text is going to integrate into the other sign systems. That is a task for the director and the actors and serves again to underline the fact that theatre is a collaborative process in which not only are different sign systems involved, but a host of different people with different skills. (Bassnett & Lefevere, 1998: 99)

The approach in *La mirada del hombre oscuro* is essentially the same as Rivera's. While the latter – as a bilingual living in a country where there are millions of Spanish-speaking residents and Hispanics are now the largest minority group – might have assumed that at least some of his spectators would, in fact, have understood some Spanish, del Moral could make no such assumption in Spain about audience familiarity with African languages. The other actors must therefore react to Ombasi's Spanish lines as if they were incomprehensible. Repeatedly interspersed for comic effect in his lines directed to the family are the one word and two names in Spanish that he does know: '¡*Viva España*! ¡*Butragueño*!' In the original text, Ombasi's Spanish is set off by italics and, according to the stage directions, are to contrast with his fluent native language by being pronounced '*con un acento endiablado*' (del Moral, 1992: 15).

In *Dark Man's Gaze*, Jartu Toles's translation of *La mirada del hombre oscuro*, the pseudo-bilingualism was easily resolved (del Moral, 1999). All Spanish simply became all English and the responsibility for conveying lack of cultural and linguistic understanding remains with the actors. On the other hand, the reference to Butragueño did pose a problem. The translator opted to change this soccer figure to a Spanish tennis player who might be better known to American audiences. In his terrible accent, Ombasi thus repeatedly says, '*Sánchez Vicario*!' Now that Arantza Sánchez Vicario has retired from competition, a director staging the play in English may well feel obliged to revise the name to that of the best known Spanish sports star of the moment.

Far removed from the Rivera and del Moral texts are plays specifically written for a bilingual audience. An excellent illustration is Dolores Prida's *Coser y cantar* (first staged in 1981), 'A One-Act Bilingual Fantasy for Two Women'. The Cuban-American author states in an important prefatory note: 'This play is really one long monologue. The two women are one and are playing a verbal, emotional game of ping pong'. Prida strongly affirms that the 'play must NEVER be performed in just one language' (Prida, 1991: 49). According to Patricia González, Prida's protagonist exemplifies what Gustavo Pérez-Firmat calls a cultural Siamese: 'neither here nor there but simultaneously coexisting in both places' (quoted in González, 2002: 84). González believes that *Coser y cantar* is the first play to reflect this hybrid reality and that 'She/Ella, with her ordinary simplicity, schematic clichés, and cultural complexities, continues to be the best and most tangible theatrical example of life on the hyphen' (2002: 84).

In essence, the roles in this two-actor play – 'ELLA, una mujer' and 'SHE, the same woman' (Prida, 1991: 49) – are not so much a divided self as the two complementary halves of the character. Each speaks in her language of preference, reflects the culture associated with that language, and, throughout most of the action, pretends that the other character does not exist. Sometimes a speech may provide a translation of the previous one or at least partially clarify its content in the other language:

SHE: (*SHE goes to her dressing table, sits down, takes pen and paper.*) I'll make a list of all the things I must do. Let's see. I should start from the inside ... Number one, clean the house ...

ELLA: (*Still eating*) Uno, limpiar la casa.

SHE: Two, take the garbage out.

ELLA: Dos, sacar la basura.

SHE: Then, do outside things. After running, I have to do something about El Salvador.

ELLA: Salvar a El Salvador. (Prida, 1991: 52)

The final line does not give a complete rendering of SHE's previous comment but rather puns on the underlying meaning in the name of the Central American country: To save The Saviour. The humour, as well as the full content of this chunk of dialogue, would be lost on a monolingual speaker of English.

Typically in *Coser y cantar*, there is no connection between a line of dialogue and the one that follows. The opening speeches, in which SHE totally ignores ELLA's exasperation at being interrupted, provide an example:

ELLA: (*With contained exasperation.*) ¿Por qué haces eso? ¡Sabes que no me gusta que hagas eso! Detesto que me interrumpas así. ¡Yo no te interrumpo cuando tú te imaginas que eres Barbra Streisand!

SHE: (*To herself, looking for her watch.*) What time is it? (*Finds watch.*) My God, twelve thirty! The day half-gone and I haven't done a thing ... (Prida, 1991: 51)

Prida's strong initial statement suggests that she would never approve a translation that removed the intentional bilingualism. ELLA is so obviously Hispanic that only a free adaptation that radically altered her national identity would permit a change from the Spanish that characterizes her, but the play, retaining Spanish as one of the languages, might work in France or some other country that has a substantial number of Latin American immigrants.[2]

The assumption that underscores Prida's more or less equal use of two languages is that her audience will understand both. This is the case with many works of Latino theatre in the United States that incorporate code-switching, as characters move seamlessly from English to Spanish and back again.[3] In his analysis of Chicano playwright Rodrigo Duarte Clark's frequently staged but unpublished monologue *Doña Rosita's Jalupeño Kitchen* (1994), Eduardo Cabrera provides excellent examples of this strategy. Worried that a developer wants to take over the neighbourhood, Doña Rosita debates whether she should sell her restaurant: 'They're taking Salsipuedes from us and like a pendeja I'm packing' (quoted in Cabrera, 2002: 70). The image of heaven that she evokes in a dream is an Anglo-Saxon white space, but her Saint Peter is a code-switching bilingual: 'Tú eres católica mujer; your husband who you married through the Church is still your husband. You may not remarry. Nunca' (quoted in Cabrera, 2002: 72).

Were *Doña Rosita's Jalapeño Kitchen* to be translated, code-switching to Spanish would be essential to retain the original play's flavour. In this respect, Saint Peter's speech in the above example poses no difficulties. If changes were considered necessary for an audience that does not understand Spanish, the addition of just two words would fully clarify the message: <u>Catholic</u> Church, <u>never</u> remarry. Doña Rosita's line is more problematic. In Spanish the name Salsipuedes, like El Salvador, has an underlying meaning: Get Out If You Can. The translator will have to decide what, if any, special efforts must be made to convey that double meaning. When Doña Rosita calls herself a dummy, 'pendeja', her choice of term reflects her Mexican roots and therefore cannot be replaced by *estúpida* or *tonta* – words that might be understood more readily by an audience of limited Spanish – unless the loss of Chicano identity in compensated for elsewhere in the script.

In plays like *Coser y cantar* and *Doña Rosita's Jalapeño Kitchen*, a substantial proportion of the dialogue is in Spanish. By contrast, in Miguel González-Pando's *The Great American Justice Game* (1987) English predominates but Spanish is introduced briefly near the end of the play. The Cuban-American playwright satirizes the conservative, intolerant English Only movement in the United States by imagining a law that carries the prohibition on use of Spanish to the extreme; he then substitutes a game show format for a trial. When the teen-age protagonist (María) wakes up and realizes that the grotesque courtroom scene was only a dream, she and her mother (Liberty) communicate through code-switching:

> **LIBERTY**: Mi amor, estamos en América! That could never happen here ... You know? It was just a bad nightmare ... Ven, déjame darte un beso. (*They embrace.*) ...
>
> **MARIA**: Mamá, qué bueno que somos americanos! I am so proud to be an American! (González-Pando, 1992: 107)

Spectators will not need to know Spanish to understand these few lines, which use relatively easy language and are adequately clarified by the characters. The potential translator would leave them in Spanish.

Unlike Prida or Duarte Clark, the Spanish playwright Juan Mayorga had no expectation that his audience would understand German, the second language he introduced in his two-character *El traductor de Blumemberg*. He has stated that for him the ideal spectator will not speak German. The actor playing Calderón has the responsibility of conveying the meaning of Blumemberg's fluent German lines through gestures and actions that clarify the context. The spectator then must fill in the blanks. Mayorga suggests that the strategy is similar to that of a telephone conversation within a monologue: the spectator hears only one side of the conversation but yet grasps what has been said on the other end of the line (Mayorga, personal interview, 2000).

The original version of *El traductor de Blumemberg* was given a professional staged reading in Madrid in March 1994. It did not receive its first full production until August 2000, in Buenos Aires.[4] Mayorga recalls that the Spanish audience did not have trouble following the text even without understanding German; the real problem in Spain is finding a cooperative actor who can deliver authentic German pronunciation with ease. That actor must also create Blumemberg's accent in Spanish: Argentine pronunciation with a German flavour.

The character Blumemberg is a philosopher whose anti-Semitic, racist ideas supposedly influenced Hitler, the only reader of his last book. After years of exile in Argentina, Blumemberg has returned to Europe where Calderón has been hired by the unseen Silesius to translate the lost book to Castilian Spanish. In Argentina, where both Jews and Nazis sought refuge before or after the Second World War, one can assume that more members of the audience than in Spain would be Spanish-German bilinguals. The role of Blumemberg was played by the German-Jewish-Argentine actor Rubén Schumacher.[5]

In *El traductor de Blumemberg*, Mayorga uses three strategies with respect to the lines in German and, to a lesser extent, in French. (In the opening scene, where the German writer and his Spanish translator meet on a train, Blumemberg is disguised as a blind French toy salesman.) For some expressions in the foreign language, the other character provides an immediate, consecutive interpretation, usually delivered as a question. For example, to Blumemberg's 'Travail', Calderón thus responds '¿Trabajo?' (Mayorga, 1993: 3); to the former's 'Noch night', Calderón's rejoinder is '¿Todavía no?' (1993: 27). At other times, the action clarifies the meaning. Such is the case in the first scene in the train:

CALDERÓN: Pues no estamos con luz eléctrica pudiendo ... (*Descorre la cortina de la ventana.*)
BLUMEMBERG: (*Reaccionando al ruido de la cortina.*) J'aime mieux la laisser comme ça.
CALDERÓN: (*Corriendo la cortina.*) Perdón, perdón. Claro, por los ojos. (Mayorga, 1993: 2)

Spectators who do not understand Blumemberg's line in French will know when Calderón closes the curtain immediately that the other man complained when he opened it to let in some light.

On the other hand, *El traductor de Blumemberg* includes some passages in German that are never directly clarified for the benefit of spectators who do not understand them. Sometimes these lines can be guessed from context but at other moments, like these when Blumemberg is dictating from the book that now exists only in his mind, no effort is made to explain. Calderón merely keeps typing.

BLUMEMBERG: Die Idee der Repräsentation ist ... von dem Gedanken persönlicher Autorität ... beherrscht. (*Calderón teclea.*)

BLUMEMBERG: Repräsentieren ... kann   nur   eine   Person ... und
              zwar ... (*Calderón teclea.*)
BLUMEMBERG: ... eine autoritäre Person ... oder eine Idee die ...
              (*Calderón teclea.*) (Mayorga, 1993: 35)

This silence does not mean that the content of Blumemberg's book is
insignificant. One main theme of the play is fascism and, by implication,
the menace of neo-Nazism in Spain as elsewhere. Through Calderón's
translation, the mysterious Silesius wants to disseminate Blumemberg's
appalling ideas to new readers.

From the perspective of translation studies, the other main theme of
Mayorga's text is of special interest. It provides an on-going discussion
of the author–translator relationship and the process of translation.
Blumemberg wishes to control Calderón entirely, but gradually Calderón
usurps the text with the intention of destroying it to protect the children
who might be affected by its venom. The dialogue relating to translation
ranges from this broad, ethical question to specifics on how to approach the
source text. The translator is understandably upset when he learns that
he will not be able to read the book in its entirety before beginning his work.

BLUMEMBERG: 'Der Feind ist unsere einzige Frage als Gestalt.'
CALDERÓN: ¿Perdón?
BLUMEMBERG: Der ersten Satz.
CALDERÓN: ¿La primera frase?
BLUMEMBERG: Es wird so gemacht werden: Satz für Satz.
CALDERÓN: Acostumbro leer el libro entero antes de traducir
              una pala ...

Blumemberg cuts him off. This translation will be done sentence by
sentence as the author dictates his book from memory.

Mayorga has marked clearly the path to be taken by any translator of
his play. The German, like the brief passages of French, should be retained
in the original language; the translator's task is thus limited to the
Spanish. Whether British or American audiences would be as receptive
to this kind of bilingual game as Argentine and Spanish audiences have
been is debatable.

In this respect, David Edney's commentary on late 20th-century
experiments in bilingual theatre in Canada are of interest. Asserting that
translation is not always necessary, he relates collaborating in a bilingual
production of Molière's *Les Fourberies de Scapin*, 'in which unilingual
spectators from both language groups were unable to understand part
of what was being said' (Edney, 1996; 234). Similarly, David Fennario's

Balconville, which features four Francophone and four Anglophone characters whose households have adjacent balconies, has been staged with no attempt to render dialogue in either language intelligible to monolingual speakers of the other: Fennario's text has been performed, without spectator complaints, in English Canada and in Great Britain (Edney, 1996: 235).

Since 1979, following the success of the experiment with *Balconville*, Edney reports that there have been other bilingual and multilingual productions in Canada: 'Robert Lepage has used not only French and English in his plays, but also other languages such as German, Chinese and Mohawk' (Edney, 1996: 235), and La Troupe du Jour, a French-language company in the predominantly English-speaking city of Saskatoon, has mounted several bilingual plays. For Molière's *Scapin*, the effect of the linguistic games was farcical, but at other times the Saskatoon company's intent has been serious, political commentary. *Romeo & Juliette*, in which the Capulets are Francophone and the Montagues are Anglophone, reflects the potentially tragic results of Canadian duality and its clash of cultures. In the case of these classic works, we may speak of free adaptations, involving some translation, rather than theatrical translation per se.

Another interesting example of a monolingual play being turned into a bilingual one is that of Samuel Beckett's *Waiting for Godot*. Shoshana Weitz discusses an Arab-Israeli version of the play that premiered in the municipal theatre of Haifa in May 1985. Spectators for the original production generally understood both languages. Vladimir and Estragon were portrayed as two Arab construction workers. Master Pozzo, on the other hand, spoke Hebrew. A survey of audience reaction revealed that Arab spectators tended to give the play a concrete political meaning while Jews were inclined to see Beckett's classic piece from the theatre of the absurd as far more abstract.

With reference to staging the bilingual text of Molière's *Scapin* in Canada, Edney describes an array of techniques, some of which we have already noted in Prida's *Coser y cantar* and Mayorga's *El traductor de Blumemberg*. When 'languages are used in alternation, a speaker sometimes repeats in translation the words just spoken while answering or commenting on them in the other language' (Edney, 1996: 236). Without breaking psychological realism, English explanations were interpolated into the original French text. For example:

ARGANTE: (*thinking he is alone*) *'Je voudrais savoir ce qu'ils me pourront dire sur ce beau mariage.'*
SCAPIN: (*aside*) We've thought of something <u>to say about this fine marriage</u>. (Edney, 1996: 236)

Edney clarifies that the company also developed two overt, theatricalist techniques for doubling: 'the instant replay and the action loop' (Edney, 1996: 237). In the former case, the actors freeze, back up to their previous location, and replay the passage in the other language. In the second case, the strategy is less opaque. The actors move naturally to the previous location and repeat, in the other language, without a break.

The experimentation in Europe of Cuban-French playwright Eduardo Manet is somewhat related to the strategies defined by Edney for bilingual theatre in Canada. Like Prida, Manet was born in Cuba, has lived in exile for most of his life, and writes primarily in his second language. No doubt because of his own divided self, he typically plays bilingual, bicultural games in his theatre. Like Mayorga, Manet often focuses directly on the role of translator or interpreter. In his _Monsieur Lovestar et son voisin de palier_ (1995), one of the two characters is a haughty literary translator and the other is a Portuguese labourer who seeks help in converting his 52-page love letter to poetic French. The unlikely and often humourous confrontation between the author of the source text and his unwilling translator leads initially to a verbal sparring match and a threat of violence.

In his boisterous, Brechtian farce, _Un Balcon sur les Andes_ (1979), Manet creates a troupe of actors who, as political refugees from France in the 19th century, escape to Latin America. In the early scenes, they do not yet speak Spanish and therefore perform in French. A spectator volunteers his services and provides a running simultaneous interpretation for the benefit of the Spanish-speaking audience. Gradually the actors become bilingual performers. The meaning of the Spanish lines, provided for the fictional audience's benefit, will be clear to the real French-speaking audience but will be played for comic effect.

In another of Manet's metatheatrical farces, _L'Autre Don Juan_ (1974), French actors are performing a translation of Juan Ruiz de Alarcón's Golden Age comedy, _Las paredes oyen_. Ignoring time and space, the character Alarcón is acting with the troupe. Outraged by the director's changes in the staging of his text, he begins delivering his lines in the original Spanish. The desperate director intervenes with consecutive and then simultaneous interpretation to French.

The French translation of the 17th-century play embedded in the modern text is Manet's own, faithful rendering. At the same time, he parodies the deliberate distortion that is sometimes introduced in crosscultural productions, ostensibly for box-office appeal. Thus he highlights his fictional director's outrageous introduction of cross-gender casting, erotic gestures and a bull-fighting scene. Were an American or British translator to tackle *L'Autre Don Juan*, the text's use of Spanish should remain in Spanish and the French would become English. The most difficult problem would be translating Alarcón's Golden Age verse drama.

Another extended use of multilingual games is present in Manet's *Lady Strass* (1977). The action takes place in Belize. His three characters are Bertrand, a middle-aged Frenchman; Manuel, a young Guatemalan; and Mrs Eliane Parkington Simpson, an elderly Englishwoman. The two men are would-be thieves who break into an apparently abandoned house, whose reclusive owner greets them with drawn shotgun. She is seated above them on a balcony, and they are trapped on the stage below that in grander times was used for amateur theatricals. The original text is written dominantly in French but with a fairly steady stream of English and Spanish expressions. Spanish is characteristically used for interjections and obscenities.

One may theorize that bilingual authors, like Duarte Clark, Prida and Manet, use both languages in their texts as a way of expressing their own divided self. In his analysis of the protagonist's flexible speech in *Doña Rosita's Jalapeño Kitchen*, Cabrera points out that the character switches to Spanish for references to food and her own culture 'and when she does a transition from one emotional state to another' (Cabrera, 2002: 73). In that respect, Manet's character Manuel Sierra may speak for his author. The Guatemalan is a native speaker of Spanish who must communicate in French. Spanish comes through when he is most puzzled or upset or hostile. An example is the dialogue in the opening scene, when the two men are breaking into the home of the eccentric British lady:

> **VOIX DE MANUEL:**   Tu es là, alors saute, <u>cojones</u>. Il pleut des cordes, je vais attraper la crève! (L'Avant-Scène Théâtre: 10; underline is mine)

Or, when they first hear the voice of Eliane, who issues her warning in three languages:

> **VOIX D'ÉLIANE:**   Don't move! Ne bougez pas! No se muevan! You are under surveillance! Estais siendo vigilados!
> **MANUEL:**   Qu'arrive-t'il, <u>madre de Dios</u>? (L'Avant-Scène Théâtre: 10)

My favourite example comes when Bertrand and Manuel discover that they are trapped inside the house:

> **MANUEL:**   Puta y reputa de la chingada de su madre! (L'Avant-Scène Théâtre: 14)

As translator of *Lady Strass*, my inclination was to leave Spanish expressions in Spanish and incorporate French expressions of comparable register but with slightly reduced frequency to compensate for the loss of English expressions within the original French text. That is the approach I took in the first published version of my translation (Manet, 1992). However, when the play was scheduled for staging at Ubu Repertory Theater in New York City, Ubu's artistic director, Françoise Kourilsky, requested that I delete all uses of Spanish and French. The now defunct Ubu Repertory, which for many years specialized in staging French and Francophone plays in translation, had a firm policy of English and English only. With respect to Manet's deliberately multilingual text, the policy resulted in a kind of acculturation.[6] Fortunately, from my point of view, play director André Ernotte, aided by bilingual actor Robert Jimenez in the role of Manuel, recommended a compromise. I was to leave the French out but could put back some Spanish (see revised translation, Manet, 1997). In performance the 'puta y reputa' line evoked loud laughter, thus putting the audience in the proper mood for the comic aspects of the tragicomedy. To my knowledge, there were no complaints in New York City about the few expressions delivered in Spanish comparable to the criticism Marcos Martínez has reported from his 1998 production of Rudolfo Anaya's *¡Ay Compadre!* in Los Angeles (Martínez, 2002: 26).[7]

It should be noted that the use of expressions in foreign languages or limited dialogue in dialect not only may be used more or less seriously to establish a character's identity but has long been a convention in comedy, for the purpose of evoking laughter. As far back as the 16th century, Spanish playwrights Torres Naharro and Lope de Rueda frequently incorporated different languages and dialects into their works for humourous effect. In plays using this device, at times the speaker is intended to be a caricature, a comic figure typical of farce. At other times, if some characters within the play do not understand the speaker but the spectators do, the result will be comic irony. US Latino theatre has been introducing such bilingual games for decades.

Even the passing use of foreign words can create headaches for the translator, particularly if that second language is the translator's target language. Two interesting examples occur in Antonio Buero-Vallejo's *Música cercana* (1989) and Roger Cornish's *Rocky and Diego* (1988).[8] In the former play, the Spanish author introduces an elderly servant who speaks occasional lines in English, much to the bewilderment of the other characters. In the latter historical play, the American playwright has Nelson Rockefeller try out his newly learned Spanish on Diego Rivera, the Mexican muralist. When Marion P. Holt translated Buero-Vallejo's play, he had to make an important

decision on what to do with the original English within the translated
English text. Similarly, in translating Cornish's play to Spanish, Antonio
Gil had to consider ways to compensate for Rocky's beginner's Spanish
within the text of a Spanish play in which the character otherwise speaks
the language fluently.

In the case of *The Music Window*, Holt opted to translate Buero-Vallejo's
sporadic use of English to Spanish, thus merely reversing the two languages.
In a prefatory note to the 1994 published translation, he clarifies that the character Lorenza 'occasionaly reveals her disgust and punctuates the moment
with a blunt comment or word in English, which is not understood by the
character she is addressing'; he assumes that the English-speaking audience
will react to the counterpart expressions in Spanish 'essentially as Spanish
audiences reacted to the unexpected English words and phrases' (Buero-
Vallejo, 1994: xii). Nevertheless, Holt places the original English lines from
Música cercana in brackets within the text should a director prefer to have
the actor deliver them as asides. In a second translator's note at the end of
the volume, he expands his suggestion: 'A director may prefer to find a
different solution by changing the expressions to French or some other
language, or by simply having them spoken in English as asides. In any
case, Lorenza's caustic interjections are essential to her character and to an
authentic performance of Buero's play' (Buero-Vallejo, 1994: 64).

Holt's suggested use of asides differs from the technique used by
Rivera and del Moral in which the same language will be understood
by the audience to be a different, incomprehensible one for the other characters. Had Holt envisioned that kind of strategy in *The Music Window*, it
would have required adaptation in consultation with the author, as well
as the cooperation of the acting company.

Holt's translation had already been submitted to the publisher before
the play was given a performance in New York City. In her review of
the 22 November 1993 staged reading of *The Music Window* (CUNY
Graduate Center, dir. Michael Rivera), Patti Firth makes several observations that might have convinced Holt that translating Lorenza's
English words to Spanish was not the ideal solution. Firth's comments,
however, were not published until after the translation was in print.

> In the original text . . . Lorenza . . . has a habit of making comments,
> usually vulgar ones, in English, amusing and sometimes confusing
> the other characters. This creates a comic effect. However, in the trans-
> lation, Holt has Lorenza make her comments in Spanish and then the
> other characters, in English, express their lack of understanding. This
> makes for a jarring effect, since the audience knows that the play

takes place in Spain, and that Spanish is normally the language spoken there. The result is one that translators generally try to avoid: the translation constantly calls attention to itself as a translation, while ideally the audience should be able to forget that fact.

Merely reversing English and French in my translation of Manet's *Lady Strass*, where the action takes place in Belize, is an easy solution; the counterpart English–Spanish reversal in Buero's *The Music Window*, where the action takes place in Spain, poses problems.

More difficult yet is the problem faced by Gil in his translation of Rocky's use of Spanish in *Rocky and Diego*. In Cornish's text, all the characters speak English. Some spectators might consciously realize that in reality the Mexican artist and his wife, Frida Kahlo, would probably have spoken Spanish to each other when alone in the United States; the playwright can count on the theatre audience's acceptance of this conventional use of English for Spanish in his dramatic world. The limited use of rudimentary Spanish by his character Nelson Rockefeller establishes the young man's desire to be friendly to this particular foreign visitor and to establish his good will toward Latin America in general. When Diego politely tells him that his Spanish is improving, Rocky enthusiastically proclaims that he is studying 'Because I see the future in Spanish-speaking America'. The intentional errors or hesitancy in Rocky's Spanish merely reinforce his status as a beginning learner of the language. For example, he says of Rivera's mural in progress: 'Lo es muy hermoso'; his incorrect insertion of the object pronoun 'lo' is consistent with an English speaker's tendency to express a subject pronoun where none exists in Spanish.

Gil, in collaboration with Cornish, arrived at a solution that is not unlike the technique that del Moral used for Ombasi in *La mirada del hombre oscuro*. Throughout *Rocky y Diego*, the Spanish-speaking audience will understand that the action of the play takes place in the United States and that the characters are speaking English even though the dialogue is in Spanish. As Gil clarifies in the introduction to his translation thesis, he distinguishes the second level of Rocky's language by incorporating three strategies: grammatical errors ('Mucho verdaderamente' and 'Está verdad'), typically Mexican expressions ('¡Qué rebién lindo!' and '¡Carajo!'), and an added comment by Diego on how Mexican Rocky sounds ('ya casi habla como un mexicano'). Rather than juxtaposing two languages, Gil's procedure juxtaposes two dialects. In a production in Spain – the target country of his translation – this strategy could be especially effective if the Rivera and Kahlo roles were played by

Mexican actors or, at the least, by actors who could effectively convey a Mexican accent. The true test of how well Gil's solution works will not come until his translation is staged.

Gil's solution points to a possible answer to the dilemma that Henry G. Schogt has identified for French translations of Chekhov's *The Three Sisters*. In the Russian play, the sister-in-law of the title characters presumes to speak French. Her use of the foreign language marks her social ambitions but her errors indicate that she does not know French well enough to speak it with any naturalness. Schogt finds unsatisfactory a French translation of the play that 'ends up with a mixture of fluent French corresponding to the Russian and bad French used in the original' (Schogt, 1988: 115). However, this solution can work well if the actors understand the function of passages of stilted French; like Gil in *Rocky y Diego*, the French translator might add a few brief words to clarify the contrast between the two levels of French.

In *The Aspern Letters* (1996), a play based on Henry James's novel *The Aspern Papers*, Cornish sets the action in Prague in 1992. Once again he introduces expressions in a second language. His unnamed American visitor to Prague asks Tina, a bilingual character, to help him learn the language. To guide the actors, for each word or phrase in Czech, Cornish provides the English translation in brackets. In context, the Czech expressions are transparent and should be readily understood by the audience. For example, when HE says 'Dobry den. [Good day.]', Tina looks at the evening sky and corrects him, 'Dobry vecer. [Good evening.]' (Cornish, 1996: 32). When HE compliments Tina on her dress, she says 'Dekuji. [Thank you.]'; trying hard, he responds 'To je v poradku. [You're welcome.]' and Tina corrects his pronunciation (Cornish, 1996: 33).

In her translation of *The Aspern Letters* (Cornish, 1997), Gloria Gastón-Dwyer simply translated the English to Spanish and left the Czech expressions in Czech but added missing diacritics to Cornish's use of Czech words. She explains in the introduction to her translation thesis that one aspect of the source play required additional research. In the character of Vaclav, a tourist guide, Cornish creates a native speaker of Czech whose otherwise fluent English is marked by errors. Gastón-Dwyer states that she discussed this aspect of dialect with the author because she felt that Vaclav, in her translation, should speak Spanish 'with a similar degree of incorrectness'. Cornish told her that he had taken a generic approach, making his character speak the way that he thought any non-English speaker might. Gastón-Dwyer felt the need to pursue a specifically Czech accent in the corresponding Spanish. As a professional linguist with years of experience teaching English as a second language, she affirms 'that the errors a Hispanic person makes are not the same as those made by an Eastern European' (Cornish, 1997: 6). Accordingly, she consulted a fluent speaker of Czech who could guide her in creating the appropriate kinds of errors for Vaclav's Spanish.

In the source text, the Czech guide's use of the second language is slightly stilted. In the Spanish translation he makes identifiable grammar errors (missing indirect object and relative pronouns, gender error, failure to use the subjunctive):

> But ... you don't know them. And you don't want them to know you come here to stay in their home. OK, I am expert in this. (Cornish, 1996: 11)

> *Pero ... Ud. no conoce a ellos. Y Ud. no quiere ellos saber Ud. viene para vivir con ellos. Ok, ok, yo soy en eso experto.* (Cornish, 1997: 23)

In their recommendations on translating passages of dialect in narrative, Sándor Hervey, Ian Higgins and Louise M. Haywood observe that the problem can be solved by using standard language and inserting a phrase like the following: 'he said, suddenly relapsing into the local vernacular' (Hervey *et al.*, 1995: 115). Cornish, as author, and Gastón-Dwyer, as translator, might have followed a similar procedure by stating in a stage direction that Vaclav speaks with a marked Czech accent, thereby transferring the problem to the actor. Instead they have, in different ways and to somewhat different degrees, provided a dialogue that guides the actor into creating the appropriate voice for the character.

At the extreme, dialect may seem like a foreign language. In his discussion of Brigitte Jaque's *Elvira 40*, Edney observes that the French-Canadian playwright inserted passages of Molière's *Don Juan* into her metaplay, including a section of act II in which the peasants 'speak a patois that is so different from the standard French of the other characters that abundant notes are necessary to enable modern readers to understand it' (Edney, 1996: 233). The solution Jaque found for her production was to have the peasants in the play-within-a-play speak in a French-Canadian accent in contrast to the standard French used by the characters in the frame play.

Problematic for the translator to English is the handling of passages of Catalan interspersed in José María Rodríguez Méndez's *Flor de Otoño* (written 1972), a play set in Barcelona in the 1930s. Although the author is not Catalan, he lived in Barcelona for many years and is well aware of how the two languages function together; the result is this bilingual

Spanish-Catalan text. Catalan, the regional language of Northeastern Spain and part of France, is not a dialect of Castilian Spanish but a separate Romance language; for that reason, the Cátedra edition provides footnotes with translations to Spanish for expressions that might not be easily guessed. To represent Catalan in English by some regional accent in contrast with 'standard' English would shift the action out of Spain and belie the fact that Catalan is the first language of the characters who are native to the city. When the original play was staged in Spain (1982) and in France (1992), the inclusion of Catalan within the text apparently did not pose major difficulties for spectators who were willing to make the leap. For an American or British audience, most of the Catalan dialogue in lines such as these would be incomprehensible:

EL SEÑOR JOROBADO:	(*Tose y carraspea.*) ¡Ai, senyó ...!
DOÑA NURIA:	Aleshores, un Serracant, tot un Serracant, barrejat amb la gent del hampa ...
LA SEÑORA REGORDETA:	¡Mare de Deu Santísima ...!
EL SEÑOR GORDO:	Y, es clar, els Teixits Serracant barretjats amb la gent del hampa ...
LA SEÑORA RUBIA:	(*Echándose a llorar.*) Ai, ai, jo em vull morirme ... ¿Com podré anarhi al Lliceu ara? ¡Quina vergonya ...! (Rodríguez Méndez, 1995: 136)

Holt's solution as translator was to transfer most of the Catalan to English but leave in some interjections and other short expressions in the original language to create the impression of a bilingual community.

THE HUNCHBACKED GENTLEMAN:	(*Clearing his throat*): Ai, Senyor!
DOÑA NURIA:	Then ... a Serracant, a true Serracant, has gotten mixed up with the underworld.
THE PLUMP LADY:	Mare de Deu Santísima!
THE FAT GENTLEMAN:	And it's quite clear then: Serracant Textiles is mixed up with the underworld.
THE BLOND LADY:	(*Starting to cry*): Oh my, I think I want to die ... How will I ever set foot in the opera house again? Quina vergonya! (Rodríguez Méndez, 2001: 10)

The result is not unlike US Latino plays that include just enough Spanish to remind the spectators of the characters' ethnic identity. For the 2001 edition of his translation, *Autumn Flower*, Holt provided a glossary of names, places and titles mentioned in the play as a guide to future directors and actors (Rodríguez Méndez, 2001: 60–61).

In general, the characters in Rodríguez Méndez's play speak either Catalan or Castilian Spanish, depending upon the circumstances, but they do not change languages between sentences or in mid sentence. Holt's solution was to introduce a limited use of Catalan in a form of code-switching. In discussing *Greenpoint Miracle*, her translation from Polish of Edward Reliński's *Cud Na Greepoincie*, Szczęsna Klaudyna Rozhin considers variations on code-switching to solve the problem of recreating in English how Polish immigrants speak.

Realistically, Redliński mixed English nouns into his characters' speech in Polish. Rozhin's first approach was to give Polish inflections and endings to English verbs, nouns and adjectives, interspersing them with Polish prepositions, conjunctions and pronouns. When actors could not handle her invented dialect, she tried mixing Polish metaphors and idioms into an English text. The language was still not clear. She then tried broken English, somewhat like the language spoken by the Czech guide in Gastón-Dwyer's translation of the Cornish play. But Rozhin quickly realized that the characters would be speaking fluently to one another and ungrammatical English was also not the answer. Ultimately she produced a translation in correct English and maintained Polish only for proper names: 'After several unsuccessful attempts to preserve the immigrants' dialect, I produced a version virtually free from Polish words, free from "bad" English and strange neologisms. I neutralized the dialect, and by doing this undoubtedly deprived the language of the play of its unique character and colour' (Rozhin, 2000: 148). Conceivably the example of Holt's translation of *Autumn Flower* might have presented other options.

The plays discussed in this chapter vary widely in the extent and impact of their use of a second language. Most of them were written by authors who are themselves fluent in two or more languages. In theatre, the bilingual author's divided self may be represented linguistically, thus posing a particular challenge to the translator. But the challenge in theatre can never be fully resolved by the translator alone. Deliberate multilingual games call upon the full and creative cooperation of director and actors, as well as a receptive audience.

Notes

1. Beatriz J. Rizk observes: 'With respect to bilingualism, the United States is perhaps the only country in the world in which speaking two languages

is not an advantage, but is almost a stigma, especially if one of them is Spanish' (Rizk, 2002: 7). She cites the examples of *The English Only Restaurant*, by Colombian-born Silvio Martínez Palau, and *The Great American Justice Game* by the late Cuban-American author Miguel González-Pando as plays that satirize the English Only movement in the United States by showing what would happen if speaking Spanish were declared illegal (Rizk, 2002: 10–11).

2. In my travels in Europe, I have encountered families with parents born in Spain and children born in France who code-switch between two languages exactly the way that Hispanic-American families do in the United States.

3. Code-switching 'occurs in the language use of speakers whose active repertoire includes several language varieties–dialects, sociolects, even distinct languages' in order to fit changing social circumstances (Hervey *et al.*, 1995: 115).

4. Mayorga has kindly made available to me both the third version of *El traductor de Blumemberg* (manuscript dated March 2001) and an intermediate version. My analysis of the play is based primarily on the third version; page numbers in the text refer to this unpublished manuscript. This playscript is shorter than the earlier versions, and the use of German has been reduced. The staging in Argentina was directed by Guillermo Heras at the Teatro Cervantes.

5. Mayorga studied German at the Goethe Institute in Spain, took courses in East Germany, and wrote his doctoral dissertation on Walter Benjamin. While he acquired his knowledge of German through the academic route, there are German-Spanish bilinguals in Spain: children of Spaniards who emigrated to Germany or Switzerland in the early 1960s to seek employment and later returned to their native country.

6. André Lefevere has observed how plays of Bertolt Brecht have been acculturated (Bassnett & Lefevere, 1998: 109–22). The process involves making the language more transparent, turning the songs into musical comedy rather than function as an alienation effect, dividing the text into acts/scenes to make the play Aristotelian in format, and deleting hints of Marxism. To a lesser degree, we do something similar when we downplay the multiple languages in a text. The result is to normalize the source play to the expectations of the American audience.

7. Martínez staged Anaya's play at Nosotros Theater, a showcase for Latino actors. He reports being reproached 'for the play's use of a few sprinkled bilingual/Spanish phrases as being "way too much Spanish". . . It was an insidious environment where personal taste must be supplanted in order to maintain professional survival' (Martínez, 2002: 26).

8. *Rocky and Diego* was the winner of the 1988 Kennedy Center Fund for New American Plays Award in 1988, has received multiple stagings, but has not been published. The late Roger Cornish was a playwriting professor at Rutgers, The State University; he graciously worked with our masters candidates in translation on various projects relating to translation and theatre.

References

Bassnett, S. and Lefevere, A. *Constructing Cultures. Essays on Literary Translation.* Clevedon: Multilingual Matters, Topics in Translation 11, 1998.

Buero-Vallejo, A. *The Music Window* (trans. M. P. Holt). State College, PA: ESTRENO, ESTRENO Contemporary Spanish Plays 5, 1994.

Cabrera, E. The encounter of two cultures in the play *Doña Rosita's Jalapeño Kitchen* (Or, the Representation of Cultural Hybridity). In L. A. Ramos-García, ed., *The State of Latino Theater in the United States*, 2002, 67–78.

Cornish, R. *Rocky and Diego*, 1988. Unpublished manuscript. Unpaginated.

Cornish, R. *Rocky y Diego* (trans. A. Gil). Masters thesis. Rutgers, The State University, 1995.

Cornish, R. *The Aspern Letters*, 1996. Unpublished manuscript.

Cornish, R. *Las cartas de Aspern* (trans. G. Gastón-Dwyer). Masters thesis, Rutgers, The State University, 1997.

del Moral, I. *La mirada del hombre oscuro*. Madrid: SGAE, 1992.

del Moral, I. *Dark Man's Gaze*. (trans. J. Toles). Masters thesis. Rutgers, The State University, 1999.

Edney, D. Translating (and not translating) in a Canadian Context. In D. Johnston, ed., *Stages of Translation. Essays and Interviews on Translation for the Stage*. Bath, England: Absolute Classics, 1996, 229–38.

Firth, P. Staged reading of Buero Vallejo's *The Music Window*. *Estreno* 22.2 (1994): 4.

González, P. Nostalgia in Cuban theater across the shores. In L. A. Ramos-García, ed., *The State of Latino Theater in the United States*, 2002, 79–92.

González-Pando, M. The Great American justice game. In L. F. González-Cruz and F. M. Colecchia, eds, *Cuban Theater in the United States: A Critical Anthology* (trans. L. F. González-Cruz and F. M. Colecchia). Tempe, AZ: Bilingual Press/ Editorial Bilingüe, 1992, 77–108.

Hervey, S., Higgins, I. and Haywood, L. M. *Thinking Spanish Translation. A Course in Translation Method: Spanish to English*. London and New York: Routledge, 1995.

Manet, E. *L'Autre Don Juan*. Paris: Gallimard, Collection Le Manteau d'Arlequin, 1973.

Manet, E. *Lady Strass*. *L'Avant-Scène Théâtre* 613 (1 July 1977): 5–31.

Manet, E. *Un Balcon sur les Andes*. With *Mendoza, en Argentine . . . , Ma'Déa*. Paris: Gallimard, 1985.

Manet, E. *Lady Strass*. (trans. P. Zatlin). *Modern International Drama* 26.1 (1992): 5–35.

Manet, E. *Monsieur Lovestar et son voisin du palier*. Paris: Actes Sud-Papiers, 1995.

Manet, E. *Lady Strass*. Dir. André Ernotte. Ubu Repertory Theater, New York City, 1 October 1996.

Manet, E. *Lady Strass* (trans. P. Zatlin). In *Playwrights of Exile. An International Anthology*. New York: Ubu Repertory Theater Publications, 1997, 1–80.

Martínez, M. Still treading water: Recent currents in Chicano theater. In Ramos-García, L. A., ed., *The State of Latino Theater in the United States*, 2002, 15–29.

Mayorga, J. *El traductor de Blumemberg*. With *Leda*, by a. Lidell Zoo. Madrid: Centro Nacional Nuevas Tendencias Escénicas, Colección Nuevo Teatro Español 14, 1993.

Mayorga, J. Personal interview, 5 June 2000.

Mayorga, J. *El traductor de Blumemberg*. Revised version, manuscript. March 2001.

Prida, D. *Coser y cantar. Beautiful Señoritas & Other Plays*. Ed. J. Weiss. Houston: Arte Publico Press, 1991, 47–67.

Ramos-García, L. A., ed. *The State of Latino Theater in the United States. Hybridity, Transculturation, and Identity*. New York and London: Routledge, 2002.

Rivera, J. *The House of Ramon Iglesia.* In E. Osborn, ed., *On New Ground. Contemporary Hispanic-American Plays.* New York: Theatre Communications Group, 1987.

Rizk, B. J. Latino theater in the United States: 'The Importance of Being the Other'. In Ramos-García, L. A., ed., *The State of Latino Theater in the United States,* 2002, 1–14

Rodríguez Méndez, J. M. *Flor de Otoño.* With *Bodas que fueron famosas del Pingajo y la Fandanga.* Ed. J. Martín Recuerda. Madrid: Cátedra, Letras Hispánicas 104, 1995.

Rodríguez Méndez, J. M. *Autumn Flower* (trans. M. P. Holt). New Brunswick, NJ: ESTRENO Plays, Estreno Contemporary Spanish Plays 20, 2001.

Rozhin, Szczęsna Klaudyna. Translating the untranslatable. Edward Redliński's *Cud Na Greenpoincie* [*Greenpoint Miracle*] in English. [Note problem of peculiar diacritics.] In C.-A. Upton, ed., *Moving Target. Theatre Translation and Cultural Relocation.* Manchester, UK & Northampton, MA: St. Jerome Publishing, 2000, 139–49.

Schogt, H. G. *Linguistics, Literary Analysis, and Literary Translation.* Toronto, Buffalo & London: University of Toronto Press, 1988.

Weitz, S. Mr. Godot will not come today. In H. Scolnicov and P. Holland, eds, *The Play Out of Context. Transferring Plays from Culture to Culture.* Cambridge: Cambridge University Press, 1989, 186–98.

Chapter 6
Titling and Dubbing for Stage and Screen

The Catalan play E. R. (Benet i Jornet, 1994; winner of Spain's National Drama Prize, 1995), along with its corresponding film version (*Actrius*, 1996, dir. Ventura Pons), portrays three mature women who in their youth studied acting together under the great Empar Ribera.[1] Two of them are now famous stars, one of stage and screen and the other of television. The third, Maria, has dedicated her professional life to dubbing films and is totally unknown. As far as audiences are concerned, she is quite literally invisible, for she is part of what Thomas L. Rowe has called the cinematic netherworld, a place filled with phantom actors (Rowe, 1960: 116).

Playwright Josep M. Benet i Jornet is author of both the original play and the film script for *Actrius*. Given his extensive experience in television and cinema as well as theatre, he is not only sympathetic to his character but also knowledgeable about her work. Maria indeed describes to Glòria the special arrangements she has put in place as director for dubbing a film that Glòria has made in Italy. Maria has scheduled the takes in four sessions to make them less burdensome for her longtime friend, who will read her part herself; she will allow Glòria to request a retake of any scene that does not satisfy her (Benet i Jornet, 1996: 24).

Catalan is a minor language, spoken by relatively few people in the world. The film industry of Catalonia, a bilingual region of Spain, therefore has ample experience with both dubbing and subtitling as means of reaching larger audiences. The original Catalan version of *Actrius* was immediately dubbed into Castilian for the Spanish-speaking world; simultaneously the original Catalan version was released for export elsewhere with English subtitles.

For more than 70 years, the international film industry has promoted these two forms of translation: subtitles (an abbreviated version of the dialogue, which is projected on the screen) and dubbing (an alternate, synchronized soundtrack of the complete dialogue). In Juliane House's typology, subtitles are overt translation whereas dubbing, which purports to be a second original, is covert (House, 1977: 188–89). Henrik Gottlieb further observes that subtitles are fragmentary but dubbing is integral translation (Gottlieb, 1994: 102).

With today's digital technology, both subtitles and dubbed soundtracks are readily available on DVD versions of movies. In Gottlieb's terms, these DVDs provide options for either vertical (same language – of use to the hearing impaired) or diagonal (different language) subtitling (Gottlieb, 1994: 104). They may also provide one or more separate soundtracks in other languages. The variety of options varies by country. In the United States, the consumer can readily find films with both options and choices of English, Spanish, and French. DVDs in Spain, France, and Germany generally resemble American ones in the quantity of options, although the language choices are different and, according to Christopher Mack, in France they can rise to eight or nine languages for particularly popular films (Mack, personal interview, 2003). In Germany, recognizing that the country is a key trade partner with Turkey, Turkish is often included among the subtitles and even, occasionally, as a soundtrack. In the United Kingdom, soundtracks typically incorporate English, French, and Italian along with subtitles that may extend to Arabic, Bulgarian, Dutch, German, Portuguese, Romanian, Spanish, and, to a lesser degree, Czech, Danish, Finnish, Greek, Hebrew, Hungarian, Icelandic, Norwegian, Polish, and Swedish. Distributors in the United Kingdom are seeking a broad international market and are willing to invest in the creation of subtitles and dubbed soundtracks.[2]

The digital revolution, however, is recent. Back in the era of silent movies, Hollywood studios reached foreign markets 'simply by supplying titles for their films in the appropriate language' (Holt, 1980: 19). With the advent of talking movies, more effort was required to reach lucrative foreign markets. Marion P. Holt credits RKO with responding immediately to the new situation by dubbing *Rio Rita* into Spanish in 1929; a few years later, the technique of dubbing became widespread.[3]

As subfields of theatrical translation, subtitling and dubbing offer real possibilities for earning a steady income, and in the future the demand for specialists should continue to grow worldwide. The application of subtitles and dubbing to film has been the subject of considerable commentary, including substantial research into how rapidly spectators may be expected to read and process titles. In recent years counterpart methods have been applied to stage productions: theatres that wish to reach an audience that does not speak the language of performance may offer open captioning for spectator viewing or 'simultaneous translation' for spectators to hear over headsets. There is still a dearth of published studies on this application of titles and dubbing for the stage.

At the personal and national levels, one can find strong preferences for one or the other of the two methods of film translation. In a special 1960 issue of the translation journal _Babel_ dedicated to cinema, editor P.-F. Caillé recounted his experiences as author of French scripts for English-language movies and weighed in strongly in favour of dubbing. He contended that subtitles block the spectators' view of the screen and that people are incapable of reading them because they pass by so quickly; besides, he questioned who would want to listen to two hours of a foreign language (Caillé, 1960: 104). At one time in France, dubbing was far more common than subtitles; in his 1998 overview of subtitling, Gottlieb states that dubbing is preferred in countries that speak French, German, Italian and Spanish.

Analogous to Caillé's argument in favour of dubbing for movies is Mark Herman and Ronnie Apter's support for their work as translators of opera librettos. They reject 'the highly abridged translation used for movie subtitles and projected English captions. For such translations, even if done well, offer only a glimpse of the original work to a person not fluent in the original language' (Herman & Apter, 1991: 102).[4] Moreover, subtitles may be distracting. Jay Boyar (1986) points out that with subtitles the viewer must simultaneously take in the visual image while reading 'a ghostly script across the bottom of the movie frame.' David Wills attributes visual damage to those ghostly words: 'by appearing at the bottom of the screen they cause the bottom of the film to fall out' (Wills, 1998: 149).

Despite such caveats, subtitles continue to be used extensively. Subtitles, rather than dubbing, dominate for movies and television in small countries, both European and non-European, and for foreign art films imported by Anglo-American nations (Gottlieb, 1998: 244). In Denmark, dubbing is reserved for children's television programmes (Gottlieb, 1994: 102); the preference no doubt stems from the difficulty beginning readers would have with subtitles. Dirk Delabastita specifically mentions Belgium, a bilingual country, and the Netherlands as preferring subtitles (Delabastita, 1989: 207). According to Ingrid Kurz, a survey of television viewers in the Netherlands revealed that 64% of adult respondents chose subtitling over dubbing (Kurz, 1990: 168); giving an even higher survey figure, Richard Kilborn reports that 82% of viewers in that country preferred subtitling for foreign television programmes

(Kilborn, 1989: 429). Jan Emil Tveit reports that after a three-week experiment with a dubbed American television series, 85% of Norwegian viewers voted in favour of subtitling (Tveit, 1998: 368).[5]

Caillé admits that dubbing seeks to create 'the illusion of an illusion' (Caillé, 1960: 108). No matter how well synchronized the lip movements of the actors on screen with the voices in the foreign language, that illusion will have its flaws. Tveit, reacting to hearing Woody Allen 'speak' in German and Leonardo DiCaprio in French, contends, 'They did not come anywhere near sounding like perfect illusions' (Tveit, 1998: 368). On the other hand, Mack remarks that in France certain actors consistently are the voices for particular Hollywood celebrities. Therefore, 'many French people recognize various popular American movie stars only in their French voices, and are shocked when they hear the "real thing"' (Mack, personal communication, 2004). One logical reason for subtitling – with its retention of the original voice – is 'its honesty' (Gottlieb, 1994: 102).

Certainly part of the division along national lines is economic: it can cost up to 15 times more to dub a film than to add subtitles (Baker & Hochel, 1998b: 75; Gottlieb, 1994: 118). Hollywood movies, even mediocre ones, are popular with audiences in many other countries; foreign films in the United States, with occasional exceptions, attract relatively few spectators. Consequently, it is cost-effective to dub American films into languages spoken by many millions of people but prudent to use subtitles for less commonly spoken languages and for films imported to the United States. Even less expensive than subtitling is a voice-over with one narrator who interprets the film's action for the audience; that method has been used in Russia and Poland (Gottlieb, 1998: 244). In Cambodia, live actors act out the movies from booths beside the screen (Rowe, 1960: 117).

The advantage of subtitles in smaller nations is not limited to the economic factor. According to Tveit, the Scandinavian countries adopted subtitles instead of dubbing because of relative expense but then discovered that access to the original dialogue, usually English, has proved to have educational value as well (Tveit, 2000: 43). In 1987, Tveit carried out a research project involving 4200 students of English from nine European nations: 'A conspicuous finding was that listening comprehension was perceived as significantly more difficult by students from "dubbing countries" than by students from "subtitling countries"' (Tveit, 1998: 366). Cay Dollerup affirms that spectators in Denmark want subtitles so they can hear the source language and thereby improve their language skills (Dollerup, 1974: 197). In contrast, in the late 1980s Kilborn suggested that the British preference for dubbing was, in fact, related to a national 'resistance to acquiring a good working knowledge of foreign languages' and a 'characteristically insular mind-set' (Kilborn, 1989: 430).

From an American perspective, Boyar says that people who love movies consider subtitling superior to dubbing or voice-over translations. His opinion is doubtless a minority view. Outside of New York, a few other major cities, and scattered foreign film festivals, it is difficult to find projections of original versions in the United States. Even well-publicized Oscar-winning foreign films, like the Italian _Life is Beautiful_ (dir. Roberto Benigni, 1998), attract relatively few spectators unless there is a dubbed version (Fukushima & Major, 2002: 74). Instead the American foreign movie fan must seek out video – or, as time passes, DVD – collections at university and municipal libraries or national cultural services, such as the Cervantes or Goethe institutes. It is not surprising that Wills suggests that Hollywood is inclined to remake popular French movies precisely for the purpose of eliminating subtitles (Wills, 1998: 148). The Hollywood remake of a foreign film, with an American cast, also shifts the action to a more familiar place: 'The remake neutralizes the otherness of the foreign film, in general, but in no way more clearly than by effacing the subtitles' (Wills, 1998: 149–50).

On any given week, _Time Out New York_ provides an array of subtitled foreign films available in the City; except for animated features, there are no listings for dubbed versions because, as Holt observes, 'New York audiences simply wouldn't tolerate it' (Holt, personal communication, 2003). But just how difficult is it to find a subtitled foreign film in movie houses outside the major metropolitan centres in the United States? _The Sunday Star-Ledger_ movie listings cover all of New Jersey, a state with a large population of bilingual and college-educated people. On 22 June 2003, the Newark paper's movie listings included 16 of the state's 17 counties with a total of 106 playhouses, most of which have multiple screens. In their movie reviews that day, Bob Campbell and Stephen Whitty evaluated 43 current films including five subtitled foreign films and one English-language movie subtitled in Spanish. At almost 14%, the representation of subtitled movies they reviewed was relatively high for the United States, but how accessible were these particular films for their readers? One of the films, _L'Auberge espagnole_ was visibly advertised as 'France's smash hit comedy' and was being shown at three theatres: in Montclair, Ridgewood, and Rocky Hill. Montgomery Cinema in Rocky Hill, not far from Princeton, is well known for its willingness to show foreign films; besides _L'Auberge_, it was also featuring _The Man on the Train_ (French) and _Nowhere in Africa_ (German, Swahili and English). The latter film could also be seen in another theatre in

Montclair. *City of God* (Brazilian Portuguese) was being shown in one playhouse, in North Bergen. For the other two of the six reviewed films – all of them rated between two and three and a half stars out of a possible four – the interested moviegoer would have to go to Manhattan.

Are the Chicago suburbs any more receptive to subtitled foreign films than New Jersey? In one respect, it is difficult to tell. The Weekend Entertainment section of the *Chicago Tribune* does not label movies as having subtitles or identify a film's country of origin. Regina Robinson's compilation of 'Movie Capsules' on 21 June 2003 includes *L'Auberge espagnole*, *Man on the Train*, and several other original version films, but the potential spectator will not find that out from reading her ratings. Five theatres Downtown or in the Near North and North suburbs were listed as showing one, two, or three movies each from those identified as subtitled in the New Jersey newspaper, but only one playhouse gave this information to readers of their announcement (a theatre in Evanston showing *L'Auberge espagnole*).

As one moves west in Illinois, away from Chicago, the presence of foreign films disappears. In 'Movies at a Glance' in Elgin's *Daily Herald* on 23 June 2003, only one of 40 films reviewed is foreign; *The Eye* (Cantonese, Mandarin and Thai) is carefully labeled as having subtitles, but the interested reader will have to travel to a distant North suburb to see it. There are no foreign films listed in this West suburb newspaper's movie section. If there is a dearth of foreign films in New Jersey, which neighbours New York City, and Illinois outside the metropolitain Chicago area, it is safe to conclude that original versions with subtitles are even more difficult to find in other regions of the country.

Both subtitling and dubbing may be considered complex, challenging variants of theatrical translation. For Caillé, dubbing places special emphasis on phonetics; subtitling, on semantics (Caillé, 1960: 109). The preparation of subtitles presupposes the same skills required for producing a stageable play translation and then adds the problem of obligatory brevity; negative criticisms of subtitles at times are directed not at mistakes but at omissions. Additionally subtitles must be synchronized with the action so that the words on the screen coincide with the image. Fortunately, as Tveit points out, state-of-the-art subtitling equipment has made the precise cueing of titles much easier than in the past (Tveit, 1998: 367). In the case of dubbing, synchronization continues to pose significant problems. Unlike the translator of stage plays, the writer of a dubbing script does not have the freedom to reorder text to facilitate natural speech in the target language. Instead, he or she must follow the fixed images of the film; for close-ups, the dubbed script should make the words fit the movement of the actors' mouths. Rowe somewhat facetiously sums the process up as the 'crossword puzzlement of the lip-synch requirements' (Rowe, 1960: 117).

Edmond Cary has asserted that dubbing should be considered the top of the translation pyramid because it must respect not only the written text, but also the life and soul of the words; among the various aspects of language the translator has to take into consideration are articulation and gestures (Cary, 1960: 112). The problem is compounded when the transfer occurs between a language with a wide range of gestures and another that 'has a much more limited gestural range' (Kilborn, 1989: 425). Caillé observes that good dubbing, which should be considered an art, all too often is disparaged (Caillé, 1960: 108). Like Benet i Jornet's character, translators who prepare subtitles and film scripts for dubbing are virtually invisible. Nevertheless, their work gives rise to very visible criticism and debate.

Howlers in subtitles are difficult to hide; anyone who knows both the language of the movie and of the captions can identify obvious mistakes. In my advanced translation courses I often project videoclips with quirky subtitles and ask my students to note errors and suggest better solutions. Finding examples of defective subtitles is easy; offering concise improvements is not.[6] Mistakes in a dubbed dialogue are harder to spot unless one already knows the source text well or can read lips in the original language. That is why dubbing is the preferred vehicle for censorship. L. Alonso Tejada reminds us that in Spain during the years of Franco's dictatorship with its concomitant National Catholicism, original versions with subtitles were prohibited under a 1941 law. The Spanish film industry perfected 'synchronization and cunning' as a way to manipulate dialogue and story lines, ostensibly to impose higher moral values (Alonso Tejada, 1977: 140). Alonso Tejada cites three particularly egregious instances of such revisions in dubbed film scripts: in *The Champion* (1949), a husband was turned into a father; in *The Snows of Kilimanjaro* (1952), an expression of desperate love was changed into a prayer; in *Mogambo* (1953), a husband and wife were presented as brother and sister to keep the wife's relationship with her lover from being adulterous (Alonso Tejada, 1977: 143). The resultant brother/sister incest in the dubbed version of *Mogambo* was readily noted by spectators, but apparently the censors considered incest a less popular sin than adultery and hence less threatening to public morals.

Even without the kind of systematic, official censorship that prevailed under the Franco regime, dubbing may give rise to deliberate manipulation. Rowe reports a time when, in conformity with Hollywood codes,

writers of American scripts for dubbed French and Italian films had to
censor 'ribald scenes of Rabelaisian candor' (Rowe, 1960: 120). Delabastita
affirms that dubbing may be used to suppress unwanted ideas; he cites a
1969 study that found all allusions to Germany's recent past had been
removed from dubbed films in that country (Delabastita, 1989: 208).

It is possible that within a particular country, the preference for
dubbing may diminish with changing circumstances. In major cities of
Spain, interested movie-goers now have the opportunity to see original
versions with Spanish subtitles. In Barcelona, the movie schedule in
La Vanguardia newspaper listed 48 films for 19 February 2003. Ten of
these were Spanish and two Argentine. Of the 36 movies filmed in
languages other than Spanish, 24 – from the United States, France, Japan,
Great Britain, and Italy, as well as co-productions including Canada,
Germany, Romania, Poland, Brazil, New Zealand, and Finland – were
available in original versions, some of them showing in more than one
theatre. Predictably *Harry Potter* (*Harry Potter y la cámara secreta*, United
States, 2002), a movie aimed primarily at children, was provided only
in the dubbed version; *The Lord of the Rings* (*Las dos torres* [*El señor de los
anillos*], United States-New Zealand, 2002), a movie of equal interest to
young people and adults, was offered in the dubbed version in several
places but was also available in the original version at one cinema
complex. In Madrid, a special section of movie listings in *LA RAZÓN*
(27 February 2003) identified ten movie houses or cinema complexes
that regularly present original versions.[7] Madrid still differs considerably
from Buenos Aires, where Argentines now understand that original versions, with subtitles, is the default; children's movies, which are clearly
labeled as being dubbed *en castellano* in the 'Cartelera/Espectáculos'
section of *La Nación*, are the only exception for foreign films in Argentina
(Werth, personal communication, 2003).

It is also possible that situations have changed in other countries, or
that generalizations offered in prior studies were not totally accurate.
Kilborn (1989: 430) has told us of a British preference for dubbing, but
when I visited London I could find no dubbed films there at all except
for children's movies. *Time Out London* for 23–30 April 2003 lists 52
first-run movies: 38 (73.1%) that were filmed in English and 14 (26.9%)
that were made in other languages. Except for an animated feature
(*The Little Polar Bear*, Germany) and a multinational film (*The Pianist*,
Great Britain/France/Germany; dir. Roman Polanski), which would
have been released with multiple soundtracks, the foreign films are
listed as subtitled or partially subtitled. They include movies from
Brazil, Denmark, Finland, France, French Canada, Germany, Greece,

Hungary, Italy, Russia, Spain, and Sweden. Some of these foreign films were being shown simultaneously in several movie houses of the West End; such visibility implies that British spectators may have a less insular mind-set than Kilborn suggested.

Foreign films, in original versions, also travel outside London, and not only to the largest cities in the United Kingdom. According to Henry Little, Head of Opera and Music Theatre for the Arts Council England, 'Most cities and large towns have an art house cinema where foreign films are regularly screened. And they are always screened in the original language with subtitles – never dubbed' (Little, personal communication, 2004). Maria Delgado clarifies that dubbing is 'largely a phenomenon of the non-English speaking world where Hollywood is dubbed to reach the widest possible global audience' (Delgado, personal communication, 2004). In that very little European television reaches the United Kingdom, very little dubbed material is shown on British television except for specialized channels.[8]

In 1960 in France, Caillé took a firm stance in favour of dubbing; in 1998, Gottlieb asserted that dubbing was preferred in France and Germany. His statement for Germany may still be true, but in France subtitled foreign films are no longer hard to find.

In Paris there are numerous foreign films listed in *L'Officiel des Spectacles* for 30 April–6 May 2003; virtually all of them, except animated features and *Harry Potter et la chambre des secrets*, are original versions. Among the 12 new releases featured that week, ten were foreign films (from Brazil, Germany/Russia, Great Britain, Iran, Japan, Mexico, Spain, and the United States). All of these, like other first-run foreign films, were being shown with subtitles (Alluin *et al.*, 2003). The situation in Paris has apparently changed in the past 15 years. By contrast, the 24–30 May 1989 issue of *L'Officiel des Spectacles* lists a number of foreign films that were available in either subtitled or dubbed versions; a full-page advertisement for *L'Ami retrouvé* (*Reunion*, United States, 1988) highlights seven Parisian movie houses that were showing the original version in English and six that were showing the dubbed version in French. Literary agent Geneviève Ulmann and her husband Pierre affirm that subtitled movies have been available in Paris over the several decades of their memories but that major films, like those of Italian director Federico Fellini and Swedish director Ingmar Bergman were also dubbed.

Outside Paris, the practice of releasing both subtitled and dubbed versions of commercial movies continues. In Grenoble, a university city in Eastern France, spectators today, like those in Madrid, may choose between foreign films in original versions with subtitles and dubbed versions in French. As revealed in *Le Petit Bulletin* of 7–14 May 2003, the former are typically found at smaller movie houses and the latter at the more commercial multiplex theatres. Spectators that week could see a variety of movies from Argentina, Italy, Japan, Mexico and Russia, as well as France and the United States. In recent years, there has been a shift from dubbing to subtitled original versions in provincial cities even though dubbing still dominates in small towns. Throughout France the classification 'Salle d'Art et d'Essai Classée Recherche' identifies a network of government-subsidized movie houses that specialize in experimental and art films; all of them show foreign films in their original versions with subtitles. At Grenoble's participating Cinéma Le Méliès, the programme for 30 April–13 May 2003 included three French, two Korean, and one Latin American films for adults. Original versions of movies are also available on cable television, Canal+, and the French/German cultural channel Arte – but only for night owls.[9] The handful of listings for original versions on the Radio-Television page of *Le Monde* do not cite any that begin until after 10 pm.

In Germany, too, the regular television channels are in German only, as are most foreign movies. But movie-goers in large cities now have the option of seeing original versions of foreign films just as they do in Madrid or Barcelona. In Frankfurt, dubbed versions are the norm, but one cineplex, the Turm-Palast, routinely offers subtitled versions.[10] The American film *Seabiscuit*, which was featured on the cover of *Kino Journal Frankfurt* for the last week in September 2003, was thus available in dubbed German at six theatres but also in subtitled English at Turm-Palast.

In his support of dubbing, Caillé asserted that subtitles pass by too quickly for movie spectators to read. Guidelines for subtitling have now been designed to prevent that problem. Subtitles, consisting of one or two lines, should be placed left or centre at the bottom of the screen. A maximum of about 35 characters, including punctuation marks and spacing between words, is typical. However, the number of characters may vary depending upon the equipment used (Hervey *et al.*, 1995: 148–49).[11] One line requires a minimum of two seconds' viewing time and a double-line subtitle requires four; no title should be shown for fewer than two nor more than six seconds (Hervey *et al.*, 1995: 147). Based on her thesis research and practical experience, Ellen Bay adopted a more conservative position than this norm. She considers '25 to 30 character lines to be optimal, as they are easily read' and recommends a range of three to five seconds of viewing time for a more balanced feel (Bay, 1998: 7). In his proposed set of subtitling standards, aimed primarily at European television, Fotios Karamitroglou advises three and a half seconds for a single line of seven to eight words and five and a half seconds for a two-line subtitle of 14–16 words (Karamitroglou, 1998: 4–5).

For television or video, the subtitler will work from videotape (original language source) to disk (titles in the target language), but Gottlieb describes the process for cinema as being paper to paper (Gottlieb, 1998: 245). Starting with a post-production script, the subtitler translates the dialogue and then reduces it to a list of subtitles that will then be transferred to the film by others. The titles must be synchronized with the movie. For that purpose, a process called spotting is implemented: 'The subtitler runs the film on a viewing/editing table, measuring the time of each phrase, sentence and shot to determine when titles should start and stop' (Hervey *et al.*, 1995: 147).

Subtitles should properly reflect not just the meaning but also the nuances and register of the language of the dialogue. Ideally a translator should be able to consult others and work collaboratively on the subtitles, but time and funding generally prevent this. Sometimes no written script is available and the translator must depend on his or her ears. Gottlieb concludes that 'a subtitler worth his salt needs to have the aural competence of an interpreter' (Gottlieb, 1994: 108). Whether working solely from the oral text or from a written script, the subtitler is challenged not only to translate interlingually but also to 'transfer the dialog from one sub-code (the seemingly unruly spoken language) to another (the more rigid written language)' (Gottlieb, 1994: 106).

Numerous conventions exist to facilitate easy reading of subtitles. When dialogue of two speakers is shown on the same screen, each line is introduced by a dash and the lines are generally left justified rather than centred. Bay found that using italics for the second speaker allowed viewers to detect the change of voice more readily. She gives this example:

– Why are you crying?
– *Because I want to!* (Bay, 1998: 6)

Bay notes that, in accord with English grammar rules, italics may be used to set off a foreign word and are also routinely used for a narrator's voice-over. Karamitroglou specifies that quotation marks should surround the italicized subtitle if the off-screen source is a public broadcast, aimed at a number of people, rather than a narrator within the text; italics, embraced by quotation marks, likewise are used for song lyrics (Karamitroglou, 1998: 9).

Bay advises against varying the colour of the titles unless there is an artistic reason for doing so or the change is needed for clear viewing (Bay, 1998: 6). In his detailed, prescriptive perspective, Karamitroglou states that subtitles should be coloured pale white, rather than the more fatiguing snow-bright white, and should be 'presented against a grey, see-through "ghost box"' (Karamitroglou, 1998: 4). The ghost box – or the occasional use of coloured subtitles – will prevent the problem of which Kilborn complains: unreadable white subtitles against a white background (Kilborn, 1989: 426). Karamitroglou adds that neither bold-face nor underlining is permitted in subtitles (Karamitroglou, 1998: 9). The font chosen should be without serifs, for clearer viewing, and with proportional distribution, to save space (Karamitroglou, 1998: 4). The use of upper- and lower-case letters follows normal rules except that all upper-case letters should be used for displays and captions (Karamitroglou, 1998: 9).[12]

Two short subtitles are easier to read than one long subtitle. Although the optimum division is two lines of more or less equal length, the segmentation must be done with care. Karamitroglou states that segmentations should be made 'at the highest syntactic nodes possible' (Karamitroglou, 1998: 9). Based on this principle, he diagrams a sample sentence, compares the segmentations

'The destruction of the
city was inevitable.'

'The destruction of the city
     was inevitable.'

and concludes that the second is easier to read even though the first contains lines of equal length (Karamitroglou, 1998: 10). In reviewing the weaknesses in their students' work as subtitlers, Fukushima and Major observe a number of instances of failure to segment in accord with Karamitroglou's syntactical guidelines (Fukushima & Major, 2002: 70).

Perhaps easier to implement than the grammatical concept of highest syntactic node is Helen Reid's suggestion for rhetorical segmentation. This Dutch television subtitler has defined three kinds of possible segmentation: grammatical, rhetorical, and visual (quoted in Gottlieb, 1994: 109). Grammatical segmentation follows semantic units; visual follows camera moves and cuts in the film. Rhetorical segmentation is guided by the rhythm of speech; cuts come 'where the speaker pauses to breathe' (Gottlieb, 1994: 110). Gottlieb is primarily concerned with breaks between screens: 'pauses are typically found at intervals of 5–6 seconds, exactly the two-line subtitle standard' (Gottlieb, 1994: 110). But the rhetorical test could also be applied to the example cited above. A pause between 'the' and 'city' would sound strange indeed; the eye is jarred by such a division just as the ear is.

Ideally sentences are contained in a single cut. If a sentence must be split over more than one title, three suspension points are placed at the end of the first one and three at the beginning of the following one. Hervey *et al.* give several examples, including this one:

It's the best exam I've ever done . . .

. . . and I got my worst mark ever. (Hervey *et al.*, 1995: 150)

A related problem occurs when the visual and audio tracks of the source film do not coincide. For her subtitling of Víctor Erice's film *El sur*, Bay had to confront cuts in which the voice-over describing the moment lagged behind the image. Her solution was to have the subtitle appear for at least a second before the cut and a second after, thus continuing the title from the visual to the audio cue (Bay, 1998: 11). Her decision complements Gottlieb's observation about public service television: 'If an important, fast-spoken utterance is followed by silence and the camera remains focused on the speaker, a TV subtitler would keep the subtitle on the air for a second or two, giving viewers the time needed to read it' (Gottlieb, 1994: 115).

Formatting rules, aimed at ease of reading, are straightforward enough that they can be imposed, or at least evaluated, more or less mechanically. Carrying the content over to the audience effectively within the restricted space is a far greater challenge. There may be occasional cuts in which the film's dialogue does not exceed in words per second the desirable reading speed, but they will be exceptional. The translator should condense without resorting to telegraphic language. Bay suggests that pronouns and conjunctions can usually be deleted 'often with the positive effects of "tightening" the text and eliminating ambiguity' (Bay, 1998: 5). Karamitroglou provides categories of linguistic items that can be omitted: padding expressions that are empty of semantic load (such as 'you know'); redundant adjectives and adverbs ('great big'); and responsive expressions ('yes' and 'no') (Karamitroglou, 1998: 12). Reductions in number of words may also be achieved through changes in syntax: active instead of passive voice, positive instead of negative structures, prepositional phrases instead of subordinate clauses, and so on. Among Karamitroglou's convincing examples are these:

'It is believed by many people.' (30 characters)
'Many people believe.' (20 characters)

'I'll study when I finish watching this movie.' (46 characters)
'I'll study after this movie.' (28 characters)

Robert Gray, who does English titles for French-Canadian movies, defines his 'task as a subtitler as giving the audience enough information to be able to follow the film' (quoted in Boyar, 1986). Optimally, that information will at least hint at differences in dialect and language register of the various characters. At the same time, the subtitler must strive to create a cohesive whole. Titles will disappear within a few seconds and it is imperative that they convey transparent continuity and cogency (Hervey *et al.*, 1995: 151). Changing the order of dialogue or inserting words like 'it' or 'this' to refer to antecedents will confuse the viewer.

In essence, the approach to preparing subtitles or a dubbed film script should be the same as for any theatrical translation. The translator should have a thorough understanding of the source text before beginning the project. That understanding includes an analysis of the text sequence by sequence while simultaneously placing those sequences within a cohesive whole. Boyar believes the subtitler should see the film at least twice to get a good feel for the characters and story; but he notes that often 'subtitling is done so quickly and cheaply that errors – sometimes amusing ones – occur.' Cary observes that it takes months and years to create original dialogue, but yet the translator will be forced to rush in writing the film script for dubbing (Cary, 1986: 70).

A specific error that Javier Marías discusses with respect to *The Patriot* is one he spotted in a Spanish subtitle of the video version, viewed through a store window: 'En el nombre del Padre, del Hijo y del Santo Fantasma.' The word 'fantasma' struck him as a blatant error in that the fixed expression, in the context of the Father, the Son and the Holy Ghost, is 'Espíritu Santo'. Later he learned that in the movie about the American Revolution, the character played by Mel Gibson is known by fellow colonists as 'The Ghost'. When a minister refers to 'the Holy Ghost', he is secretly alluding to the Gibson figure but with the expectation that British soldiers will miss his double meaning. Out of context, Marías obviously missed it as well, and he correctly points out that the character's nickname throughout the movie should have been 'Espíritu' so that the minister's comment would have passed by the British without drawing attention to itself. Had the subtitler viewed the movie twice before beginning the translation, the problem would have been anticipated and the error avoided.

Subtitles at the movies or on video versions are permanently on the screen. Modern teletext technology and DVDs provide viewers with the option of turning titles on or off, perhaps even choosing between levels of speed and complexity. In this respect, such subtitles are like the closed captioning that is available to hearing-impaired television viewers who have the proper access codes.[13] Open captioning, like traditional subtitles, is in constant view; this is the system that is used by opera companies, at times for intra- as well as interlingual titles, but has only recently been introduced for stage productions.

A frequent method for captioning at the opera might be called 'supertitles' – open captioning projected above the proscenium.[14] That is the system that Ellen Bay observed at the New York City Opera and that I saw at the Opéra de Monte-Carlo in May 2000 during the premiere production of Charles Chaynes's *Cecilia* (libretto by Eduardo Manet). The opera *Cecilia*, although based on the Cuban novel *Cecilia Valdés*, is written in French, as were the captions projected during the sung passages. Director Jorge Lavelli considers captions essential even if the spectators speak the same language because he believes that opera lyrics are always hard to understand. With respect to *Cecilia*, the cast included American singers; Lavelli feared their foreign accent might lower audience comprehension (Lavelli, telephone interview, 2000).

The underlying motivation behind captioning in the theatre is no doubt the same as for opera: expanding the audience by making the text more accessible. Among the first Hispanic theatres in the United States to implement open captioning in English for Spanish-language productions is Teatro Avante in Coral Gables, Florida. There the titles are projected like slides; the size of the letters varies depending upon the particular equipment. According to Mario Ernest Sanchez, Producing Artistic Director of Teatro Avante and of the International Hispanic Theatre Festival, the program they use is quite simple: it only requires that a person be proficient with a computer keyboard. More difficult is knowing how to divide the segments of dialogue; that decision resides with the stage director. Sanchez says that some directors prefer abbreviated titles; others want to have the complete text projected and then let the audience choose to read or not.

Live theatre poses major difficulties in comparison with movies or even opera. With film, the images are fixed; in opera, the orchestra will perform predictably so that the music will continue even if a singer flubs a line. On the other hand, actors on stage may omit or improvise words; they may unintentionally change the order of dialogue. Claude Demarigny, a translator in Paris who works from Spanish, has prepared captions for performance; he explains that he has handled the equipment himself so that he can make rapid adjustments if necessary. In Germany, translators Almuth Fricke and Susanne Hartwig have similarly operated the equipment themselves to project captions they created in Microsoft Powerpoint.[15] These translators may derive titles for plays they have already translated or may directly create captions for a source text.

Demarigny prepared French titles for a work by Gabriel García Márquez that was performed by a group from Bogotá, Colombia. For their staging at the Odéon Theatre, the system used was that of supertitles. He observes that it is challenging to keep within the limit of 40 characters and yet retain the meaning, tone, and spirit of the original author's text.

Fricke, who resides in Cologne and specializes in Latin American theatre, and Hartwig, a resident of Giessen who concentrates on plays from Spain, each indicates that open captioning in the theatre requires abbreviation. Their respective e-mail messages (Fricke, 2002; Hartwig, 2003) repeat the concepts already enunciated for film subtitling. Fricke explicitly compares titles for theatre and movies: both involve limited space and a fixed number of characters. Based on her captioning for performances in Berlin and Marburg, Hartwig sets forth the following guidelines: project a maximum of two lines of titles at a time; avoid long sentences by shortening text; simplify grammatical structure without splitting phrases between screens; maintain suspense. She further observes how German syntax complicates the goal of achieving concise language.

Bay's experience with open captioning in Spanish for a 2002 production at George Street Playhouse in New Brunswick, New Jersey, stands in radical contrast to the experience and advice of Demarigny, Fricke and Hartwig. Not taking into consideration ease of reading, the theatre directors required her to prepare the complete text. In the Miami area, Teatro Avante may assume that many of their spectators are bilingual, do understand Spanish, and need not rely heavily on rapid English captions if the complete text is projected. While New Brunswick is also in a bilingual area and has a growing Hispanic population, George Street was aiming at a monolingual audience: recent Spanish-speaking immigrants who have not yet learned English. Through a grant-funded Bridge Project, this regional, professional theatre specifically reached out to the Hispanic community for designated performances of *Public Ghosts–Private Stories*, a play by Ain Gordon that draws on oral history about the city.[16] The playhouse has a thrust stage rather than a proscenium. Accordingly, Spanish-speaking spectators were seated in a particular section of the theatre so that they could view a large monitor mounted over the playing space.

There is no question that the goal of the George Street Playhouse management was laudable, but the results of their first-time experiment were less than satisfactory. There is not yet a tradition of captioning in New York area Hispanic theatres, so they were basically inventing the process. Their mistakes provide a number of insights on how open captioning does and does not work well. In the field of theatrical translation, tension between theatre practitioners and translators is not unknown. In subtitling and dubbing, there are always technical restraints. In this case, the theatre people and technicians dominated. With hindsight, translator Bay realizes that she should have asserted herself and not agreed to the requirements (Bay, personal communication, 2002). Certainly those in charge must have been unaware that a Spanish translation normally is 25% longer than its source text in English.

From the outset, George Street's decision to translate the dialogue to Spanish in its entirety predictably made it difficult, if not impossible, for spectators both to watch the play and to keep up with the reading. Rather than one or two lines of stationary text, for *Public Ghosts–Private Stories* three lines of scrolling text were visible at a time. Karamitroglou correctly warns us that this kind of overlay – a technique for presenting a dynamic text, often to avoid revealing surprises too quickly – 'should be used cautiously' (Karamitroglou, 1998: 6). As spectator, I considered the process a frustrating test in speed reading.

At George Street, serious problems resulted from arrangements with the company that rented the captioning equipment. The technician who would operate the keyboard did not read Spanish and therefore indicated he would project the captions by following the parallel English text. To make his work easier, he told Bay to produce a literal translation, broken down into fixed lines of 32 characters that would correspond to the source text. Neither the system nor the technician's capabilities allowed for adjustment if the actors in performance made changes in the dialogue.

Moreover, the equipment was not installed before opening night, so there was no opportunity to preview the captions. During actual performance, Bay discovered to her dismay that the technician had reformatted her Spanish captions using his English-language spell check. Inadvertently, he 'prompted several words to bounce back into English' and 'he deleted a few lines, and as he did not speak Spanish, did not realize that they were missing.' Even if there were no such accidental errors, Bay strongly feels that preview was essential: 'Although the text was proofread various times, captioning is a visual art, and its effect is not solely based on the quality of the translation, but also upon the physical appearance of the words on the screen' (Bay, personal communication, 2002).

In his responses to my questions about captioning at Teatro Avante, Sanchez indicated that no special training is needed to project titles during performance. But Teatro Avante not only has years of experience with the process and appropriate equipment, but no doubt also can draw upon bilingual technicians. It is essential that the technician – like the translators in France and Germany who work the keyboard themselves – understand both the language of the play in performance and the language of the titles. Also, if the purpose is to make the performance accessible to monolingual spectators, the titles must be designed for ease of reading.

Although Caillé's categorical rejection of subtitling is extreme, it is true that dubbing for films, despite its greater cost, offers significant advantages. The viewer does not have to divide attention between image and words; the need to abbreviate dialogue is eliminated. Historically, criticism of dubbed films has focused primarily on the problem of synchronizing lip movements between source and target languages. Caillé states that dubbing's initial bad reputation resulted from a total disregard of that issue: films were cut into a series of sequences to guide the actors reading the translated script but no effort was made to synchronize the movement of the lips. The translator should work with the text in juxtaposition with the images.

One-for-one substitutions seldom exist. Caillé cites the problematic word pairs of the English 'hat' and the two-syllable French *chapeau*, and the two-syllable French *amour* and the three-syllable Italian *amore* (Caillé, 1960: 104). Cary provides the example of the simple German negative *nicht* and the divided French equivalent *ne . . . pas* (Cary, 1960: 112). Matching two languages syllable by syllable is never an easy matter.

According to Rowe (1960: 116), some viewers are more concerned about lips than about literature. On the other hand, total fidelity to synchronization can yield results as unsatisfactory as literal translation. Although the goal is to produce natural language that is synchronized with the visual cues, Caillé thus wisely affirms that the sense of the dialogue should be more important than lip movement (Caillé, 1960: 107).

Cary recalls seeing a film version of *Hamlet* that ignored synchronization but was so admirable that within ten seconds the audience accepted it (Cary, 1986: 70).

As previously mentioned, Spain has a long tradition of dubbing films and has perfected the strategy. Sally Templer's detailed description of the process followed by Estudios de Doblaje Sonoblok in Barcelona is especially valuable for understanding how dubbing is implemented. By 1995, when she presented her discussion as part of a seminar in Valladolid, Templer had translated 130 feature length movies.[17] Theoretically the writer of the dubbed script has the opportunity to play and replay the film (Cary, 1986: 69). In practice Templer has an average of four days to produce her translated dialogue. Generally she sees the movie before beginning her work but on occasion she has had to start with just the written script.

Templer's contribution as author of the translated script is only the first step. The translated dialogue is divided into 'takes', a term derived from filming movies that Templer says is a misnomer when applied to dubbing, where it really refers to 'loops' of celluloid. These takes, or loops, are projected over and over for actors to speak the lines in accord with the image until the dubbing director is satisfied. Next a specialist sets about adjusting the dialogue so that the text '"fits in the mouths" of the characters on screen' (Templer, 1995: 153). The distributor, who has commissioned the dubbed version, may supervise the adjusting process and also offer corrections. Once the adjusted script has been approved, a copy of the movie is cut into takes to coincide with new soundtrack takes. The corrected, translated dialogue is typed into corresponding sequences; the format, to facilitate reading, includes indications of pauses, gestures, and so on. The dubbing actors assemble in a recording studio to 'put the text in the mouths of the actors on screen' (Templer, 1995: 154). At this point, the dubbing director may introduce additional adjustments. Technicians then mix the Spanish dialogue into the original soundtrack. The client is given the opportunity to view the movie in *Interlock*, a technique in which visual and sound tracks are still separate. If further corrections are needed, there will be retakes and a new mixing of the soundtrack. As a last step, a negative and copies of the dubbed movie are produced.

Cary suggests that, because the writer of the dubbed script can view the film over and over and follow the facial expressions and gestures of the actors, it is possible to create the new script with the help of a literal translation even if one does not know the original language at all (Cary, 1986: 69). The question, however, as Joseph Farrell has noted in the context of translation for the stage, is 'precisely what a literal translation might mean'; the translator needs to interpret, to decide obscure points, and to make choices as to 'the meaning that fits into the overall context' of the script (Farrell, 1996: 284). It is likely that a dubbed filmscript of *The Patriot*, prepared from a literal translation in the narrow sense, would repeat the 'Santo Fantasma' error that Marías detected in the subtitled version. From Templer's description of how she lives each film intensively and feels each character's role, it is clear that she believes translations should go far beyond the 'literal'. Certainly for a dubbed film to come fully alive, the script must be created by a talented writer. Rowe, lamenting how some comic movies fall flat in translation, astutely presents this basic principle: 'dubbing of comedy requires above all a writer capable of writing a funny line in his own language' (Rowe, 1960: 120).

Templer clarifies that the actors doing the dubbing at her studio often do not know the source language, usually English. They are guided by the translated script, coupled with the original actors' facial expressions and tone of voice, which they do hear several times before beginning their own recording. The adjusters also generally do not understand the source movie but rely on the same written text and visual/auditory cues to guide their work. Templer emphasizes the fact that in this kind of situation the real responsibility for avoiding errors in meaning resides with the translator (Templer, 1995: 154).

In a theatrical translation for the stage, one option is to move the action entirely to a different time and place. For a translated filmscript, that option obviously does not exist: the locale is fixed. The translator, in cooperation with the dubbing director and actors, nevertheless must still consider how to handle the linguistic aspects of local colour, such as dialect and slang. Rowe questions the wisdom of having actors speak with a foreign accent in an attempt to retain the film's foreign flavour, or, worse yet, of having French cops speak pidgin English in the English-language version of a French film (Rowe, 1960: 119). Of course a translation that only carries over surface meaning without regard to register or idiolect also has its shortcomings.

Templer states that American films pose particular problems for dubbing because the country has so many different ethnic and social groups and such a propensity for slang, some of it incomprehensible even to many American viewers. She suggests avoiding equivalents that are conspicuously regional or colloquial; for obscenities, she recommends evaluating the social and emotional situation of the character to determine the proper register (Templer, 1995: 156–57). Her philosophy does not differ radically from advice for theatrical translators in general.

There are major differences between dubbing films and 'simultaneous translation', the equivalent process for live theatre. The writer of the dubbed filmscript in essence is dealing with a single performance of the work; working in collaboration with a large crew of people, the translator produces a version that will become an immutable soundtrack. For theatrical translation in general, the writer of the translation, like the original author, may contemplate a text that is open to varying interpretions by different directors and casts. For simultaneous translation, because it relates to a specific live performance, the text may have to be adjusted, on the spot, to coordinate with what is happening on the stage.

At first glance, 'simultaneous translation' – the term used by two of the major Hispanic theatres in the United States, Repertorio Español in New York City and Teatro Hispano Gala in Washington, DC – is a misnomer, an oxymoron. Translation normally refers to written work and hence cannot be produced at the same time as the performance; the corresponding word for oral presentation is 'interpretation'. Indeed Teatro de la Luna, another theatre in the Washington, DC, area, began publicizing their option as 'simultaneous English interpretation' and now calls it 'live English dubbing'.

The word 'interpretation' with its two meanings – oral translation and the creative expression of actors – would seem apropos but poses a difficulty.[18] For the uninitiated, simultaneous interpretation may imply that the actors in the second language ad lib their text. The former management of George Street Playhouse had precisely that idea when they first considered providing a simultaneous Spanish version of Bernardo Solano's English-language play *Entries* for performance in 1996: they started with the false assumption that bilingual actors could readily interpret the play in progress. In reality, few actors have training in the extraordinarily difficult and demanding field of simultaneous interpreting and few professional simultaneous interpreters have any training as actors. Besides, if the actors interpret independently of each other, the foreign language text will not form a cohesive whole. The point of departure has to be a careful, written play translation. Fortunately, the directors of the theatre were open to suggestions and ultimately implemented a more effective approach.

The dominant strategy in the United States is the one used in 1992 by Teatro Hispano Gala when they staged Jaime Salom's *Una hoguera al amanecer*, a Brechtian historical drama about Bartolomé de las Casas. My translation, *Bonfire at Dawn*, was also scheduled for publication by ESTRENO Plays in conjunction with the centennial marking the arrival of Spaniards in the New World. Using this existing translation, director

Hugo Medrano hired four actors, two men and two women, to synchronize a reading of the English dialogue with the action on stage. Special equipment allowed their voices to be transmitted directly to interested spectators, who heard the English version over headsets. Although the limited cast required more doubling in roles than is true of the source text, the four voices were sufficient to clarify the interaction of characters in dialogue. The actors read their roles with appropriate expression, much as they would have done at a staged reading or in a radio production. Medrano decided to shorten Salom's play by eliminating the epilogue; for this and other changes, he altered the English text accordingly, but it was the function of the actors to improvise if the onstage performers transposed lines.

At the other extreme, the procedure that Susanne Hartwig describes for simultaneous translation in Germany is more cost-effective. The equipment required would be about the same, but the extra cast of four professional actors is eliminated. Hartwig explains that the counterpart convention in German television is for the translator/interpreter to sound like a robot: to read with no voice modulation. Spectators in a German theatre do not expect to hear a real performance over their headsets. For a production in Bonn, Hartwig read all of the roles, both male and female, from her own translation. She reports that timing the reading with the action on stage is extremely difficult (Hartwig, personal communication, 2003).

Difficult and challenging are doubtless the best words to describe the various procedures that we have considered in this chapter. In the wide domain of theatrical translation, both the forms requiring abbreviation – subtitling for movies and open captioning for plays – and the forms that focus on synchronization – dubbed filmscripts or simultaneous translation – are genuine jigsaw puzzles. Getting the pieces to fall into place will call into play all the experience and talent the translator can muster.

Notes

1. The initials of the fictitious Empar Ribera, used as the title of the play, refer intertextually to *Plany en la mort d'Enric Ribera*, a play by another Catalan author, Rodolf Sirera. In that audiences outside the region would miss the connection, Pons changed the movie title to *Actrius* (Actresses), and the French translation is likewise called *Actrices*. Holt calls his American translation of the text *Stages*.
2. In 2003 I checked a sample of DVDs in stores in Central New Jersey, Madrid, London, Paris, and Frankfurt. If there were any foreign movies available at my video rental store in New Jersey, I did not spot them; foreign films – primarily

but not exclusively American – abounded in other countries. The traveller should be alerted, however, that the same problem of incompatibility of format exists in DVDs as in videos: PALS in Europe versus NTSC in the United States. A DVD purchased on one side of the Atlantic will not play on regular machines on the other side.

At a large 'video rental' store in New Jersey, I found a number of American movies with English, French and Spanish options; typically these included one of the foreign languages as a soundtrack and the other as subtitles. In the case of *My Big Fat Greek Wedding*, an independent film that achieved unexpected popularity in 2002, only English was offered as a soundtrack but the subtitle options included Greek as well as the usual three languages. In Germany, the DVD of this same film offered soundtracks and subtitles in both German and English but did not include other languages. This limited pattern of source and target languages as soundtracks and as subtitles was one I found frequently in my sampling except in London.

Mack, an American director and actor who currently resides in Paris where he frequently does dubbing into English for documentaries, alerts me that dubbing and translation are also important for video games, which represent an expanding entertainment market (Mack, personal communication, 2004).

3. Major Hollywood studios initially rejected dubbing in favour of filming parallel Spanish-language versions of American movies for their largest foreign market. They hired Spanish playwrights to serve as scriptwriters. Once the English-language movie was completed, they used the same sets to film the translated versions with Spanish-speaking casts (Holt, 1980: 19–20).

4. The translation of opera is an area requiring special talents. Herman and Apter provide this summary: 'The theory behind opera translation is easily stated: translate the libretto so as to preserve the drama, poetry, and music of the original. But all three depend on the complex interplay of words and notes. The words are part of the music; the drama results from them both. If a translator mistakenly tries to sacrifice the words to the music or the music to the words, the result will be the sort of disaster all too commonly heard in contemporary opera houses' (Herman & Apter, 1991: 100). They affirm: 'Only a full *performable* translation of the libretto, re-creating the subtleties of plot, the nuances of character, and the *interplay* of words and music can carry an opera across the language barrier' (Herman & Apter, 1991: 102).

5. The use of subtitles, dubbing, and voice-over for news broadcasts and other television programming lies outside the scope of this study. For commentaries on the subject, see Delabastita (1989), Dollerup (1974), Gottlieb (1994), Kurz (1990) and Tveit (1998, 2000). Tveit predicts that subtitles will be used more and more: 'Providing teletext alternatives will also be a must for the satellite television companies with their multilingual audiences' (Tveit, 1998: 369). In 1994, Gottlieb reported that almost half of the existing television sets in Europe still lacked teletext facilities for receiving subtitles but that the situation was temporary: 'except for portables, all TV sets sold in (Western) Europe nowadays come with teletext' (Gottlieb, 1994: 118).

Another area worthy of research is the cross-Atlantic borrowing of television and film ideas. Among websites that provide information on American TV programmes based on British series is http://www.eskimo.com; their comprehensive guide, which I consulted in March 2004, had 40 listings. I am grateful to Steven Capsuto for pointing this subject out to me.

6. One graduate student, Ellen Bay, was intrigued enough by this class exercise that she arranged to do her required translation/interpretating internship at the two opera companies in New York City in order to learn more about captioning. As part of her masters thesis in translation (1998), in collaboration with Rutgers University's Office of Television and Radio, she created English subtitles for the video version of a Spanish film. In 2002, she wrote the Spanish captions for an English-language stage production at a regional theatre. In the preparation of this chapter, I am indebted to Bay's thesis research and to her recent, helpful responses to my questions.

7. I did not find newspaper listings in small Spanish cities I visited in 2003 for movie houses that similarly present subtitled rather than dubbed foreign films.

8. I did not travel outside the London area enough to verify personally the presence of subtitled versus dubbed foreign films in the United Kingdom in general. I am grateful to Little and Delgado for responding to my follow-up inquiries on this subject. Kilborn's 1989 assessment of the British situation – at least as I understood it – seems far off the mark for current reality.

9. I am grateful to Benoit Mitane for answering my questions about foreign films available in movie houses in provincial cities and on television. During my stay in Grenoble he kindly lent me movie schedules from several sources.

10. Randall Browne, an Australian who works in Frankfurt, told me that, in addition to film festivals, one can find subtitled versions at two movie houses. He also kindly referred me to *Kino Journal Frankfurt* for movie listings. In the issue I consulted, Turm Palast was clearly the place to find subtitled films. The other theatre, Kinopolis-Main-Taurus was showing *The Quiet American* in both languages but all other films were in German.

11. Bay edited a NTSC Beta version of the video with a PALTEX ES/D Edit Controller; she created and edited the subtitles on a 20K Dubner Character Generator.

    Hervey, Higgins and Haywood's *Thinking Spanish Translation* is the only textbook of Spanish translation among the several I have used in my courses that mentions dubbing or subtitling as aspects of the field. They include a eight-page section on the subject of subtitling with suggested practice exercises (Hervey *et al.*, 1995: 146–53). For an informative and detailed discussion of how subtitling has been taught in Japanese courses in the United States, see Fukushima and Major (2002).

12. Swedish subtitler Jan Ivarsson defines displays as texts, such as letters or newspaper headlines, that are recorded by the camera during the creation of the movie and captions as texts that are imposed on the finished film (quoted in Gottlieb, 1994: 107).

13. I wish to thank Lindsay Polumbus, of Caption Colorado, for a clarification of captioning and subtitling as well as services offered by this company. In their system, subtitling is more flexible in terms of font, colour, and placement, but is also more expensive than captioning. In an informational brochure, Caption Colorado identifies itself as the largest real-time captioning company in the United States. It serves 80 television stations, has ten years experience in captioning for the deaf, and has now added Spanish captioning to its offerings.

In addition to real-time captioning for television, the company can provide delayed/pre-recorded closed captioning offline. With appropriate screen and technical setup, they can facilitate captioning in theatres.

14. The system of 'MetTitles' developed at the Metropolitan Opera in New York City is closed captioning: it uses a screen, on the back of the seat in front of the spectator, that the individual can turn on or off. The screens 'are angled in such a way that you really are not bothered by the light coming from the screen of the person next to you' (Bay, personal communication, 2003). Captions for opera must be coordinated with the music even more than with the onstage action; music substitutes for the cuts considered in designing film subtitles. 'Think of the music in the same way that you would think of the movie screen ... You could not work doing subtitles for the Met or the CONY unless you can read and understand a musical score quite well' (Bay, personal communication, 2003).
15. Fricke specifies that she has worked with a PC and videobeam (to project Powerpoint titles on a screen), using Focon, a machine that is favoured by opera companies.
16. George Street Playhouse has a tradition of reaching out to special audiences. Audio-described performances with Braille programs are offered to blind patrons, open-captioned performances are offered for the hearing impaired, and on occasion they have offered sign language interpreting for designated performances.
17. I am grateful to a former student, Ana Ángulo, for providing me with relevant published materials as well as some related notes from this course.
18. To avoid the ambiguity presented by the double meaning of the word 'interpretation', professional interpreters in the United States now refer to their field as interpreting.

References

Alluin, P. _et al._ Nouveaux films. _L'Officiel des Spectacles_ (Paris). 2940 (30 April–6 May 2003): 57–63.

Alonso Tejada, L. _La represión sexual en la España de Franco_. Barcelona: Biblioteca Universal Caralt, 1977.

L'Ami retrouvé (Reunion). Dir. Jerry Schatzberg. Advertisement. _L'Officiel des Spectacles_ (Paris) 2213 (24–30 May 1989): 70.

Baker, M., ed. _Routledge Encyclopedia of Translation Studies_. New York & London: Routledge, 1998a.

Baker, M. and Hochel, B. Dubbing. In _Routledge Encyclopedia of Translation Studies_, 1998b, 74–77.

Bay, E. Subtitling the Spanish Film _El sur_. Masters thesis in translation. Rutgers, The State University of New Jersey, 1998.

Bay, E. E-mail, 22 October 2002.

Bay, E. E-mail, 3 February 2003.

Benet i Jornet, J. M. _E.R._, 2nd ed. Barcelona: Edicions 62, 1996.

Boyar, J. Subtitles: An art, not a science. From the _Orlando Sentinel_. Reprinted in _The Home News_ (New Brunswick, NJ), 11 September 1986.

Browne, R. Personal interview, 25 September 2003.

Caillé, P.-F. Cinéma et traduction. Le traducteur devant l'écran. *Babel* 6 (1960): 103–109.

Campbell, B. and Whitty, S. Movie capsules. *The Sunday Star-Ledger* (Newark, NJ), 22 June 2003, Section 4: 11.

Cary, E. (Cyrille Znosko-Borovski). La Traduction totale. *Babel* 6 (1960): 110–15.

Cary, E. *Comment faut-il traduire?* Introduction Michel Ballard. Presses Universitaires de Lille, 1986.

Cinéma Le Méliès. Program (Grenoble, France). 169 (30 April–13 May 2003).

Delabastita, D. Translation and mass-communication: film and T.V. translation as evidence of cultural dynamics. *Babel* 35.4 (1989): 193–218.

Delgado, M. E-mail, 4 February 2004.

Demarigny, C. Personal interview, 6 May 2003.

Dollerup, C. On subtitles in television programmes. *Babel* 20 (1974): 197–202.

Farrell, J. Participant in Round Table on Translation. In D. Johnson, ed., *Stages of Translation*. London: Absolute Classics, 1996, 281–94.

Fricke, A. E-mail, 28 November 2002.

Fukushima, T. and Major, D. L. Translation course in film subtitling. *Translation Review* 64 (2002): 59–77.

Gottlieb, H. Subtitling: Diagonal translation. *Perspectives: Studies in Translatology* 2.1 (1994): 101–22.

Gottlieb, H. Subtitling. In M. Baker, ed., *Routledge Encyclopedia of Translation Studies*, 1998, 244–48.

Hartwig, S. E-mail, 9 February 2003.

Herman, M. and Apter, R. Opera translation. In M. L. Larson, ed., *Translation: Theory and Practice. Tension and Interdependence*. American Translators Association Scholarly Monograph Series 5 (1991). State University of New York at Binghamton, 1991, 100–19.

Hervey, S., Higgins, I. and Haywood, L. M. *Thinking Spanish Translation. A Course in Translation Method: Spanish to English*. London and New York: Routledge, 1995.

Holt, M. P. *José López Rubio*. Boston: G. K. Hall, Twayne World Authors Series 553, 1980.

Holt, M. P. E-mail, 6 October 2003.

House, J. *A Model for Translation Quality Assessment*. Tübingen: TBL Verlag Gunter Narr, 1977.

http://www.eskimo.com/~rkj/weekly/aa102500a.htm Dateline, 25 October 2000; updated, 3 March 2004.

Karamitroglou, F. A proposed set of subtitling standards in Europe. *Translation Journal* [On-line serial] 2.2 (1998). Retrieved 13 April 2003 from http://accurapid.com/journal/04stndrd.htm

Kilborn, R. 'They Don't Speak Proper English': A New Look at the Dubbing and Subtitling Debate. *Journal of Multilingual and Multicultural Development* 10.5 (1989): 421–34.

Kino Journal Frankfurt. 39/3 (25 Sept.–1 Oct. 2003).

Kurz, I. Overcoming language barriers in European television. In D. Bowen and M. Bowen, eds, *Interpreting – Yesterday, Today, and Tomorrow*. American Translators Association Scholarly Monograph *Series* 4 (1990). State University of New York at Binghamton, 1990, 168–75.

Lavelli, J. Telephone interview, 23 May 2000.

Le Petit Bulletin. L'hebdo gratuit des spectacles (Grenoble, France). 436 (7–14 May 2003).

Little, H. E-mail, 3 February 2004.

Mack, C. Personal interview, 16 May 2003.

Mack, C. E-mail, 7 March 2004.

Marías, J. Por la felicidad de los lectores. *El Semanal* 23 December 2001: 8.

Mitane, B. Personal interview, 10 May 2003.

Polumbus, L. E-mail, 3 February 2003.

Radio-Télévision. *Le Monde* (Paris), 7 May 2003: 31.

Robinson, R. Movie capsules. *Chicago Tribune*, 21 June 2003: Section 1: 13, 16, 17.

Rowe, T. L. The English dubbing text. *Babel* 6 (1960): 116–20.

Sanchez, M. E. E-mail, 16 December 2002.

Templer, S. Traducción para el doblaje. Transposición del lenguaje hablado (casi una catarsis). In *Perspectivas de la traducción inglés/español. 3er curso superior de traducción*. Coordinated by Purificación Fernández Nistal and José Mª Bravo Gozalo. Universidad de Valladolid: Instituto e Ciencias de la Educación, 1995, 153–65.

Time Out London. Film: Current releases A–Z. No. 1705 (23–30 April 2003): 75–79.

Tveit, J. E. The role of translation in the film and television industries. In A. G. Macfarlane, ed., Proceedings of the 39th Annual Conference of the American Translators Association. Alexandria, VA: ATA, 1998, 365–69.

Tveit, J. E. The challenges of subtitling. *ATA Chronicle* 29.6 (June 2000): 43–45, 47.

Ulmann, G. and Ulmann, P. Personal interview, 5 May 2003.

Werth, B. E-mail, 6 October 2003.

Wills, D. The French Remake *Breathless* and Cinematic Citationality. In A. Horton and S. Y. McDouglas, eds, *Play It Again, Sam. Retakes on Remakes*. With an Afterword by Leo Braudy. Berkeley, Los Angeles, and London: University of California Press, 1998, 147–61.

Chapter 7

On and Off the Screen: The Many Faces of Adaptation

A quick glance at the most celebrated American movies of late 2002 reveals the continuing importance of adaptation. Heading the list of Oscar nominees in 2003 was *Chicago* (dir. Rob Marshall); a dazzling film adaptation of Bob Fosse's 1975 musical (revived on Broadway in 1996), it simultaneously paid tribute to other Fosse stage productions, most notably *All That Jazz*. Also at the top was *The Hours* (dir. Stephen Daldry), an adaptation of Michael Cunningham's novel that in turn weaves Virginia Woolf's 1925 novel, *Mrs. Dalloway*, into a complex narrative of the lives of three women who are removed from one another in time and space. The list of 2002 movies includes one specifically titled *Adaptation* (dir. Spike Jonze). This ingeniously metatheatrical film portrays both Charlie Kaufman – the real-life scriptwriter who is struggling to adapt a real non-fiction book, *The Orchid Thief* – and Susan Orlean – the author of that study who, in the world of the movie, becomes obsessed with her subject.

Although adaptation has been practised since the days of silent movies, its pervasiveness does not mean that it has been universally accepted. Some theorists have even rejected the strategy per se. Numerous commentaries have given absolute preference to fiction over film or to film over drama. Such dogmatic positions overlook the complexities of interchange. Sources for films are not limited to literature: they may include a range of texts from real life to comic books. Robert Stam correctly states that film adaptations 'are caught up in the ongoing whirl of textual reference and transformation, of texts generating other texts in an endless process of recycling, transformation, and transmutation, with no clear point of origin' (Stam, 2000: 66). Academic criticism that focuses narrowly on the transformation of novels, particularly ones considered great literature, overlooks this broader range of adaptation. Luca Somigli shows, for example, how comic books, the epitome of low culture, have been transformed into film.

With regard to theatre, many commentators have found drama too wordy and too static for screen adaptation. Such criticism tends to overlook the fact that theatre is performance as well as dramatic literature. Progressively theatre has adopted cinematic techniques in staging.[1] At the extreme is *Cegada de amor* (Blinded by Love), a 1996 production of the Barcelona group La Cubana that melded the two genres: actors in a movie about making a movie stepped through vertical slits in the screen to enter the theatre and interact with the audience. In more conventional ways, exchange works in both directions: plays have frequently been adapted as movies, but film scripts can also be transformed into stage plays. And, as Nia Vardalos's *My Big Fat Greek Wedding* attests, a single text or idea may be translated to various media.

Vardalos, as actor and author, portrays the comic conflicts that arise when a young woman, from a close-knit Greek-American family, falls in love with a man who is not Greek. Vardalos created a comedy routine in 1996 and then turned it into her own one-woman play. By 2002, her screenplay version (dir. Joel Zwick), starring herself, had become the most successful independent film in history. In 2003 it was spun into a television comedy series, *My Big Fat Greek Life*. In transposing a basic story across media, Vardalos is following a well-worn trajectory.

An outstanding predecessor to Vardalos's play/movie/television progression is Neil Simon's *The Odd Couple*, which over a period of four decades has undergone a variety of transformations, not all initiated by the playwright. This ever popular American comedy deals with two mismatched men whose efforts to live together in New York City, following their separation from their wives and children, meet with humourous failure. The Broadway production, starring Walter Matthau as the sloppy Oscar and Art Carney as the fastidious Felix, won for Simon the Tony Award for best play in 1965. The Broadway production ran through 1967, with Jack Klugman eventually taking over the role of Oscar. The text is now firmly established as part of theatre repertory around the world.

Simon's screenplay for the 1968 film version of *The Odd Couple* (starring Matthau and Jack Lemmon, dir. Gene Saks) was nominated for an Academy Award. A subsequent television series, produced by Garry Marshall without involvement from Simon, featured Klugman and Tony Randall; it entertained audiences for several seasons, 1970–1975. On the other hand, the translation of the characters from white to black in *The New Odd Couple*, also produced for television by Marshall and starring Demond Wilson and Ron Glass, survived only one season, 1982–1983. In 1985, Simon decided to do his own gender-switch rewrite. The female version of his stage play, starring Sally Struthers and Rita Moreno, enjoyed a year's run on Broadway and, like the original text, has become a favourite of regional and academic theatres. Simon, declaring that women are more likely to reveal their real feelings than men, expressed particular pleasure in creating Olive and Florence.

In 1993, Klugman and Randall reunited for a TV movie called *The Odd Couple: Together Again*; the plot centred on the marriage of Felix's daughter. Felix, ever picky on details, goes to help with the wedding arrangements. He is such a nuisance that he is kicked out and ends up living once again with Oscar. In 1998 Simon created *Odd Couple II* (dir. Howard Deutch), a sequel movie starring Matthau and Lemmon that contradicts the story of the television film. Thirty years have passed since the action of the original play; Oscar and Felix are now in their 70s, and Oscar lives in Florida. The first reunion in 17 years of the former apartment mates is prompted by the engagement of Oscar's son to Felix's daughter, in California. The two old friends embark on a series of wild adventures before they, and Felix's suitcase, finally arrive at the wedding. The sequel nevertheless retains not only the characters' personalities but such elements as Oscar's weekly poker party and Felix's moving back in with him. Simon then rewrote his play once again, this time to update the text for the new millenium. According to the author, about 70% of the material was new. *Oscar and Felix: A New Look at the Odd Couple* premiered in 2002 and starred John Larroquette and Joe Regalbuto.[2]

There is no doubt that adapation continues to be a widespread, popular strategy. A reflection on how transformations like those of *The Hours* and *The Odd Couple* are elaborated, and why some work well and others do not, is more constructive than a rigid rejection of adaptation on a par with the infamous *traduttore, traditore* comment about translation.

In his introduction to *Film Adaptation* (2000), James Naremore summarizes past commentaries by citing a 'cartoon that Alfred Hitchcock once described to François Truffaut: two goats are eating a pile of film cans, and one goat says to the other, "Personally, I liked the book better"' (Naremore, 2000: 2). Naremore observes that academic critiques of adaptation all too often have been similarly

> narrow in range, inherently respectful of the 'precursor text,' and constitutive of a series of binary oppositions that poststructuralist theory has taught us to deconstruct: literature versus cinema, high culture versus mass culture, original versus copy. (Naremore, 2000: 2)

Several contributors to Naremore's anthology of critical essays emphasize this same point. Stam notes, 'Much of the discussion of film adaptation quietly reinscribes the axiomatic superiority of literary art to film, an assumption derived from a number of superimposed prejudices' (Stam, 2000: 58). As a result, 'The language of criticism dealing with the film adaptation of novels has often been profoundly moralistic, awash in terms such as *infidelity, betrayal, deformation, violation, vulgarization,* and *desecration,* each carrying its specific charge of outraged negativity' (Stam, 2000: 54). Robert B. Ray asserts that such criticism has yielded little distinguished work. It would have been more fruitful to analyse 'how stories travel from medium to medium' (Ray, 2000: 41).

Patricia Santoro, who takes precisely the tack recommended by Ray in her 1996 book on Spanish novel into film, finds excitement 'in the discovery of how a verbal text takes a concept and works to create a mental image, and how a cinematic text utilizes technology and visuals to translate those concepts onto the screen' (Santoro, 1996: 9). Stam clarifies what is meant by that mental image: 'We read a novel through our introjected desires, hopes, and utopias, and as we read we fashion our own imaginary mise-en-scène of the novel on the private stages of our minds' (Stam, 2000: 54). The mental mise-en-scène for the reader of a dramatic text is similar to that of the reader of a novel; the spectator of a theatrical text in performance will, of course, have a visual image already developed for his or her viewing. This difference aside, we shall follow the approach suggested by Ray and Santoro in the chapter 'From Stage to Screen': a practical look at how adaptation is accomplished rather than a judgemental consideration of 'fidelity'.

Various writers included in Naremore's anthology propose that film adaptation be analysed not in terms of fidelity but by using the critical framework of translation or intertextuality. Among these are André Bazin and Dudley Andrew. In an essay written in 1948 but not translated to English until a half century later, Bazin used terminology akin to Eugene Nida's concept of dynamic equivalence or equivalent effect in translation to recommend a method for examining film adaptation: 'faithfulness to a form, literary or otherwise, is illusory: what matters is the *equivalence in meaning of the forms*' (Bazin, 2000: 20). In *Concepts of Film Theory* (1984), Andrew provided a list of elements to be evaluated in judging equivalence.

In his attempt to set aside superficial approaches to the analysis of film adaptations, Andrew developed what have become classic definitions. He defined three modes of relation between film adaptations and source text: 'borrowing, intersection, and fidelity of transformation' (Andrew,

1984: 98). Borrowing is the most frequent of these modes: it makes more or less extensive use of the material, idea or form of a prior work, usually a successful one that is cherished by the potential audience, but does so in a 'vast and airy' way (Andrew, 1984: 98–99). Intersecting is the opposite of borrowing; a refraction, rather than an adaptation of the original, it leaves the source text unassimilated. Transformation is the middle ground: it will retain the skeletal story while also finding stylistic equivalents in film for 'the original's tone, values, imagery, and rhythm' (Andrew, 1984: 100).

Andrew's test for equivalence calls into play the concept of intersemiotic translation, the conversion of verbal signs to nonverbal sign systems.[3] In his 1992 analysis of American detective films, Patrick Cattrysse extends the translation metaphor. He proposes a theory of film adaptation based on a polysystemic approach to translation. Translation of verbal texts is regarded as interlinguistic, intrasemiotic transposition. Film adapation may or may not involve interlinguistic translation but, according to Cattrysse, should always be judged in terms of intersemiotic transposition (Cattrysse, 1992: 15). Stam cites Cattrysse's analysis when he submits that translation should replace fidelity as the trope for addressing film adapation: 'The trope of adaptation as translation suggests a principled effort of semiotic transposition, with the inevitable losses and gains typical of any translation' (Stam, 2000: 62).

Less known but comparable in perspective to Andrew's modes of relation are three types of transition of fiction into film that Geoffrey Wagner described a decade earlier, in 1975. Basing himself on a thesis of Béla Balázs, Wagner offered definitions of analogy, transposition, and commentary. Analogy, like Andrew's concept of borrowing, represents a 'considerable departure for the sake of making *another* work of art' (Wagner, 1975: 227); examples include movies 'that shift a fiction forward into the present, and make a duplicate story' (Wagner, 1975: 226). He places within this category such films as *Candide* (1960), *The Trial* (1962), *Cabaret* (1972), *Death in Venice* (1971), and *Contempt* (1963). In transposition, 'a novel is directly given on the screen, with the minimum of apparent interference' (Wagner, 1975: 222). Although he found this method, which we might equate to Andrew's intersecting, to be dominant in Hollywood, Wagner declared it to be the least satisfactory. He gives as illustrations *Wuthering Heights* (1939), *Jane Eyre* (1944), *Madame Bovary* (1949), *Lord Jim* (1965), *Hunger* (1966), and *Last Year at Marienbad* (1961). Wagner's definition of commentary is somewhat removed from Andrew's concept of fidelity of transformation but nevertheless overlaps it. For Wagner, in commentary 'an original is taken and either purposely or inadvertently altered in some respect. It could also be called a re-emphasis or re-structure' (Wagner, 1975: 222). Wagner does not view the 'commentary' films he has studied to be a tribute to their sources but states that an authentic reconstruction could be a creative restoration. 'Sometimes a change in character or scene may actually fortify the values of its original on the printed page' (Wagner, 1975: 224). His examples of commentary are *The Heiress* (1949), *Catch-22* (1970), *A Clockwork Orange* (1972), and *The Stranger* (1967).

Wagner, like most theorists on film adaptation, generally concentrates on the novel, but his taxonomy may also be applied to theatre. We can identify transformations of *The Odd Couple* that fall into each of his categories. Simon's screenplay based on the original comedy is a transposition because of its minimal changes. The movie sequel that ages the characters and moves the action forward may be considered an analogy. Simon's female version of his own comedy or his updated version, which shifts the setting to our present, are stage adaptations but otherwise might be seen as fitting Wagner's definition of commentary. Certainly they are reconstructions that alter characters or setting but retain the values of the original work. In *Interpreting Shakespeare on Screen* (2000), Deborah Cartmell makes effective use of Wagner's concepts for analysing film adaptations of drama (Cartmell, 2000: x–xi). She considers Kenneth Branagh's *Hamlet* (1996) to be an accurate adaptation and hence identifies it as transposition. Because Baz Luhrmann's *William Shakespeare's Romeo and Juliet* (1996) alters the original in terms of line order and ending, she labels it commentary. According to Cartmell, John Madden's *Shakespeare in Love* (1998), which freely adapts both *Romeo and Juliet* and *Twelfth Night*, is an example of analogy.

The goat in the Hitchcock anecdote preferred the book to the film. The facile idea that literature is superior to movies has surely been the thrust of many objections to film adaptations of fiction. As for film adaptations of theatre, the argument has often gone the other way, despite the unquestionable popular success of such close film adaptations of stage plays as *The Odd Couple* and *Harvey* (dir. Henry Koster). The latter 1950 film, starring Jimmy Stewart, was based on Mary Chase's Pulitzer Prize-winning play. (In the next chapter we shall place *Harvey* along the spectrum from unassimilated transposition to fidelity of transformation.)

Carlos Gortari and Carlos Barbáchano, authors of an introductory manual on cinema, succinctly highlight the apparent conflict between the two art forms from a historical perspective. Silent films, breaking away from 19th-century melodrama, had just developed their own narrative methodology when the advent of the talkies once again imposed drama on movies.[4] Overnight, playwrights were converted into screenwriters. Movies were in danger of becoming filmed theatre. But, happily, the threat was soon overcome (Gortari & Barbáchano, 1983: 53).

In essence, Gortari and Barbáchano, along with many other critics, oppose movies that are merely 'canned theatre'. For television, stage plays may be filmed with the use of two or three cameras and accompanying close-ups as their only modification; the procedure has generally ceased to be acceptable for the big screen.[5] Thus editor Béatrice Picon-Vallin carefully chooses the title *Le Film de théâtre* for her beautifully illustrated 1997 volume. In her introduction, she clarifies that 'filming the performance is an activity that falls within the contemporary context of interartistic practices' (Picon-Vallin, 1997: 19). The implication is that theatrical performance on film does not purport to be a movie per se and therefore should not be confused with filmed theatre.

Far more sympathetic to drama than Gortari and Barabáchano, Susan Sontag attempts to deconstruct simplistic cinema/theatre comparison in an essay first published in 1966. Nonetheless, she finds it impossible to deny the validity of the perceived dichotomy.

> The history of cinema is often treated as the history of its emancipation from theatrical models ... Movies are regarded as advancing from theatrical stasis to cinematic fluidity, from theatrical artificiality to cinematic naturalness and immediacy. (Sontag, 1985: 340)

Criticism of film adaptations of narratives have tended to value those movies that remain most faithful to their source. The opposite has been true of film adaptations of stage plays:

> The success of movie versions of plays is measured by the extent to which the script rearranges and displaces the action and deals less than respectfully with the spoken text ... the basic disapproval of films which betray their origins in plays remains. (Sontag, 1985: 344–45)

Over the years, a number of theorists have outlined what they deem to be irreconcilable differences between theatre and cinema. At an extreme, Balázs in 1945 emphasized the effect of the close-up in silent movies that could not be paralleled either in stage drama or in talking movies. Balázs felt that the close-up had both widened and deepened our vision of life (Balázs, 1985: 255). Close-ups of facial expressions 'revealed to us a new world – the world of microphysiognomy' (Balázs, 1985: 261). Sound only detracted from the impact. For Balázs, silent film presented 'a drama of the spirit closer to realization than any stage play has ever been able to do' (Balázs, 1985: 264). In reviewing the early arguments against equating sound film with recorded stage drama, Bruce Morrissette cites another comment by Balázs: contrary to the effect created by filming and editing techniques, theatre is presented at a fixed distance from the spectator, who sees the scene as a whole, always from a fixed point of view (Morrissette, 1985: 14).

The differences between the two art forms go beyond questions of montage and angle or distance of vision. In his 1936 book, *Film and Theatre*, Allardyce Nicoll affirmed that there are basic laws that govern stage drama and cinema. 'The theatre rejoices in artistic limitation in space while the film demands movement and change in location'; for that reason, 'a film can rarely bear to admit anything in the way of theatricality in its settings' (Nicoll, 1936: 173). According to Nicoll, painted sets are out of place in film, which should not be shot in a studio. Although the practice that Nicoll deplored gradually disappeared from cinema to a large extent, it is worth observing that films may still be shot in studios. For example, the enchanted, moonlit forest in *A Midsummer Night's Dream* (1999, dir. Michael Hoffman) was created on a huge soundstage, complete with live trees and plants, ponds and bubbling water, and wandering pathways. The unreal – and hence theatrical – quality of the enclosed, magical forest contrasted effectively with the exterior world of daylight.

As Russell Jackson notes, Nicoll's attitude was widespread: 'From its early days, the narrative cinema proclaimed its ability to show a dramatic action's physical surroundings more vividly, spaciously and accurately than the illusionist theatre' (Jackson, 2000: 19–20). On the other hand – in contrast to the more flexible Elizabethan theatre – 'realistic, scenic theatre, such as those of Wilde or Shaw' proved problematic for film adaptation: 'Here the difficulty is more acute, because an organising principle of the original is that as many significant turns of event as possible should take place in a limited number of locations within a given period of time' (Jackson, 2000: 19).

Despite this problem in practice, Nicoll predicted in theory that cinema, given its superior realism, would totally displace naturalistic drama:

The film has such a hold over the world of reality, can achieve expression so vitally in terms of ordinary life, that the realistic play must surely come to seem trivial, false and inconsequential. The truth is, of course, that naturalism on the stage must always be limited and insincere. (Nicoll, 1936: 183)

Whatever the validity of Nicoll's comparisons, his skills as a prophet were limited. On the Anglo-American stages, into the 21st century, realism and naturalism still dominate.

Nicoll likewise asserted that theatrical dialogue is 'too rich and cumbersome for cinematic purposes' (Nicoll, 1936: 173). Despite the greater development of dialogue on stage, he paradoxically affirmed that stage characters are types whereas cinema demands individualization. Other commentators, while still maintaining that stage and film characters are basically dissimilar, have come to the opposite view. Sontag reminds us that Erwin Panofsky, in an essay written in 1934, held that cinema, contrary to drama, requires flat or stock characters (Sontag, 1985: 345). Writing 15 years after Nicoll, Bazin affirmed that in theatre 'the drama proceeds from the actor, in the cinema it goes from the decor to man' (Bazin, 1985: 361). Bazin concluded that the essential element of theatre is the text, and of cinema, 'realism of space' (Bazin, 1985: 369).

Gerald Mast has defined three basic problems in filming a play: the verbal text must be converted into sights and sounds, the theatrical decor must be changed into a cinematic decor, and the dramatic work must be converted into an 'epic' (that is, a narrated) work (Mast, 1982: 290). More recently, contemporary Spanish playwright José Luis Alonso de Santos has affirmed:

> The sea in the theatre is a blue cloth; the sea in movies is the sea ... The underlying drama in theatre is the struggle of ideas; in movies, it is the struggle of human beings. For that reason movie drama is transmitted as violence: it is translated as violence. (Alonso de Santos, 1997: 78)

Alonso de Santos observes that in movies the action is what counts, but in theatre what underlies the action may be more important. He says that spectators leaving a play may ask what did it mean, while movie audiences are more likely to ask what happened (Alonso de Santos, 1997: 82).

Informing early theoretical debates about adaptation of theatre are the assumptions that the adaptation will be aimed at popular audiences and that the play is conventionally realistic, with a representational set and the careful, linear structure of the well-made play. Some of the supposedly irreconcilable differences between the two forms disappear or change considerably when these assumptions are set aside. For this purpose, the distinction that Noël Carroll makes between 'movies' and 'films' is useful. The former are popular, narrative works – ones that tell a story – while the latter are modernist, art films (Carroll, 1988: 170). A play that resists adaptation as a movie might work well as an art film. Jackson reminds us that cinema has used diverse strategies for story-telling:

> In the study of film techniques a broad distinction can be made between films in which story-telling is effected by the montage of images, and which foreground the means by which this is done; and others which conceal the art which places dramatic scenes before the camera with an illusion of unobstructed and privileged access for the audience. (Jackson, 2000: 15)

For adapting stage plays, the latter strategy, associated with the continuity editing that dominated in Hollywood before the 1960s, might be less effective than a self-conscious technique.

Despite the continued dominance of realism/naturalism on the American and British stages, more imaginative, non-illusionist kinds of theatre are prevalent elsewhere and theatre everywhere has evolved over time. Taking into consideration theatricalist modes of staging, Linda Seger even remarks that theatre, unlike film, may make use of abstract sets and fluid spaces (Seger, 1992: 36–40). She fails to mention that such spatial fluidity on stage may well be a cinematic device, as is the use of temporal fluidity in the form of flashbacks and simultaneous action.

In her 'how-to' book on screen adaptations, Seger gives practical advice. She says that theatre resists film because it is more thematic, its themes are human-centred, it uses dialogue to explore ideas, and character is more important than story. In choosing a play for film adaptation, one should look for a realistic context that can be opened up, a story line that can be developed, and cinematic images to give expression to the human themes (Seger, 1992: 42).[6] In that she is focusing on popular movies, Seger would no doubt agree with Erskine and Welsh's assertion that the 'more theatrical and abstract the design of a play, the less likely it is to be adapted successfully' (Erskine & Welsh, 2000: xiii).

Sontag, in 1966, suggested that the dichotomy between the two art forms was beginning to disappear as theatre adopted cinematic strategies. Morrissette agrees, pointing out that 'more modern forms of staging have undermined the universal application of Balázs's principles of mise-en-scène' (Morrissette, 1985: 14). Martin Esslin argues persuasively that today live theatre and cinematic types of drama (movies and television) have more similarities than differences (1987).[7] Somewhat more restrictively, Jackson asserts that some film strategies have equivalents in theatre but that others, such as camera angles, 'construction of spatial relationships between characters' and 'rhythm of shots in the edited film' are specific to cinema (Jackson, 2000: 18).

Spanish film and theatre director Josefina Molina declared in 1981 that the relationship between cinema and theatre is symbiotic (Molina, 1981: 29). Her own stage productions invariably incorporate cinematic strategies. Such work across genres has obvious implications for film adaptation. Andrew Horton and Joan Magretta observe that there is a spirit of creative adaptation in European cinema where it 'is not uncommon for filmmakers themselves to be novelists, dramatists, or essayists' (Horton & Magretta, 1981: 4). To a lesser extent, in the United States some professionals also move seamlessly between various functions and media. The case of Nia Vardalos, who has moved from comedy club to small theatre to big screen to television, in her dual role as author and actor, is by no means unique.

Although much criticism of film adaptations of stage plays has simply taken a negative stance toward theatre, the situation with respect to a prestige author like Shakespeare has more closely approximated the attitude toward great novels. Stephen M. Buhler observes: 'Most studies of Shakespearean film have understandably concentrated on what the medium of cinema reveals or obscures about Shakespeare: productions are evaluated in terms of fidelity to the text, compromises between Elizabethan stagecraft and changing filmic convention, actors' performances and directors' achievements in "realizing" the playtext' (Buhler, 2002: 2). Buhler himself is more interested in determining how filmmakers realize their adaptations.

Discussions that in one way or another disparage adaptation fail to recognize the ascendancy of the strategy. Citing from a 1998 article in *Variety*, Naremore indicates that, in addition to the 20% of American films the previous year that were adaptations of books, another 20% 'were derived from plays, sequels, remakes, television shows, and magazine or newspaper articles. This means that only about half of the pictures seen by the public that year originated from scripts' (Naremore, 2000: 10). Any in-depth study of film history inevitably uncovers what Erskine and Welsh have called 'creative cross-fertilization' (Erskine & Welsh, 2000: xv).

Television series, novels, musicals, plays and other verbal texts may be turned into screenplays, but original screenplays may also reappear as fiction, drama or television series. Frederick Knott's *Dial M for Murder* began as a TV special and then became a successful stage play before Alfred Hitchcock transformed it into his famous 1954 film. Federico Fellini's 1963 movie $8\frac{1}{2}$ inspired Maury Yeston and Arthur Kopit's 1982 Broadway musical *Nine*, winner of five Tony awards. Harper Lee's 1960

novel *To Kill a Mockingbird* won the Pulitzer Prize in 1961 and was transformed into a superb movie the next year. The film (dir. Robert Mulligan)
won Oscars for Horton Foote's adapted screenplay and Gregory Peck's
portrayal of Atticus Finch, a small-town Southern lawyer in the 1930s
who bravely defended a black man falsely accused of rape. Christopher
Sergel's stage adaptation of Lee's novel premiered in 1970 and has
become a favourite with regional and academic theatre companies in
the United States. Joseph Mankiewicz's *All About Eve* (1950), an Oscar-
winning film about an ambitious young actress who competes with an
aging star, inspired the musical *Applause* (1970) and, in 2002, was
adapted for the stage by playwright David Rambo. Although Rambo's
text has not yet received a full production, it was given a professional
staged reading as a fundraiser for the Actors' Fund of America; the
event was prominently featured in the journal of The Dramatists Guild
(Hirschhorn, 2003).

Examples of this kind of creative recycling abound in Spain and Latin
America. Jaime Salom's *La casa de las Chivas* (The House of the Jezebels) is
a moralistic play that defied Franco-era censorship to deal with life
behind the front lines on the Republican side during the Spanish Civil
War. It opened in Barcelona in 1968, enjoyed a record-breaking run of
1343 consecutive performances on the Madrid stage starting in 1969,
was made into a movie, transformed into a novel (written by Elisabeth
Szel and published, in 1972, by Planeta, a major trade press) and in
1978, shortly after Franco's death, was adapted for Spanish television.
Fernando Fernán-Gómez – director, author, and actor of stage and
screen – has reworked his own texts across media. His novel, *El viaje a
ninguna parte* (The Trip to Nowhere, 1985), which deals with the life of a
travelling theatre company, had previously been aired on radio; in 1986,
he directed and starred in his successful movie version. Two versatile
Latin American works that have triumphantly crossed national and
genre borders are Manuel Puig's *El beso de la mujer araña* (*The Kiss of the
Spider Woman*) and Antonio Skármeta's *Ardiente paciencia* (*Burning
Patience*). Puig's novel in dialogue was published in Argentina in 1976.
Skármeta originally wrote his tribute to Chile's Nobel Prize winning
poet Pablo Neruda as a play, in 1982, while living in Berlin.

When Puig received a request from Europe to authorize a stage
adaptation of *The Kiss of the Spider Woman*, he elected to prepare the
play himself (Puig, personal interview, 1987). Ultimately he prepared
two versions: a subdued one that left the audience in the dark – quite
literally in the 1987 Paris production – as to the physical relationship
between the two men in a prison cell and one that portrayed more

openly a scene of tender lovemaking between Molina, a gay window dresser with a strong passion for old movies, and Valentin, a political activist. The latter version was staged in Madrid in 1981; the former gave rise to both the French and American translations. In 1985, Puig's novel was turned into a movie that shifted the action from Argentina to Brazil. Starring William Hurt as Molina and Raul Julia as Valentin and directed by Hector Babenco with screenplay by Leonard Schrader, this United States – Brazilian production was nominated for four Oscars, including best picture, and won for Hurt the best actor award. Puig's *The Kiss of the Spider Woman* subsequently inspired a musical version, directed by Harold Prince, with a book by Terrence McNally. The stage musical played in Toronto and London in 1992 and enjoyed a Broadway run of 906 performances from 1993–1995; it won seven Tony Awards, including best musical and best score.[8]

Skármeta's *Burning Patience* similarly establishes the viability of cross-genre adaptation. Skármeta quickly adapted his play and directed it for cinema; it won prizes at film festivals in France and Spain in 1984. Obeying historical accuracy, the author's film version placed the action in Chile and reflected the political situation there; its slow rhythm allowed for numerous sequences of walks on the beach and ocean views. He next transformed the work into a novel (1986); expanding on the original title, which alludes to a line of poetry by Rimbaud, he fore-grounded Neruda's postman by calling his narrative *El cartero de Neruda*. A new film version, *Il Postino* (*The Postman*), directed by Michael Radford in 1994, achieved international acclaim. This French/Italian/Belgian production was based on the novel and featured Massimo Troisi as Mario, the postman, and Philippe Noiret, as Neruda. It won an Oscar for Luis Bacalov's original score and was nominated in four other categories, including best picture, best director, best adapted screenplay (by Radford, Troisi and three collaborators) and best leading actor (Troisi). Among other changes, the second movie shifted the action from Chile to Italy. As we shall observe in the following chapter, it is not unusual for movie adaptations to alter political background.

Recycling in one form or another is not a new invention. In the late 19th century in Spain, Benito Pérez Galdós began writing stage versions of his realistic novels as a way of reforming the Spanish stage. One of these projects, *El abuelo* (The Grandfather) has recently formed the basis for a critically acclaimed film. A precedent for Puig's *El beso de la mujer araña*, *El abuelo* (1897) was written as a novel in dialogue. Galdós's stage play, first performed in 1904, was a predictably abbreviated version of the novel. The author reduced the number of named characters from

15 to 11 and decreased the number of scene changes by eliminating some of the secondary action or moving it offstage. Borrowing primarily from the novel but also, to some extent, from the play, in 1999 director José Luis Garci created a 147-minute movie adaptation. Predictably he reintroduced and expanded the changes of locale suggested in the novel but continued to suppress certain minor characters. Fernán-Gómez, in the title role of the grandfather, received a Goya award at the San Sebastián film festival for best actor. Garci's _El abuelo_ was nominated in a total of 12 categories for Goya prizes, as well as for an Oscar as best foreign film.

Another example of a work recently adapted anew for the screen is Edgar Neville's _La vida en un hilo_ (Life by a Thread). Neville's text pursues the opposite path of _El abuelo_: the film preceded the stage play.

Neville was the first in a group of Spanish authors to make contacts in Hollywood; he spent several years there preparing Spanish-language scripts for Metro Goldwyn Mayer before returning to Europe, where he directed 22 movies between 1935 and 1960, including a number of adaptations of his own plays and other works. Pointing out that 80% of Spanish films made in the 1940s were comedies, John Hopewell singles out Neville as a dissident director during the Franco regime who should not be ignored (Hopewell, 1989: 23–24). Ángel A. Pérez Gómez and José L. Martínez Montalbán identify _La vida en un hilo_ as one of the best comedies in postwar Spanish cinema (Pérez Gómez & Martínez Montalban, 1978: 222).

Neville's original movie version of _La vida en un hilo_ reached the screen in 1945; the stage play came years later, in 1959. The action revolves around two possible lives for Mercedes: the boredom of her marriage to the humdrum Ramón, recounted through flashbacks, and the excitement she would have found with the artist Miguel. The latter scenario is revealed to her by Doña Tomasita, a woman capable of looking into one's eyes and discovering what might have been. Fortunately Mercedes is now widowed, and fate brings her back in touch with Miguel; after the contrasting sequences of remembered tedium and imagined happiness, the audience may anticipate that fantasy will become reality. Surely the memory of _La vida en un hilo_ lingered on, thus inspiring the 1992 remake, _Una mujer bajo la lluvia_ (A Woman in the Rain). Directed by Gerardo Vera, who also co-wrote the new screen play, the recent film featured a stellar cast, headed by Angela Molina, Imanol Arias, and Antonio Banderas.

In the field of literary translation, relatively few commentaries explore theatre, as opposed to narrative and poetry. Similarly adaptation theory has tended to concentrate on fiction into film rather than transformations from stage to screen.[9] Case studies have likewise bypassed drama to concentrate on narrative. The most notable exception is the growing list of books that focus on film adapations of Shakespeare. In this chapter we have cited four of these, all published in 2000 or later (Buhler, 2002; Cartmell, 2000; Coursen, 2002; Jackson, 2000). Recent books by Juan Antonio Ríos Carratalá (1999) and María Asunción Gómez (2000) view the subject in general terms and then analyse in depth eight case studies each of film adapation of Spanish plays.[10]

Because of their emphasis on novel, many commentaries on film adaptation specifically highlight the two genres' respective narrative strategies. Gómez, who provides an excellent overview both of the historical relationship between theatre and film and of the accompanying theoretical debates, concludes that, because cinema is itself a narrative genre, film adaptation of plays is in fact more difficult than adaptation of narrative. The latter merely implies transferring a verbal narrative mode to a visual one.

> On the other hand, from a structural point of view, turning dramatic action into narrative requires substantial changes that complicate the adaptor's work. A good adaptation does not consist of mechanical reproduction of the play in question ... On the contrary, one should take maximum advantage of the wealth of possibilities of the cinematographic medium ... (Gómez, 2000: 51)

In the next chapter, through concrete examples we shall identify the strategies that various film directors have used to translate stage plays for the screen. In the process, we shall determine what transformations we can generally expect when we see a movie adaptation of a play.

Notes

1. Teresa García-Abad García provides a review of relationships between cinema in theatre. She concludes that the influence of film has been beneficial in the development of modern theatre (1997: 481).

2. For information on the ongoing history of *The Odd Couple,* see the website maintained by Jaclyn Mussehl. For additional examples of texts that have been translated from one medium to another, see the section titled 'The Recycling of Drama: Stage to Screen and Screen to Stage' in Erskine and Welsh (2000: xiv–xviii). In his interesting taxonomy of kinds of remakes, Robert Eberwein provides examples like these: a film remade as television film, *Sweet Bird of Youth* (1962, 1989); a film remade as a television miniseries, *East of Eden* (1955, 1981); a television series remade as a film, *Maverick* (1994) (Eberwein, 1998: 29).

3. In *Film Adaptation*, Naremore (2000) approvingly foregrounds Andrew's groundbreaking modes of relation. Quite opposite is the reaction of Erskine and Welsh in their volume on video versions of plays, also published in 2000. Labelling Andrew's approach as semiotics, they find it to be 'less fashionable now than it was when he pontificated on it so absurdly in his *Concepts of Film Theory* in 1984' (Erskine & Welsh, 2000: xiii). I consider the concepts outlined by Andrew and the related ones of Wagner to be useful and will refer to them in my discussion of specific film transformations.

4. Brewster and Jacobs have dealt extensively with the impact of theatre on silent movies in their *Theatre to Cinema*. They report that over half of Paramount's feature films produced between 1913 and 1915 were theatrical adaptations but observe that 'the popular nineteenth-century stage was intimately concerned with the metaphor of the stage picture' (Brewster & Jacobs, 1997: vi). The thrust of their comparison therefore is the 'abstract conception of the theatrical and the pictorial, and how it impinged on filmmaking' (Brewster & Jacobs, 1997: vii).

5. In a book on recent productions of Shakespeare on screen, H. R. Coursen suggests reasons why television is receptive to canned drama. While movie scripts are generally condensed in comparison to stage plays, television 'can contain more dialogue than film and needs more dialogue to augment its image' (Coursen, 2002: 4). Moreover, television 'duplicates our living space' (Coursen, 2002: 4). Conventional drama fits comfortably into this kind of set but movies prefer the greater freedom of cinematic reality.

6. Jackson cites Syd Field's suggestions for mainstream movies. Screenwriters should concentrate on 'strong and active characters, combined with a unique, stylized visual narrative that constantly moves the story forward' (quoted in Jackson, 2000: 17).

7. In the next chapter I will note in passing some differences between television adaptations and those for the big screen. Naremore expresses regret that his critical anthology does not include writings that compare made-for-television adaptations and movies (Naremore, 2000: 11). Geoffrey Nowell-Smith believes that the gap between the media is not as great as some believe: 'cinema in the pure sense remains central to the experience of the moving image even in the complex world of multimedia' (Nowell-Smith, 1996: 763). Nowell-Smith affirms that, video and television are not self-sufficient markets for feature-length films. Films can 'be made electronically, without recourse to celluoid' but 'theatrical release in 35 mm. is still a necessity for most films of any importance' (Nowell-Smith, 1996: 763).

8. The website theatre-musical.com, omitting any reference to the stage play, cites Puig's novel along with the movie and musical versions. For a comparison of novel, play and movie, see Santoro (1977). The American translations of *The Kiss of the Spider Woman* (trans. Michael Feingold) and *Burning Patience* (trans. Marion Peter Holt), accompanied by brief but helpful introductions, appear in *DramaContemporary: Latin America* (Holt & Woodyard, 1986).

9. There are 38 items in Naremore's annotated bibliography (Naremore, 2000: 239–43). Only three allude directly to theatre in their titles: two books on Shakespeare and A. Nicholas Vardac's *Stage to Screen: Theatrical Method from Garrick to Griffith*, which deals with the influence of 19th-century melodrama. One other entry, on André Bazin's *What Is Cinema?*, refers to theatre in the

annotation. Similarly Sally Faulkner's 2004 book on literary adaptations in Spanish cinema highlights nine novels and only one play: Ventura Pons's 1998 adaptation of Sergi Belbel's *Caricies*.

10. Of interest is Emerterio Diez's review essay of studies published in Spain 1930–2000 on cinema and theatre. The first book he considers a real commentary on the relationship and influence between the two genres is Fedor Stepun's *Theater und Film* (1953), translated from German to Spanish in 1960. Diez's essay contains an extensive bibliography.

References

Alonso de Santos, J. L. De la escritura dramática a la escritura cinematográfica. *Cine y Literatura*. Monographic issue incorporating papers from X Ciclo Escritores y Universidad, 7 November–5 December 1995. *República de las Letras* 54 (1997): 77–82.

Andrew, D. *Concepts in Film Theory*. Oxford: Oxford University Press, 1984.

Balázs, B. The close-up. In G. Mast and M. Cohen, ed., *Film Theory and Criticism*, 1985, 255–64.

Bazin, A. Theatre and cinema. In G. Mast and M. Cohen, ed., *Film Theory and Criticism*, 1985, 356–69.

Bazin, A. Adaptation, or the cinema as digest (trans. A. Piette and B. Cardullo). In J. Naremore, ed, *Film Adaptation*, 2000, 19–27.

Brewster, B. and Jacobs, L. *Theatre to Cinema. Stage Pictorialism and the Early Feature Film*. Oxford: Oxford University Press, 1997.

Buhler, S. M. *Shakespeare in the Cinema. Ocular Proof*. Albany, NY: State University of New York Press, 2002.

Carroll, N. *Mystifying Movies. Fads and Fallacies in Contemporary Film Theory*. New York: Columbia University Press, 1988.

Cartmell, D. *Interpreting Shakespeare on Screen*. New York: St. Martin's Press, 2000.

Cattrysse, P. *Pour une théorie de l'adaptation filmique. Le film noir américain*. Berne: Peter Lang, 1992.

Coursen, H. R. *Shakespeare in Space. Recent Shakespeare Productions on Screen*. New York: Peter Lang, 2002.

Diez, E. Relaciones teatro y cine: El estado de la cuestión. *Acotaciones. Revista de Investigación Teatral* 5 (July–Dec. 2000): 73–89.

Eberwein, R. Remakes and cultural studies. In A. Horton and S. Y. McDouglas, ed., *Play It Again, Sam. Retakes on Remakes*, 1998, 15–33.

Erskine, T. L. and Welsh, J. M. *Video Versions. Film Adaptations of Plays on Video*. With John C. Tibbetts and Tony Williams. Westport, C and London: Greenwood Press, 2000.

Esslin, M. *The Field of Drama. How the Signs of Drama Create Meaning on Stage & Screen*. London and New York: Methuen, 1987.

Faulkner, S. *Literary Adaptations in Spanish Cinema*. London: Tamesis, 2004.

García-Abad García, T. Dos estéticas en contacto: lo cinético y lo dramático. *Revista de Literatura* 59.118 (July–Dec. 1997): 465–81.

Gómez, M. A. *Del escenario a la pantalla. La adaptación cinematográfica del teatro español*. Chapel Hill: North Carolina Studies in the Romance Languages and Literatures, 2000.

Gortari, C. and Barbáchano, C. *El Cine. Arte, evasión y dólares.* 1st reprinting. Aula Abierta Salvat: Temas Clave 16. Barcelona: Salvat Editores, 1983.

Hirschhorn, J. *All About Eve* finally onstage. *The Dramatist* 5.6 (July/August 2003): 28–31.

Holt, M. P. and Woodyard, G. W., eds. *DramaContemporary: Latin America.* New York: PAJ Publications, 1986.

Hopewell, J. *El cine español después de Franco 1973–1988* (trans. C. Laguna). Madrid: Ediciones El Arquero, 1989.

Horton, A. S. and Magretta, J., eds. *Modern European Filmmakers and the Art of Adaptation.* New York: Frederick Ungar, 1981.

Horton, A. and McDouglas, S. Y., eds. *Play It Again, Sam. Retakes on Remakes.* With an Afterword by Leo Braudy. Berkeley, Los Angeles, and London: University of California Press, 1998.

http://theatre-musical.com/Spiderwoman/movie.html.

Jackson, R., ed. *The Cambridge Companion to Shakespeare on Film.* Cambridge: Cambridge University Press, 2000.

Mast, G. Literature and film. In J.-P. Barricelli and J. Gibaldi, eds., *Interrelations of Literature.* New York: The Modern Language Association of America, 1982. 278–306.

Mast, G. and Cohen, M., eds. *Film Theory and Criticism*, 3rd ed. New York and Oxford: Oxford University Press, 1985.

Molina, J. Interview with Carla Matteini. *Pipirijaina* 18 (Jan.–Feb. 1981): 28–31.

Morrissette, B. *Novel and Film. Essays in Two Genres.* Chicago and London: University of Chicago Press, 1985.

Mussehl, J. http://odd_couple.tripod.com/history.html.

Naremore, J., ed. *Film Adaptation.* New Brunswick, NJ: Rutgers University Press, 2000.

Nicoll, A. *Film and Theatre.* London, Bombay & Sidney: George G. Harrap & Company, Ltd., 1936. (Reprint Edition, Arno Press, 1972).

Nowell-Smith, G., ed. *The Oxford History of World Cinema.* Oxford: Oxford University Press, 1996.

Pérez Gómez, Á. A. and Martínez Montalban, J. L. *Cine español 1951/1978. Diccionario de directores.* Bilbao: Mensajero, 1978.

Picon-Vallin, B. *Le Film de théâtre.* Avant-propos par Élie Konigson. Paris: CNRS Éditions, 1997.

Puig, M. Personal interview, 9 April 1987.

Ray, R. B. The field of 'literature and film'. In J. Naremore, ed., *Film Adaptation*, 2000, 38–53.

Ríos Carratalá, J. A. *El teatro en el cine español.* Alicante: Instituto de Cultura Juan Gil Albert, 1999.

Santoro, P. J. *Novel into Film. The Case of La familia de Pascual Duarte and Los santos inocentes.* Newark: University of Delaware Press; London: Associated University Presses, 1996.

Santoro, P. J. *Kiss of the Spider Woman*, novel, play, and film: Homosexuality and the discourse of the maternal in a third world prison. In A. M. Stock, ed., *Framing Latin American Cinema. Contemporary Critical Perspectives.* Minneapolis and London: University of Minnesota Press, 1977, 120–40.

Seger, L. *The Art of Adaptation: Turning Fact and Fiction into Film.* New York: Henry Holt, 1992.

Somigli, L. The superhero with a thousand faces: Visual narratives on film and paper. In A. Horton and J. McDouglas, eds, *Play It Again, Sam. Retakes on Remakes*, 1990, 279–94.

Sontag, S. Film and theatre. In G. Mast and M. Cohen, eds, *Film Theory and Criticism*, 1985, 340–55.

Stam, R. Beyond fidelity: The dialogics of adaptation. In J. Naremore, ed., *Film Adaptation*, 2000, 54–76.

Wagner, G. *The Novel and the Cinema*. Cranford, NJ: Associated University Presses, Inc; London: The Tantivy Press, 1975.

Chapter 8

From Stage to Screen: Strategies for Film Adaptation

In their categorization of approaches to film adaptation, both Geoffrey Wagner and Dudley Andrew include a method that transfers the source text to the new genre with virtually no change. Because it incorporates the original dialogue word for word, we might find the process analogous to literal translation. Wagner uses the term 'transposition' to label this strategy, which involves 'the minimum of apparent interference' (Wagner, 1975: 222). Describing the same phenomenon, Andrew calls 'intersecting' an attitude so respectful of the source that the original text 'is intentionally left unassimilated' (Andrew, 2000: 30).

Drama is far more accessible than narrative to unassimilated transposition. Stage plays have frequently been filmed for television directly from the theatre, using the original dialogue, sets and cast. The major difference from a regular performance will likely be the absence of an audience. Adequate lighting and camera work – medium or panning shots alternating with close-ups – serve to translate the text to the new medium by controlling the television spectator's gaze, a technique identified with film. Ideally the production will use three cameras, thereby facilitating not only variations in distance but also a shifting point of view. In editing, shots from one character's angle may be cut to show the reaction shot, from the other character's perspective. Setting up one stationary movie camera or camcorder in the theatre may provide a record of the production but inevitably yields unsatisfactory results. The single camera carries to the extreme the rigidity of distance and angle that Béla Balázs associated with the individual theatre-goer. Successful stage-to-television production requires special skills, equipment, lighting and editing. Even if the original dialogue is maintained in its entirety, some adjustments are needed to place that dialogue into the form required by the target medium.[1]

Gerald Mast points out that the critical objection to canned theatre in movies does not extend to television:

The physical characteristics of the television image (small screen, a picture reduced in brilliance, subtlety, and resolution, viewed in the light at home rather than in the dark in public) may lead us to expect less of it as a powerful artistic entity in its own right, and the cultural role that television has come to fulfill as our primary means of recording or transcribing preexisting events (sports events, news events, concerts) may also make it acceptable for recording productions of plays. (Mast, 1982: 291)

Television audiences are accustomed to action that takes place in a static location: sitcoms have often been filmed on a production set that reveals a particular kitchen or living room or that moves back and forth between just two rooms. Plays with one or two sets may readily be translated to television through the use of multiple cameras and appropriate editing.

An example of transposition or intersecting that goes beyond this basic strategy is the 1985 stage-to-television production of Arthur Miller's *Death of a Salesman*. The original stage play, starring Lee J. Cobb as the aging travelling salesman Willy Loman, was first performed in New York City in 1949 (dir. Elia Kazan). For his masterful tragedy, Miller made innovative use of a multi-leveled stage setting whose partial transparency facilitated spatial fluidity. The author's detailed stage directions indicate how the action flows from the Lomans' yard to rooms inside their house – established by imaginary wall-lines – and to various other locations, all indicated by minimal props. When some scenes are projected from Willy's consciousness, the shift from present reality to remembered or imaginary past is indicated by special lighting and by the actors' failure to observe the wall-lines. *Death of a Salesman*, a protypical work of psychological expressionism, clearly breaks from the traditional, realistic play. Gone is the conventional living room with its invisible fourth wall. On the contrary, its staging is overtly theatricalist, and the play's spatial and temporal fluidity verges on the cinematic.

The 1984 Broadway production (dir. Michael Rudman) won a Tony award for best revival. The television version (dir. Volker Schlöndorff) retained almost all of the members of this stage cast, including Dustin Hoffman (Willy), John Malkovich (Biff), Stephen Lang (Happy), and Kate Reid (Linda). The widely circulated video release is described as impressive and given four out of a possible five stars by Mick Martin and Marsha Porter in their video movie guide (Martin & Porter,

1998: 273). For his television role as Willy, Hoffman garnered Golden Globe and Emmy awards.

The television version of *Death of a Salesman* is faithful to the stage play in its use of the source text, but there are some modifications for the small screen. During the initial credits, we see Willy behind the wheel of a car and hear screeching brakes and the sound of a crash. The addition of this sequence both opens the play to more realistic space and gives it circular structure by anticipating Willy's suicide. In the theatre, lighting is used to guide the audience into following the characters from one stage area to another. In the television version, cameras accompany the actors into individual rooms or outside the Loman house or into the house next door, thus creating a greater sense of movement and space. Additionally, there are high angle shots of city apartments on the backdrop and views taken through windows. While these perspectives involve theatrical sets, they nevertheless enhance the production's realistic scope.

Were *Death of a Salesman* to be made into a movie, what further changes would we anticipate to meet cinematic expectations for realism and for fluidity of movement and space? Certainly some sequences would be shot on location, not on a production set. We might see Willy's car in traffic on the highway. In keeping with cinema's tendency to show not tell, his comments to his wife that reveal his increasingly inattentive driving would be converted from words to images. Other dialogue would also be replaced by visual effects, and the flashbacks would be more fully developed. We would have a glimpse of Biff's famous high school football game and would see Willy's Chevy headed to Ebbets Field for that event. When Biff surprises his father and the latter's female companion in a hotel room in Boston, we would see the young man's arrival outside the hotel and follow him up the stairs to the room, perhaps with cross-cutting between the action within and out-side the hotel room. We might have panoramic shots of Boston and New York. In the dramatic present, when Biff returns from Texas, we would first see him out West and then witness his travel home. These strategies would translate the stage play to big screen conventions without significant modification to the source text.

Fidelity is in the eyes of the beholder. The video cover for *Les Mains sales* (*Dirty Hands*) in the René Chateau Collection Les Années Cinquante asserts that the 1951 film (dir. Fernand Rivers) is scrupulously faithful to Jean Paul Sartre's important existentialist play (1948). For the dialogue, that may be generally true, but the director has not failed to add outside locations, movement, images and characters to the film. The stage play requires four sets, all of them interior. The action begins with Olga alone, listening to the radio inside her little house. She is soon joined by Hugo, who has just been released from prison after serving a term for murdering Hoederer – perhaps for the right political reasons, perhaps for the wrong personal ones. The film eventually gets to this point in the action but only after a series of added sequences: a panorama of a street, Olga entering various places, Hugo being released from prison while Olga secretly watches him, Hugo fleeing from men who pursue him in a car, soldiers speaking German to girls in the street. In the play, Hugo tells Olga that his wife cut off communication with him while he was in prison. In the film, we see Hugo tear up his wife's picture as he leaves the prison. In the film, but not the play, Olga has had Hugo's photo next to her radio but hides it when he knocks at the door. The gesture visualizes a romantic attachment not explicit in the play. Also in the film, but not the play, there is a flashback scene between Hugo and his father as the younger man explains his political commitment by expressing his desire to help those less privileged than he. Hugo's father does not appear in the stage play. While these added cinematic elements do not distort the tone of the source text, collectively they move the movie well beyond transposition.

The changes I have suggested for a movie version of *Death of a Salesman* are hypothetical. Quite different is the case of Carlos Arniches's *La señorita de Trevélez* (1916), for which we have contrasting examples of a literal translation for television and a free adaptation for the big screen. Arniches's grotesque tragicomedy portrays insensitive small town wags who ridicule a sentimental spinster by making her believe that one of them wants to marry her. The 1984 televised version of *La señorita de Trevélez* (dir. Gabriel Ibáñez) adds 'offstage' sets to the three (one per act) required by the stage play; it thus allows for cutting between shots and reaction shots (Galán, the supposed admirer, looking at Flora from the casino window, followed by Flora's perspective on Galán, from her balcony). This modest change notwithstanding, the play remains intact. The television version has little in common with Juan Antonio Bardem's internationally acclaimed 1956 film, *Calle Mayor* (*Main Street*). Bardem's film stands diametrically opposed to the model of canned television plays. Indeed it distances itself so much from its source that some spectators may not have realized that Bardem's bitingly satirical portrayal of small towns in the 1950s was based on Arniches's 1916 play.

Bardem's *Calle Mayor*, recipient of the International Critics Award at the Venice Film Festival, is an example of Andrew's concept of borrowing (analogy, in Wagner's terms). From Arniches's 'grotesque tragicomedy', the film takes only the skeletal story. Gone from the movie version is the spirit of the original text, most notably its use of the classic devices of farce. The film is less grotesque than bittersweet – with emphasis on the bitter; it has the potential for tragedy but no comedy. As Stephen Roberts observes, Bardem – an outspoken critic of Francoist Spain who was subjected to censorship and imprisonment by the regime – gives a prominent role to the social setting (Roberts, 1999: 28). The criticism of stagnant provincial life is far stronger than that of the Arniches text, and the solution it offers – escape – is not present in the original work. Susan Sontag states that the success of movie adaptations of plays is measured by the distance the script places between itself and the source (Sontag, 1985: 344). The success of Bardem's _Calle Mayor_ could serve to prove her point.

How well spectators would accept my proposed, faithful transformation of _Death of a Salesman_ is, of course, debatable. Making a movie of a 'sacred text' can be risky, as noted Spanish director Mario Camus discovered with his 1987 film adaptation of Federico García Lorca's _La casa de Bernarda Alba_ (_The House of Bernarda Alba_; written 1936, first staged 1945, in Buenos Aires). In her review essay on film adaptations of Lorca's tragedy, García-Abad (2001: 4) reports that the task has generally been considered impossible. Camus's stellar cast was headed by Irene Gutiérrez Caba as the despotic Bernarda and Ana Belén as Adela, the rebellious youngest daughter, but García-Abad affirms that some spectators, measuring the movie against José Carlos Plaza's magnificent 1984 stage revival (starring Berta Riaza and Belén), found the film less effective (García-Abad, 2001: 6). Some critics and spectators felt that Camus's movie was too faithful to the play; for others any alteration to the original was unacceptable.[2] At least part of the disapproval Camus experienced may be explained by the fact that he was dealing with a text that is revered both in Spain and abroad. There is certainly equal reverence for _Death of a Salesman._

Potentially the most static aspect of a stage play is the exposition. Lorca's _The House of Bernarda Alba_ is marred by a first act in which La Poncia tells the younger servant in detail about the family history and then recounts what she has just seen at the funeral service for Bernarda's second husband. Camus predictably moves his camera into the church and the street. We are not limited to hearing La Poncia (Florinda Chico) tell the younger servant about the funeral; we attend it with her. Our first image, in the opening sequence within the church, is of Bernarda Alba's cane, symbol of her authority. A series of close-ups identifies the several daughters. We see Magdalena sobbing and overcome with grief for her father's death rather than merely hear La Poncia tell the other servant about it. A sequence with La Poncia walking home from the church depicts the architectural features of a small Andalusian town: narrow streets, white-washed walls, and windows protected by iron grillwork. The image of the younger servant busily dyeing clothes and shoes black alerts us to the coming years of mourning when Bernarda's daughters will be shut in behind barred windows.

In terms of translation theory, Camus's conversion of the wordy exposition to movement and images is obligatory. As Gerardo Vázquez-Ayora has forcefully pointed out with respect to 'el genio de la lengua' (1977: 85), comparative linguistics informs us that each language has its own unique characteristics. To say 'Portuguese is spoken in Brazil' in Spanish, the passive voice must be converted to a reflexive verb form and the subject–verb order must be inverted: 'Se habla portugués en Brasil.' Camus's translation of Lorca's words to the language of images is similarly obligatory. Thus we look out the windows with the captive daughters to see the village streets and Pepe el Romano on horseback; when the villagers stone Librada's daughter, we witness the horrifying scene. Camus has also visualized aspects only hinted at in Lorca's subtext, such as the abusive treatment of Bernarda's elderly mother (tied to her bed); Angustias's coquettish concern about her appearance (standing before her mirror); and Adela's erotic desires (her sensual position in bed). Verbal references to oppressive summer heat are reinforced in images (La Poncia putting ice at the back of her neck to cool off). La Poncia's accusation that Adela had stood suggestively at her bedroom window to entice Pepe is shown: Adela looking down at him in the street and the matching low angle shot of her, from his perspective.

Although more frequent on television than in movies and less common now than in the early days of cinema, transpositions of stage plays have continued to appear on the big screen. Despite negative commentaries by various theorists, even unassimilated transpositions have often met with considerable popular and critical acclaim. To demonstrate how the strategy works, we shall consider a selection of successful film adaptations of plays, both contemporary and classic, that fall along a spectrum from relatively unassmiliated transposition to faithful transformation. If we equate film adaptation to translation, all of these examples, like Camus's *The House of Bernarda Alba*, function primarily as semantic (focused on the source text) rather than communicative translation (focused on reader or audience response).[3]

Edgar Neville's *El baile* (*The Dance*, 1959) represents an intermediate phase between a televised play, which makes no effort to open up the source text, and a transformation, which more aggressively translates the text to the narrative language of film. Directed and adapted by the playwright, *El baile* was made into a movie three years after the original stage production won Spain's National Theatre Prize. Although it goes beyond mere shifts in distance and angle of vision resulting from camera work, Neville's film version retains his source play virtually intact. Two of the three actors who formed the original cast of *El baile* (Conchita Montes and Rafael Alonso) repeat their roles in the movie; the cast has been modestly expanded, primarily through the addition of servants. A soundtrack has been added, with music to build atmosphere and underscore changing moods.[4]

Most of the action of *El baile* takes place inside the home of an unusual ménage à trois: a married couple (Adela and Pedro) and Julián, the wife's ardent but chaste admirer who is Pedro's best friend. The single set of the original play revealed the couple's living room. In the movie, the number of visible rooms in the household has been increased to facilitate camera movement and parallel action. Cross-cutting provides movement: from the library where Adela, unaware that she has a fatal illness, is writing a letter, to a balcony, where the grieving Pedro and Julián are noisily sacrificing their insect collection, which Adela hates; from upstairs, where the granddaughter Adelita (also played by Conchita Montes) prepares for a dance, to downstairs, where the two elderly men await her. Neville thus constructs for the film version of his relatively static play the sense of movement between locations that Miller built into the original script of *Death of a Salesman*. Not surprisingly, in *The House of Bernarda Alba*, film director Camus similarly opens up the static, interior setting to realistic space so that action may occur, sometimes simultaneously, in various locations within the house.

The most predictable and obvious change in *El baile* is that from theatrical to cinematic decor, that is, from static interiors to exterior scenes with ample use of tracking shots. The movie begins in Madrid's Retiro Park, where horse-drawn carriages, a few vintage cars, and colourful costumes establish the time (1900). Adela's pink dress and parasol, coupled with light music (flutes and violins), set a happy mood. The camera turns upward and the title credits are written against a background of treetops and blue sky. The scene cuts to a city street, where Adela and Julián are returning to the house from a shopping excursion.

Given his fidelity to his stage play, Neville uses exterior scenes primarily as markers between the three acts of the source. The play is episodic, with gaps of 20 or 25 years between acts; exterior sequences effectively

convey both mood and this passage of time. In the second Retiro sequence
of the film, children are playing, the sky changes colour, and the action
shifts from summer to winter snow; the scene cuts to Adela, sitting in
front of her mirror and examining her grey hair. Adela's death is visualized through cypresses (the tree of Spanish cemeteries) outlined against a
rainy sky. A final scene in the Retiro shows people dressed in modern
(1950s) clothes and the two old men sitting on a bench; a chauffeur
waits to drive them home, repeating the street sequence from the
movie's beginning. It should be noted that all of these devices evolve
from implicit aspects of the source text; they do not significantly
amplify or distort the author's original work.

Neville's *El baile* is a period piece, entertaining but a bit quaint by
contemporary standards. Only in temporal transitions and a few scenes
of parallel action has it replaced the original dialogue with cinematic
signifiers. There is a certain realism of space, but the film runs counter to
André Bazin's dictum that in theatre 'the drama proceeds from the
actor, in the cinema it goes from the decor to man' (Bazin, 1985: 361). In
Neville's movie version of his own play, decor and story are subordinate
to character. On the other hand, Neville has used film techniques
to convey the passage of time and the aging of his protagonists and has
thus successfully exploited the play's episodic structure. As an experienced
film director, he has not hesitated to go on location in the Madrid streets.

The movie version of *El baile* reflects an approach to film adaptation
that was common in the 1950s, but four decades later *Actrius* (*Actresses*,
1996) uses similar strategies and falls even closer to the transposition/
intersecting end of our spectrum. The distinguished Catalan director
Ventura Pons has recently tackled a series of stage plays, including
E. R. by Josep M. Benet i Jornet. The title has been changed radically,
but the screenplay, co-authored by Pons and Benet i Jornet, leaves the
original script essentially unaltered.[5] Contrary to general patterns in
film adaptation, the four-character cast of the source text is not expanded.
The original dialogue is maintained without noticeable additions or
omissions. The camera moves outdoors for brief interludes and provides
us with realistic detail on the several interior settings, but the film makes
no effort to break the talky quality of the original play. Indeed three of the
characters narrate their lives, without conversion of their stories to visual
images. The film is far removed from the action mode of Hollywood
movies; spectators leaving the theatre will be led to discuss the film's
underlying meaning, not what happened. *Actresses* nevertheless is a
strong film, thanks to the compelling dramatic interest of the text and
the splendid performance of relative newcomer Mercé Pons and three

of Spain's most accomplished actresses: Núria Espert (as Glòria, a famous actress), Rosa Maria Sardà (as Assumpta, a television star), and Anna Lizarán (as Maria, whose professional career has been limited to dubbing films).

Actresses is a highly metatheatrical work: theatre about theatre. The aspiring young actress is in competition with three others to play the role of the young Empar Ribera on stage. To prepare herself for tryouts, she interviews individually the three middle-aged friends who had been students of the legendary Ribera and who had once been rivals for the role of Iphigenia in a production Ribera would direct. Although not to the extent of *El baile*, the action of Benet i Jornet's play is episodic, taking place over a period of some months.

In the opening sequence of *Actresses*, prior to the titles, Pons visualizes the acting student's memory of receiving a toy theatre when she was a child; the flashback as such is not present in the stage play. The text is opened to cinematic decor by a view of cars passing in the street; the camera follows the young woman as she walks toward and enters a theatre for her interview with Glòria. While the play could be performed on an almost bare stage, with minimal props to suggest a change of location, Pons uses realistic sets to represent the three places of employment and the three homes of the older women. In the manner of *El baile*, he also uses sequences of the young woman in the street to serve as markers between scenes. On occasion dialogue is shifted to exterior locales to create a sense of movement: the aspiring actress and Maria chat, in dialogue taken directly from the source text, as they walk down the street.

Going outside so that the characters may talk while in motion is a common cinematic device, one we also find in films with historical settings: Pilar Miró's 1996 adaptation of Lope de Vega's *El perro del hortelano* (The Dog in the Manger), Jean-Paul Rappeneau's 1990 movie version of Edmond Rostand's *Cyrano de Bergerac*, and Jaime Chávarri's *Las bicicletas son para el verano* (Bicycles Are for Summer, 1984). Miro's visually stunning adaptation of the early 17th-century comedy garnered seven Goya prizes. Rappeneau's sumptuous screen version of Rostand's historical drama, starring Gérard Depardieu in the title role, was a box-office hit. Also meeting with popular success, Chávarri's movie is an adaptation of Fernando Fernán Gómez's prize-winning play about life in Madrid during the prolonged siege of that city by fascist forces during the Spanish Civil War (1936–1939).

As we noted in the previous chapter, no aspect of film adaptation of theatre has received greater scholarly attention than transformations of Shakespeare. Russell Jackson points out that Elizabethan texts invite a certain latitude. Dialogue must be translated to action and images and may be used outside the original framework. Shifts between locations is common. The text is usually cut substantially. Because the ideal running time of a movie is under two hours, most Shakespeare films use only 25–30% of the source text. Condensing Shakespeare, also a common practice for contemporary stage productions, is achieved by 'cutting within speeches and scenes, making the dialogue leaner but (mostly) preserving the scene's original shape' (Jackson, 2000: 17). Jackson further observes that such modification of the original text 'is not so much an unavoidable and regrettable consequence of filming, as an opportunity the director forgoes at his or her peril' (Jackson, 2000: 19). As British playwright Alan Bennett has stated, 'Film is drama at its most impatient' (quoted in Erskine & Welsh, 2000: xvi). These same observations are relevant to Golden Age drama in Spain.

Director Miró's 1996 film version of *El perro del hortelano* is an outstanding achievement and, as Pilar Nieva de la Paz states, all the more so in that Miró's script remained faithful to the verse form of Lope's original text (Nieva de la Paz, 2001: 259). An obvious rupture with common practices in adaptation of theatre, the resulting film script is very verbal and is marked by very rapid speech. Soliloquies are delivered in voice-off. *El perro del hortelano* starred Emma Suárez as the countess Diana and Carmelo Gómez as the secretary Teodoro who loves her, despite their supposed differences in social class. When the conflict is resolved at the end by the discovery that Teodoro is the long lost son of an elderly count, Miró treats the classic device in playful, parodic tone.

Lope de Vega, like the contemporaneous Shakespeare, was not limited by realistic stage settings; his audience would accept and imagine spatial fluidity in the developing action of the play. In filming *El perro de hortelano*, Miró creatively drew from hints in the text to open up cinematic space. Action is frequently cross-cut between exterior and interior shots of the countess's castle. The opening sequence, before and during the projection of the titles, takes place at night: someone is running outside the darkened castle while agitated people inside respond by lighting candles. During an extended sequence, the following morning Teodoro is seen walking in the garden with a friend. As Teodoro confesses that he no longer loves the servant Marcela, the two men take longer steps; the physical action underscores the secretary's emotional state. Miró finds a variety of unexpected ways to shift the background for long dialogues: one early conversation between Diana and Teodoro takes place in a rowboat on the castle pond. Elegant period costumes add to the visual pleasure of the film; the bright colours of Diana's gowns provide notes of vivid contrast to black clothing worn by other characters. Miró takes time for wordless sequences that take full advantage of the beautiful countryside or the elegant castle grounds with its fountains. These interludes, focusing on images, compensate for excessive dialogue. Music and dance, culminating in a final outdoor wedding celebration, add to the joyous spirit.

In discussing approaches to film adaptation of texts in verse, José Antonio Pérez Bowie cites *El perro de hortelano* as an outstanding example of 'naturalization'. With this method, an appropriate setting is used so that verse will seem natural within the context; dynamic acting and a playful mise-en-scène are also essential (Pérez Bowie, 2001: 329). Care must be taken in editing the source text and in casting actors who are skilled at handling verse drama. Pérez Bowie reports that Miró's script, based on a version by Rafael Pérez Sierra, has reduced the original Lope de Vega play by about 25%; by eliminating digressions, she helped the action flow gracefully (Pérez Bowie, 2001: 331). In that modern stage productions also abbreviate 17th-century texts, *El perro del hortelano* may be placed at the transposition end on our spectrum.

Both Pérez Bowie (2001: 330) and Ángel Luis Hueso (2001: 58) identify Rappeneau's *Cyrano de Bergerac*, along with Kenneth Branagh's several film adaptations of Shakespeare, as a significant antecedent for Miró's *El perro del hortelano*. The action of Rostand's late 19th-century, neo-romantic, verse drama begins in 1640 and centres on the historical Cyrano, a minor but well-known writer of the period. Rostand's classic work inspired a silent movie in France (1925, dir. Augusto Genina), as well as a black and white American film (1950, dir. Michael Gordon) that won an Oscar for José Ferrer in the title role. Rappeneau's lavish new version, using a script the director co-authored with Jean-Claude Carrière, outshines these earlier movies. Martin and Porter give four stars to the 1925 and 1950 films and their highest rating, five stars, to the 1990 version. Depardieu received the award for best actor at the Cannes Film Festival for his portrayal of the gifted poet and swordsman who, because of his absurd, long nose, suppresses his love for Roxanne to woo the young lady on behalf of the handsome Christian.

Rappeneau exploits the source text in creating a number of locations to enhance the movement and action of the stage play. In the early scenes, *Cyrano de Bergerac* uses interior and exterior views of Roxanne's home, but Rostand's drama allows for a wide range of settings, including city streets, a theatre, the salon where Cyrano practises his dueling skills, battle fields, open countryside, and a convent garden. There are exquisitely beautiful, peaceful moments that could be compared to impressionist paintings: a medium shot of Cyrano and Roxanne framed by an open window through which we see lovely trees; Roxanne reading a letter by the light of her fireplace and a candle. There are also desolate scenes on the battlefield, where riderless horses run loose, carriages are burning, and survivors take guns from the fallen. Carlos Aguilar finds this superproduction, the most ambitious in the history of French cinema, to be so ostentatious that it subordinates the acting (Aguilar, 1992: 306). Hueso believes that the movie achieves an admirable balance between the difficult task of maintaining Alexandrine verse and the goal of presenting rich interior settings and natural landscapes (Hueso, 2001: 58). Given the popular success of the movie, most spectators would doubtless agree with Hueso.

Miró's *El perro del hortelano* shortens Lope de Vega's text and moves some dialogue to more dynamic, outdoor locations, but basically her movie does not write in additional scenes. Rappeneau's *Cyrano de Bergerac*, while generally faithful to Rostand's play, introduces action scenes that have no counterpart in the source: Christian and other soldiers departing for battle, desperately hungry soldiers roasting a rat and fighting over the morsels, Christian rescuing Roxanne when she visits the battlefield to bring supplies to the men, the French circling their wagons as the Spaniards prepare to attack. These added battlefield scenes are more reminiscent of Westerns than of Rostand and hence move *Cyrano* to the transformation end of our spectrum. Also at the transformation end is Michael Hoffman's 1999 film adaptation of Shakespeare's *A Midsummer Night's Dream*. Hoffman retains Shakespeare's language, albeit with cuts, but he moves and modernizes the setting. Although Hoffman's movie shifts the fiction forward, because it does not depart from the original story, it does not classify as an analogy in Wagner's terms.

As many critics have noted, director Kenneth Branagh has remained as close as possible to Shakespeare's texts in such movies as *Much Ado About Nothing* (1993) and *Hamlet* (1996). Deborah Cartmell, who uses Wagner's concepts for analysing film adaptations, cites Branagh's *Hamlet* as a clear example of transposition. By contrast, Hoffman, who both directed and adapted *A Midsummer Night's Dream*, let his imagination run wild. As noted in the previous chapter, Hoffman created the magical, moonlit forest – realm of the fairies ruled by Oberon (Rupert Everett) and Tatiana (Michelle Pfeiffer) – on a huge soundstage. Panoramic shots in the daylight of the town, in Italy, and of nearby countryside stand in bright, realistic contrast to the misty forest. Helena (Calista Flockhart) and other human characters ride from the real town into the bewildering, enchanted space on their bicycles.

Consistent with the time of the original author, Miró keeps a 17th-century setting for *El perro del hortelano*. Hoffman prefers to move his action forward to the late 19th century. The duke, who is up to date with the latest inventions, owns an early phonograph; the dwarves who serve him steal the magical machine and some records and give them to the fairies, who happily toss them into a pond. The music chosen for the soundtrack likewise comes from the 19th century: Mendelssohn's 'A Midsummer Night's Dream' and selections from Italian operas. Modern adaptations of classic texts, whether for stage or screen, often move the action forward to a period other than that of the original author. *A Midsummer Night's Dream* in particular invites such innovation. When Jorge Lavelli staged Shakespeare's comedy for the Comédie Française, he shifted the action to the 1920s; the climax of his lavish production was a tango scene that included all of the cast, humans and fairies alike. Transformations like those of Hoffman and Lavelli involve a double dislocation in time: taking a 17th-century text and shifting the action to a more recent past, while still making it a period piece relative to the time of performance.

Movie versions of plays by both classic and contemporary authors may range widely along the scale from transposition to faithful transformation. The 1968 movie version of *The Odd Couple* (dir. Gene Saks) is freer in its approach to adaptation than the made-for-television *Death of a Salesman* and either *El baile* or *Actresses* but is likewise respectful of the source text. As was true in *El perro del hortelano* and *Cyrano de Bergerac*, the realistic context has been opened up but consistently seeks cinematic equivalences for what Andrew has defined as essential elements: the 'original's tone, values, imagery, and rhythm' (Andrew, 2000: 32). This level of fidelity is not surprising given that Neil Simon himself wrote the screenplay for *The Odd Couple*.

In Simon's original comedy, there are allusions to Felix's desire to commit suicide when his marriage breaks up. Throughout the comedy, the less than agile Felix is prone to physical ills. These allusions are visually developed in the movie in the sequences that precede and immediately follow the film titles: Felix in the New York streets, Felix checking into a seedy hotel room, Felix writing a suicide note, Felix unable to open the window to jump out, Felix pulling his back, Felix returning to the street, Felix entering a burlesque show, Felix leaning back and hurting his neck, Felix looking up at Oscar's lighted apartment window. With only minimal dialogue but underscored by Neal Hefti's music, these early sequences, none of which have direct counterparts in the source play, visually establish Felix's situation and personality and set the comic tone for the movie.

The action of Simon's comedy takes place in the living room of Oscar's apartment; the set includes doors and a hallway that lead off to other rooms. The movie adaptation opens up this set to realistic space: the outside of the building, the elevator, the door to Oscar's apartment from both sides, the inside hallway in its full extension, the interiors of several rooms. As was true in Pons's *Actresses*, some of the dialogue is placed in motion: Oscar and Felix go walking in the New York streets, enter a restaurant, sit down in a park, go bowling. Their friend Murray is a policeman; action is shifted to his police car when the poker-playing buddies are out searching for Felix along Riverside Drive. Oscar is a sportswriter; in the movie, this allusion is visualized by placing him at work in a stadium sports box. A sequence is added in which a phone call from the ever-fussy Felix prevents Oscar from seeing a spectacular triple play; while the scene does not appear in the play, it is certainly consistent with the source text's tone. Perhaps the only deliberate change from stage play to screenplay is culinary. In the original, Felix, an expert cook, has problems with the London broil that he prepares when Oscar invites the Pigeon sisters to dinner. Not only does Felix have to call his wife for the recipe, but he burns the London broil to a crisp when Oscar changes the dinner time without telling him. The switch in the movie to meatloaf works better: London broil requires no recipe and, because it cooks quickly, would have been put in the oven while the guests were being served their appetizers, not prior to their arrival. Just as translators of stage plays may on occasion suggest improvements to the text, in preparing his screenplay Simon has corrected a minor problem in his original text.

A key component of any film adaptation is the approach to opening sequences and titles. Jackson recommends that the opening sequences establish the principal characters, indicate the milieu, and serve as a springboard for the story (Jackson, 2000: 30). In *El baile*, Neville transfers his original text with few changes but unleashes his visual imagination at the beginning. Pons's most creative moment in *Actresses* comes in the opening moments. Saks and Camus freely translate verbal to visual language in the early sequences of *The Odd Couple* and *The House of Bernarda Alba*. In related fashion, in *Las bicicletas son para el verano* Chávarri forcefully establishes historical context before a word is spoken. The first image of his film is the Republican banner 'No pasarán' (They shall not pass), stretching across the screen. He cuts to two teenagers, walking down the street and looking at a poster for a war movie. The boys reach a desolate open field where they begin playing at war as the titles appear on the screen. The sequence is filmed in sepia, like old documentaries. Freeze-frames give to the boys the grimace of death. Slow cello music, in a minor key, underscores the titles. The opening moments present both an anti-war statement and an elegy to the Republican cause. There is no exact counterpart for these sequences in the source text, but hints for them are clearly found there. The play's prologue takes place in a field and focuses on the teenage Luisito and a friend, who talk about war movies.

Opening sequences, as well as development of cinematic decor, are also skillfully handled in film adaptations of two time-honoured, Pulitzer Prize winning American plays: Tennessee Williams' *A Streetcar Named Desire* (1947) and Mary Coyle Chase's *Harvey* (1944). Williams wrote his own screenplay and Elia Kazan directed both the Broadway production and the 1951 movie, recipient of four Academy Awards. Marlon Brando (Stanley), Kim Hunter (Stella), and Karl Malden (Mitch) repeated their stage roles on the screen while Vivien Leigh replaced Jessica Tandy as Blanche. Stanley is the role that made Brando famous. *Harvey* was directed on Broadway by Antoinette Perry and on screen, in 1950, by Henry Koster, with a screenplay co-authored by Chase and Oscar Brodney. The movie *Harvey* provided Jimmy Stewart with one of his most memorable roles (Elwood P. Dowd) and won the best supporting actress Oscar for Josephine Hull, who also appeared in the original stage cast as Elwood's sister. In their video movie guide, Martin and Porter give *A Streetcar Named Desire* five stars and *Harvey*, four and a half. While neither production is a transposition, once again the authors were directly involved and the results fall into the category of faithful transformation.

Reminiscent of Miller's *Death of a Salesman*, Williams' stage directions for *A Streetcar Named Desire* describe a multiple set that includes both exterior and interior space: a two-storey corner building on Elysian Fields in New Orleans and a first-floor flat. When the action moves inside, the outside areas dim and the interior is lighted to reveal two rooms and a bathroom door. During the first scene of the play, Blanche arrives at the house to visit her sister Stella, who mentions that her husband Stanley has gone bowling. In the opening sequences, the movie understandably introduces a series of images to visualize and amplify the verbal exposition: a train coming into the station, Blanche's arrival, the offer of a handsome young sailor to help the lost traveller and Blanche's coquettish response, a view of a streetcar going to Desire, and finally Blanche's arrival at Stella's house. Picking up on a clue from the source, the two sisters go to the bowling alley, where they see Stanley get into a brawl. Kazan has added elements here that quickly denote character: the appearance of the sailor points to Blanche's sexuality and the fight indicates that Stanley is prone to physical violence.

Although the movie follows the play's dialogue to a large extent, there are other changes. Curiously, Kazan eliminates one of the play's most powerful images, from the beginning moments of the opening scene. Stanley appears outside the house, bellows for Stella, and tosses her a package of meat; she protests, but manages to catch it, and laughs as Stanley continues on his way to the bowling alley (Williams, 1972: 13–14). With great economy, the brief moment establishes Stanley's role as breadwinner, his crude nature, and Stella's submissiveness.[6] Perhaps Kazan justifiably suppressed the moment to concentrate more on Blanche and to develop his cinematic use of the city, but we might consider the omission to be a translation loss. In partial compensation, Stanley's controlling nature is highlighted later in the movie in an added sequence with Mitch, shot at the plant where they work, when Stanley divulges Blanche's sordid past.

As we would anticipate, the film opens up realistic space in various ways. It also adds sequences in the street and in Eunice's upstairs flat, thus allowing for greater movement and parallel action. It shifts Blanche's long scene with her admirer Mitch from the enclosed flat to a club on a lake (probably Lake Pontchartrain, a precise reference to the New Orleans setting found in the stage directions of the source text).

Less predictably – unless we recall Hollywood's self-censorship of the period – the story of why Blanche's young husband committed suicide is altered radically. In the play, Blanche tells Mitch that she precipitated the death of her lost love by confronting him on the dance floor at a lakeside club with her knowledge that he is involved in a homosexual relationship: 'I saw! I know! You disgust me . . .' (Williams, 1972: 96). The distraught young man left the club, went down to the lake, and killed himself. In keeping with the Motion Picture Production Code still in force in the 1950s, the movie removes the allusion to homosexuality and has Blanche merely accuse her husband of being weak. On the other hand, the outdoor setting for Blanche's narration represents a certain compensation.[7] As Erskine and Welsh observe, 'In contrast to the play's limited set, the misty lakeside where Blanche confesses her past to Mitch evokes the original scene where her sexually tormented husband killed himself' (Erskine & Welsh, 2000: 331). This aspect of the verbal description from the source play is now developed visually in the film.

Koster's movie version of *Harvey*, like Kazan's film adaptation of *A Streetcar Named Desire*, maintains a balance between fidelity to the source and conformity to cinematic language. Chase's stage comedy has a cast of 11 and two interior sets: a library in the Dowds' old family mansion and an office at Chumley's Rest, where Veta hopes to confine her brother Elwood. The opening sequence is shot outside the mansion. Elwood comes out of the house and through the gate; very politely he greets the mailman (an added character) and then rips up a letter, unread. Veta and her daughter, Myrtle Mae, anxiously watch Elwood from a window. The relationships between these three main characters, Elwood's exquisite courtesy but propensity toward unusual behaviour, and the fact that the women are eager to have him leave the house are established visually before the dialogue begins. The movie adds other new scenes, secondary characters, and locations, both exterior and interior.

All of these additions are consistent with the comic tone and rhythm of the original and most of them derive from references in the source text. In Act I of the play, Veta has invited a number of society ladies to the house so that Myrtle Mae may meet them as a step toward finding a husband; in the movie, we are placed in the middle of this social gathering, we see the guests and are subjected to the dreadful singing of one of them. In the play, the staff at Chumley's Rest mistakenly believe that it is Veta, not Elwood, who should be locked up; Wilson, the orderly, whisks her off upstairs where she is forced to take a bath. The movie set includes several rooms within the mental hospital and hence we see Veta resisting the nurses. A secondary character in the play is a cab driver; in the movie there are street scenes with the cab. The film version shows the grounds at Chumley's Rest where Elwood happily picks flowers and where an elderly and increasingly confused guard is in charge of the gated entry. The play suggests that Elwood has a drinking problem. The movie includes sequences in Elwood's favourite bar, where the bartender and regular customers are well acquainted with Elwood's tall, long-eared, friend Harvey. Indeed one of the major gains in the translation of *Harvey* from stage to screen is the added illusion of reality accorded the invisible pooka. The movie provides more opportunities for Elwood to interact with the big rabbit: holding the gate open for him, pushing him out of the way of a fire truck when they are crossing the street. And the movie gives greater emphasis to the belief in Harvey shared by Dr Chumley and Veta.

I consider Chávarri's film version of Fernán Gómez's *Las bicicletas son para el verano* (screenplay by Lola Salvador Maldonado) to be as respectful of the source text as Saks's *The Odd Couple* and Koster's *Harvey* are of their original comedies, but with respect to the Spanish film, the playwright did not agree. In his book on Spanish theatre into film, Juan Antonio

Ríos Carratalá labels the section on *Las bicicletas son para el verano* 'a polemical adaptation'. Much of the controversy came directly from Fernán Gómez, who objected to the decision of the director to make the dining room of his principal characters less central by moving some action to the outside (Ríos Carratalá, 1999: 160). Spectators had a different opinion. Survey results from a Gallup poll for the Spanish Film Institute, released at the end of 1986, named *Las bicicletas son para el verano* fourth among the best-liked films of the preceding six years. In his guide to movies on video, Carlos Aguilar proclaims that the movie was an important critical and audience success (Aguilar, 1992: 142). Its all-star cast was headed by Agustín González (Don Luis), the one carryover from the stage production.

Fernán Gómez was a famous film actor and director long before he wrote his play (winner of the 1978 Lope de Vega Prize; first staged 1982). *Las bicicletas son para el verano*, like Miller's *Death of a Salesman*, is an example of cinematic theatre. The episodic action, covering a three-year period, shifts among seven locations: the dining room in the home of Don Luis, where eight of 17 scenes occur; Luisito's bedroom and that of the maid María, in the same apartment; the neighbours' dining room, the building basement, a park, and a field. The latter, on the western edge of the city where much fighting takes place during the war, is the scene of both prologue and epilogue. Director José Carlos Plaza used a multiple stage setting and emphasized the text's temporal and spatial fluidity in a deliberately cinematographic staging.[8]

One might anticipate that adaptation of Fernán Gómez's text for the screen would require far fewer changes than would a small-cast, well-made play with a single set, but Chávarri does rearrange and displace the action to some extent. For example, he takes Luisito's key conversation with his father about buying a bicycle and cross-cuts it with the preparations for celebrating Julio's new job. Both sequences come from the original text but are now rearranged through editing. At the same time, Chávarri is perhaps too respectful of the source dialogue; the result is often talky. Unlike Camus, who shortens speeches and deletes whole passages from Lorca's *La casa de Bernarda Alba*, Chávarri draws dialogue almost directly from the play. But conversations between members of Don Luis's family, particularly in the early sequences, take place as the characters stroll through the streets or sit at an outdoor café. The shift to exterior locations not only is a standard strategy for meeting the requirements of cinematic decor but provides a contrast with the later scenes of enclosure during the protracted siege of Madrid. Ríos Carratalá accurately says, 'All of the locations of the cinematographic adaptation are suggested in the theatrical text' (Ríos Carratalá, 1999: 165).

In his review in *Variety*, Peter Besas attacks *Las bicicletas son para el verano* on thematic grounds. He concludes, 'Even local audiences must by now be tiring of subjects dealing with the Civil War' (Besas, 1984: 20). Curiously, in a passing reference to the same film in *Behind the Spanish Lens*, he asserts that it is 'totally devoid of any ideological thrust' (Besas, 1985: 256). Besas is demonstrably wrong on both counts. Spanish audiences clearly did not find the subject tiring. The original stage production of Fernán Gómez's play enjoyed unprecedented success; people lined up for hours to buy tickets. Statistics released at the end of 1985 identified Mario Camus's *Los santos inocentes* (Holy Innocents) as the top-grossing Spanish film in history; *Las bicicletas son para el verano* placed sixth on the list. Nor is the film 'totally devoid of ideological thrust'. Indeed one of the significant transformations is precisely the shift from a fairly softened, neutral stance in the play to an overtly pro-Republican message in the movie.

The 'No pasarán' banner in the street from the prologue is seen again when the soldiers march off to defend the city and, as in the case of Manolita's lover, to die. The irony is enhanced in a later sequence, when a group of children play with the fallen banner. Near the same street location, Nationalist soldiers accost Manolita (Victoria Abril) and beat her brother Luisito (Gabino Diego), who tries to protect her. While there is an earlier counterpart scene to reveal Republican abuses (destruction of religious statues), the impact at the end, coupled with the political and economic aftermath of 'Victory', is stronger. The conservative landlady's well-lit, elegant living room and her radiant daughter's plans for going abroad to study contrast vividly with the deteriorating situation of Don Luis's family, as does the merry-go-round in the background when the father tells his son what the future holds for them and others not allied with Franco's winning side. In his programme note for the original stage production, Fernán Gómez declared that he was looking back without anger. The film adaptation has introduced a veiled anger or, at least, a heightened pathos.

Only five years separate the award of the Lope de Vega Prize to Fernán Gómez's play and the release of the film version, but those years were crucial in Spanish history. In 1978, during the transition from dictatorship to democracy, many Spaniards yearned for reconciliation, not recrimination, even as many feared the possible return of a repressive regime. But an attempted military coup in February 1981 was quickly overcome and the socialists achieved an overwhelming triumph in the October 1982 elections. If there is a modest ideological shift from play to movie, it is readily explained by historical context.

Theatre in performance has always been responsive to the context of the audience. Jean-Louis Barrault chose to stage Cervantes's *La Numancia* in Paris in 1937 because he knew that the Golden Age historical drama, which deals with the Roman siege of a Spanish town, could function for his spectators as a commentary on the ongoing Spanish Civil War. In 1944, during the German occupation, Jean Anouilh chose to adapt the Greek tragedy of *Antigone* because he knew that his French spectators would perceive the contemporary application of the protagonist's resistance to tyranny. Similarly the 2003 revival in Madrid of *Las bicicletas son para el verano*, on the eve of the invasion of Iraq and siege of Baghdad, conveyed a double message: a collective memory of their own national tragedy and sympathy for another people who were about to suffer in the same way. Throughout the winter and spring of 2003, Spanish actors in all theatres appeared for curtain calls wearing antiwar tags. At performances of Fernán Gómez's play about the siege of Madrid, those 'No a la guerra' tags were greeted with deep emotion.

Theatrical translators and authors of film adaptations should be aware that once a text is removed in time or space from its original context, it has the potential for transmitting new meanings, intentional or not, to some if not all spectators. María Asunción Gómez points out that the political situation in Spain changed radically between the stage premiere of Antonio Buero-Vallejo's *Un soñador para un pueblo* (A Dreamer for a People, 1958) and Josefina Molina's film adaptation, *Esquilache* (1988). When Buero-Vallejo wrote his historical drama about the failed efforts of the progressive minister Esquilache to modernize 18th-century Spain, Franco's long dictatorship was at its peak of repression. Molina's film comes at the height of power of PSOE, the Spanish Socialist Workers Party. The contemporary movie audience might well interpret *Esquilache* in terms of three sociohistorical contexts: the reign of Charles III (setting for the action), the repressive 1950s (intertextual reference to Buero's play, which used the historical setting as a means of subverting official censorship), and their own present (democratic Spain). Using cateogories outlined by George Szanto, Gómez astutely observes that *Un soñador para un pueblo* in 1958 functioned as dialectical propaganda, intended to make spectators think and hence take a stand against an authoritarian regime; under democracy, *Esquilache* functions as integration propaganda, indirectly reinforcing the status quo (Gómez, 2000: 123). Molina did not alter Buero-Vallejo's text; it is the historical context of the spectators that provides the new interpretation of the same story.

A shift in potential meaning for spectators from stage to screen may be more deliberate on the part of movie producers and directors. As mentioned in the previous chapter, the Chilean playwright Antonio Skármeta wrote and directed his own film version of *Ardiente paciencia* (*Burning Patience*) in the early 1980s. The better known movie, based on the same text about a humble postman and his friendship with poet and diplomat Pablo Neruda, is *Il Postino* (*The Postman*) (1994, dir. Michael Radford). The new title, eliminating the intertextual reference to Rimbaud, indicates a desire to attract a popular audience. Such a title change is common and does not necessarily indicate a lack of fidelity to the source. Nelly Fernández-Tiscornia's *Made in Lanús* was renamed *Made in Argentina* (1986, dir. Juan José Jusid) because few people outside the Buenos Aires area would recognize Lanús as a working class neighbourhood in that city. Jusid's movie about political exiles returning to Argentina after their forced exile during the Dirty War is basically a transposition of the source. By contrast, *The Postman*, the French/Italian/Belgian production based on Skármeta's play, moved the action from Chile to Italy and substantially altered the underlying political message. Perhaps the change was prompted by the passage of time but more likely it was done to soften the message for an international audience.

Skármeta's *Ardiente paciencia* is often poetic in tone and beautiful in cinematography, but it remains close to the life of the historical figure and emphasizes the political situation in Chile. The action of the original play, as well as Skármeta's own transposition, takes place from 1969 to 1973, when a military coup toppled Salvador Allende's government and Allende and many of those allied with him were executed.

In Skármeta's film, Neruda, an active member of the Communist Party, is seen involved in a political campaign himself and then becoming a strong supporter of Allende, who wins the presidential election. When Neruda is given the Nobel Prize for literature in 1971, the residents of the little town of Isla Negra gather in the local bar to watch his acceptance speech on television. When news breaks about the military coup and assassination of the president, telegrams of concern for Neruda's safety arrive from around the world. Mario, the postman, memorizes those messages and surreptitiously crawls up a hill to reach Neruda's house to relay them to the elderly, ill poet. The intervention of Sweden and Mexico to rescue Neruda is shown through the arrival of an ambulance and a departure by plane. In a final sequence, when officials take Mario from his home, ostensibly to ask him a few routine questions, the expression on his face confirms what we already know: those routine questions will lead to his execution. Mario also dies in Radford's movie, but he is killed by police at a large communist rally, probably in Rome; no link is made to repression in Chile, and Mario is caught up in a huge crowd, not singled out to be punished because of his friendship with a political figure. As a consequence, *The Postman* lies beyond faithful transformation to approach borrowing/analogy on our spectrum.

Another example of deliberate shifting in political message is *Bwana* (1996, dir. Imanol Uribe), based on Ignacio del Moral's *La mirada del hombre oscuro* (*Dark Man's Gaze*). The original play, winner of the first annual Sociedad General de Autores de España prize in 1991, was first staged in 1993. Uribe's movie adaptation (screenplay by del Moral and Francisco Pino) won a variety of major prizes at international film festivals in San Sebastián and Miami and was Spain's nominee for a foreign film Oscar. Del Moral's satire on racism takes place on an isolated beach on the Mediterranean coast and has a six-character cast: a Spanish mother and father with their two children and two illegal immigrants, Ombasi and his dead companion, who nevertheless has a speaking role. After an evening and night of comic misunderstandings, the father and Ombasi engage in physical fighting and the Spaniards abandon the black man. Through an epilogue with a conversation between the two Africans, we learn that Ombasi was captured and deported, but, desperately seeking a better life, later returned to Spain where he died on a city street. At play's end, the two dead men, to the sound of drums, go off to an African fiesta. The oneiric scene evokes the religious spectacles of Yoruba.[9] Typical of del Moral's theatre, the play is marked by humour and fantasy.

The movie *Bwana* predictably expands the number of locations to develop cinematic decor and adds new characters: groups of smugglers and of skinheads, both of which threaten to rape the mother. There are no hints for these violent characters within the source text. In a final sequence, the frightened family escapes in their car, leaving Ombasi alone to face the savage treatment of the menacing Neo-nazis. As Gómez observes, in that two of the skinheads are German, the responsibility for Ombasi's death is thus shifted from middle-class Spaniards, who fail to extend a sympathetic hand to strangers, to foreign representatives of the radical right (Gómez, 2002: 31). Because of these changes in tone and ideology, *Bwana*, like *The Postman*, must be considered closer to borrowing than faithful transformation.[10]

When stage directors or theatrical translators wish to make significant changes to a play by a living author, it behooves them to consult the playwright. Depending upon the contract, there may not be a comparable legal reason for such consultation in preparing movie versions of plays, but authors would doubtless prefer not to be surprised by overly free adaptations. From discussions I have had with Spanish playwrights, I conclude that most authors are likely to be dismayed by screen versions that edge away from transposition and faithful transformation even if the film proved to be a popular success and even if they had a hand in preparing the film script.[11] Del Moral, despite being credited with co-authoring the screenplay, does not approve of the violence superimposed on his *Dark Man's Gaze* (del Moral, personal interview, 2003).

Small casts are common in stage plays and unusual in cinema. The small-cast play has the advantage of a less expensive payroll, of being appropriate for little theatres and experimental spaces, and of being easier to take on tour. But if the small cast is retained in a film version, the resulting movie runs a strong risk of looking like canned theatre. Consequently, in the process of opening up to realistic space, film adaptations tend to expand as well to a realistic number of people. There are exceptions, however. One notable example is *Who's Afraid of Virginia Woolf?* (1966, dir. Mike Nichols), based on the 1962 play by Edward Albee. Like Pons's movie of Benet i Jornet's *Actresses*, Nichols's *Who's Afraid of Virginia Woolf?* stays with the original four characters. All four actors – Elizabeth Taylor (Martha), Richard Burton (George), Sandy Dennis (Honey), and George Segal (Nick) – were nominated for Academy Awards; Taylor and Dennis received Oscars as best actress and best supporting actress. The movie was also nominated in nine other categories, including best picture, director and screenplay adaptation; it won Oscars for B&W cinematography, B&W art direction, and B&W costume design. By not adding characters or using colour cinematography, *Who's Afraid of Virginia Woolf?* focused with dramatic intensity on the longstanding love–hate relationship of Martha and George, the underlying marital conflicts of the younger couple, and the interactions among the four characters.

The screenplay, written by producer Ernest Lehman, is respectful enough of Albee's text that the movie should be considered a transposition. As is often true with contemporary stage productions of Shakespeare, Lehman tightens the dialogue by judicious cutting within scenes. A comparison of the movie dialogue with the original play reveals a number of short omissions, of a few lines or a page, and some cuts that eliminate several pages of text. The only substantial change that Lehman introduces relates to Martha's age.

When plays move from the page to the stage or screen, modifications are often required because of the flesh and blood actors who have been cast in the roles. Although the strategy is routine, results may vary greatly. Irwin Shaw's screenplay for Eugene O'Neill's *Desire Under the Elms* (1958, dir. Delbert Mann) required a major rewrite to allow Sophia Loren to make her American film debut. Her character becomes 10 years younger, is turned into a recent Italian immigrant, and is given new dialogue to talk about her previous life in Naples. Each of Loren's appearances reminds the audience of her national origin; her accent constantly calls attention to itself. Because of this and other major deviations from the source, Erskine reports that 'O'Neill scholars were appalled by how much was lost and how little gained' (Erskine & Welsh, 2000: 88). Popular audiences agreed. The movie, which also starred Burl Ives and Anthony Perkins, was a flop.

Lehman's change in *Who's Afraid of Virginia Woolf?* is far more discrete; most spectators would not know that it occurred, and it does not affect the basic story. In Albee's play, Martha is 52, six years older than her husband; they have been married for 23 years and their imaginary son is 21. In the movie, gone is the age difference between Taylor and Burton – known widely at the time as the Battling Burtons because of their own marital problems. In the film version, the son is 16. Martha's precise references to the number of years they have been married are undertranslated: 'For twenty-three years!' (Albee, 1983: 153) becomes year after year; 'Twenty-three years of you has been quite enough' (Albee, 1983: 156) becomes a thousand years of you. Unlike changes in dialogue in *Desire Under the Elms*, the text flows smoothly without jarring the audience.

Albee's four-character play has a single set: the living room of a house on the campus of a small New England college. In keeping with patterns in film adaption, we would correctly anticipate that Nichols would open this interior space to several rooms and would move as much action outside as possible. He implements this anticipated process with consummate skill.

The opening sequence is indeed exterior: a low-angle shot of the moon, sky and trees; then a panoramic shot captures people leaving a house. As the titles are shown, the camera shifts to a high-angle shot of a man and woman walking across a kind of park toward their own house. Her raucous laughter and their unsteady gait establish both her personality and the fact that they have been drinking. Most of the action of the film takes place inside the house; a sense of movement is achieved not only through focusing alternately on several locations in the living room but also by going into the kitchen, out on the porch, and up the stairs to the bedroom. The campus shown in the opening sequence is used in several scenes, and a swing that hangs there from a tree takes on vague symbolic values, representing George's frustrations or perhaps the non-existent son. The long confessional conversation between the two men is transferred to this outside location: George swings while Nick leans against the tree; finally both of the drunken men are lying on the grass.

The movie version of *Who's Afraid of Viriginia Woolf?* breaks open the play's static location in another way that also draws on hints in the source text. In the play, there are repeated references to an automobile accident in which a beginning driver killed his father; that adolescent may or may not have been George. Whether the story is reality, illusion, or the mix that typifies Martha and George's seesawing relationship, the introduction of car rides – and reckless, drunk driving – follows logically after Martha's suggestion that George drive their guests home. In the play, the couples switch partners and dance in the living room. In the movie, the action shifts to a roadside restaurant and bar, with open dance floor, empty bandstand, and jukebox. The dance scene takes place here in a large space that provides greater opportunity for movement and camera work than would the enclosed house. Martha, climbing on the bandstand, is able to punctuate her remarks by beating the drums. Additional sequences take place outside: Nick and Honey leaving the club to walk home; George and Martha fighting in the parking lot.

The scene in the restaurant and bar is the only moment in the movie that adds to the four-actor cast. The old couple who run the place appear briefly, as part of the background. The man enters to say that they are closing. The woman wordlessly serves them a last round of drinks. The presence of the bar owners enhances cinematic reality without altering the dramatic intensity of the source text.

Two small-cast plays that have been opened up to additional characters with the full cooperation of their playwrights are Benet i Jornet's *Testament* (*Legacy*, 1996), which has a three-character, all-male cast, and Robert Harling's *Steel Magnolias* (1986), which has a six-character, all-female cast. In both cases the authors wrote screenplays that maximized cinematic decor while putting before the camera characters who had been limited to verbal allusions in the original plays. *Amic/Amat (Beloved/Friend*, 1998), Ventura Pons's film version of the Catalan play, set in the city of Barcelona, won acting, directing, and script awards at several European film festivals.[12] *Steel Magnolias* (1989, dir. Herbert Ross), set in a small town in Louisiana and starring Sally Field, Julia Roberts, Dolly Parton, and Shirley Maclaine, achieved popular acclaim; it is rated four and half stars by Martin and Porter.

In part *Beloved/Friend*, like *Actresses*, is a transposition. The text of *Legacy* is incorporated into *Beloved/Friend* without altering significantly either the original order of scenes or dialogue of the central characters: two university professors (the gravely ill gay philosophy Professor and his heterosexual Friend) and a student (the bisexual Young Man, who supports himself as a prostitute). Time in both versions is one action-packed day. Unlike *Actresses, Beloved/Friend* is also a transformation that expands the cast: it gives roles, of importance equal to that of the men, to the Friend's wife and daughter, who are mere voices on an answering machine in the play. In keeping with the greater realism of movies, the characters all have names: Jaume (Josep Maria Pou), the student David (David Selvas), Pere (Mario Gas), Pere's wife Fanny (Rosa Maria Sardà), and their daughter Alba (Irene Montalà).

In her 'how-to' book on screen adaptations, Linda Seger advises choosing a play that has a realistic context that can be opened up, a story line that can be developed, and cinematic images that can give expression to the human themes (Seger, 1992: 42). *Beloved/Friend* is a model of what Seger proposes. The three settings in *Legacy*, suggested with minimal props, are the characters' apartments; in the film, the three apartments are each distinctive and are shown in realistic detail. Predictably, many sequences are shot outside; realistic space is invented to serve as a dynamic background to otherwise static dialogue. For dialogue between two characters, there are close-up shots and reverse shots of the speakers. A long conversation between mother and daughter is played against the moving background of Barcelona and is cross-cut with scenes between the male characters. The cross-cutting device not only gives greater dynamism to dialogues retained from the original play text but also provides a deeper understanding of David's conflicted behaviour. The juxtaposition of mother–daughter and professor–young man sequences underscores Jaume's increasingly paternal feelings toward David and explains the younger man's shifts between respect and hostility.

Although the answering machine remains, the play's anonymous off-stage voices, whose stories do not relate directly to the central characters, disappear – along with the metaphorical level of the stage version that underscores the central themes: loneliness, love, pain and fear. Instead, *Beloved/Friend* adds new, realistic characters who play secondary roles in the lives of the protagonists: the doctor who will help Jaume out of his pain when it becomes unbearable; Alba's apartment mates.

Legacy, the play, presents homoerotic moments and harsh situations. The defiant Young Man beats the Professor, who has chosen him as his philosophical heir, and apparently destroys both disk and hard drive copies of the older man's life's work. The young woman, who is pregnant with the Young Man's child, perhaps shares the Professor's wish that she oppose the abortion her parents favour. The final scene is ambiguous. The Young Man undresses and prepares to receive a client, but the last unidentified voice on his answering machine speaks of salvation in lines reminiscent of the mystic Ramon Llull, subject of the Professor's culminating research project.

In *Beloved/Friend*, David's other life, as a hustler, is suggested visually even as the titles roll: close-ups of parts of his body reveal his sadomasochistic gear. The next sequences are shot at the university: the camera moves from an idyllic panorama of green lawn to inside a classroom building. Alba accidentally opens a door and intrudes on Jaume's medical evaluation; she quickly exits as Jaume asks his friend to help him die when the time comes. Out in the hallway, Alba confronts a dismayed David, and we are left with the image, more than the words, that imply she is pregnant. Jaume leaves the room and sees Alba and David together. Much more quickly than in the play, through images *Beloved/Friend* establishes the relationship between David and Alba and the likelihood that he is Jaume's student. We may not yet realize that David is the sexy male figure from the sequence behind the titles, but we are prepared for that revelation. We are also aware of Jaume's illness and impending death. With far greater economy than in the play, these human themes are expressed visually in the opening minutes of the movie.

If we are looking for a completely faithful film adaptation of *Legacy*, our conclusion may be that the women in *Beloved/Friend* detract from the main story. Certainly the development of Fanny and Alba's stories contributes significantly to the altered tone, that is, the shift from the metaphorical to the realistic plane. The central situation of the stage play, involving a hustler and a gay professor, is softened by the addition of a story that is closer to the experience of women spectators and perhaps commercial audiences in general. Curiously, the only heterosexual male among the protagonists, is transformed in the film to become insensitive, egocentric, and prone to anger. We are therefore not surprised that Alba would rather talk to her mother than to her father and that Fanny, after reminiscing with Alba about her own youth, decides to leave Pere after 20 years of marriage. In other ways, the film is still open-ended but less so than the play. We are more prepared to believe that Alba will have the baby and that David will change his life. In the play, the final lines are spoken by one of the anonymous voices; in the film, from which the anonymous voices have been deleted, the voice-over may mean that David is thinking of Llull's idealistic philosophy even as he dresses for his next client.

The film adaptation of Harling's *Steel Magnolias* uses the same strategies as *Beloved/Friend* to open up cinematic decor and expand the cast but does so more broadly. *Beloved/Friend* represents one action-packed day; time in *Steel Magnolias* is extended over several years, not ending with Shelby's death as the play does. All of the action of the source text takes place in Truvy's beauty salon. Realistic space, among other locations, includes town streets; interiors of Truvy's home and that of M'Lynn, where preparations are under way for Shelby's wedding; the backyard scene of the wedding and reception; the interior of Shelby's home, at Christmas, where she prepares the nursery for her baby; the hospital where Shelby works as a nurse and later dies; the grave-yard at her burial; the park where Shelby's baby, now a toddler, enjoys an Easter egg hunt. The play focuses on the sense of community among six women: Truvy, her young assistant Annelle, two older customers, the patrician Clairee, and the acerbic Ouiser, who provide emotional support for M'Lynn when Shelby, a diabetic, opts for motherhood and as a result dies, despite having received a kidney transplant from her mother.[13] On the other hand, the movie introduces Truvy and M'Lynn's respective husbands and sons as well as romantic interests for the elderly Ouiser and for Annelle, who radically changes her appearance and outlook on life, marries, and is about to give birth to her own baby at movie's end. In general, these expanded elements are hinted at in the play but the secondary stories in the movie, like the emphasis on wife and daughter in *Beloved/Friend*, tend to dilute the tone and spirit of the original play.

In her advice on screen adaptations, Seger recommends introducing a closed, preferably happy ending. Popular movies should not end with a death – unless the final scene compensates by showing others grieving the death (Seger, 1992: 7). The movie version of *Steel Magnolias* goes beyond this practical suggestion. The play ends with Shelby's death, as M'Lynn's friends, in their shared grief, try to help her find the courage to go on. The film ends with an emphasis on life: we see M'Lynn's love for her little grandson; Annelle is about to have a baby. The fact that it is the season of rebirth is visualized in the Easter egg hunt and panoramic views of a spring landscape.

Seger's advice is also relevant to *¡Ay, Carmela!*, Carlos Saura's 1990 version of José Sanchis Sinisterra's 1987 stage triumph. In the movie adaptation (screenplay by Saura and Rafael Azcona), the death of Carmela (Carmen Maura) by assassination during the Spanish Civil War is compensated for in an added final sequence: her long-time companion, Paulino (Andrés Pajares), and Gustavete (Gabino Diego), the mute boy they have quasi adopted, stand grieving at her graveside. In his sorrow, Gustavete recovers his voice.

Sanchis Sinisterra's ¡*Ay, Carmela!* has a two-actor cast: Carmela and Paulino. The single set is a bare theatre stage. At play's beginning, Paulino is alone, for Carmela has already been killed; her ghost returns episodically to tell him what she has learned in the great beyond and to provide the opportunity to relive the events that led to her death. Although temporal fluidity and flashbacks are part of cinematic codes, Saura chooses instead a linear narrative. He takes us behind the Republican lines, where the rhythmic music of the title song, emanating from the entertainers' truck, contrasts with the town's bombed-out buildings. In the movie, we travel through war-torn Spain with Carmela, Paulino, and Gustavete, we meet the condemned soldiers of the International Brigades, and we witness the preparations for Carmela's final performance, under the direction of a caricatured Italian officer.

The exchange of one metafictional device for another is not infrequent when stage plays are turned into films. Saura's movie does not attempt to duplicate the theatre-within-the-theatre convention of the play but compensates by locating the final performance in a theatre converted into a movie house, with a projector's white light used as a spotlight. The film otherwise takes the theatricalist plays-within-the play that require active audience imagination, and, as might be expected, transforms them into realistic performances complete with their respective playing spaces, spectators, and accompanying musicians. Saura expands on the musical component of the stage play, giving it fuller development and adding other vaudeville-style numbers.

Sontag's comment on the success of a movie adaptation depending upon the distance it places between itself and the source play may partially explain the enthusiastic response to ¡*Ay, Carmela!*. Like Bardem's *Calle mayor*, Saura's ¡*Ay, Carmela!* thoroughly rearranges and displaces the action, even to the point of borrowing, rather than transformation. The resulting creative adaptation differs considerably from the source text but is its equal in quality.

Our review of effective movie adaptations of stage plays from several countries and over a period of several decades suggests a wide range of strategies. Negative commentaries notwithstanding, screen versions of theatre have often been welcomed by critics and spectators alike even when the movies remain surprisingly faithful to their source. Although some devices are predictable given the nature of cinematic codes, there is no single answer on how a play might best be translated to the screen. Successful film versions of plays represent a full spectrum, from transposition (the equivalent to a literal translation that carries over the source text, more or less verbatim), to transformation (the equivalent of semantic translation that more aggressively converts verbal texts into visual screen language while remaining loyal to the source), to analogy (a kind of free, communicative translation that rearranges material and even changes tone as it more or less completely adapts the source to the requirements of a different genre). From Lope de Vega, Shakespeare and Rostand to Albee, Arniches and Williams, playwrights continue to inspire film directors to create some of their finest productions.

Notes

1. Changes made to correspond with television form might be compared to the requirements of text-bound translation. Albrecht Neubert points out that a patent application must not only be translated accurately but must also be put into the required format of the target country. In the same way, the stage play carried over to television must introduce the anticipated 'construction of spatial relationships between characters' and 'rhythm of shots' described by Russell Jackson as specific to film (Jackson: 18).
2. Barcelona critic Alex Gorina protested that Camus's film was canned theatre; he concluded that Almodóvar would have been more creative. Carlos Aguilar finds Camus's film to be leaden and unrecognizable; he laments both its facile theatricalism and the lack of spatial fluidity (Aguilar, 1992: 202). On the other hand, American critic Peter Podol asserts that Camus 'undermines the dramatic effects sought by the playwright' when he cuts or changes the order of scenes or moves sequences outside (Podol, 1995: 43). *La casa de Bernarda Alba* proved to be popular with audiences and was among the films most frequently selected to represent Spanish cinema in 1988 international film festivals.
3. For a detailed commentary on semantic versus communicative translation, see Newmark (1981).
4. Noël Carroll offers a useful framework for the analysis of the multiple functions of movie music (Carroll, 1988: 213–25).
5. Pons has adapted plays by both Benet i Jornet and Sergi Belbel. For an analysis of the movie versions of Belbel's plays, see David George (2002).
6. I am grateful to Sharon Carnicke for pointing out to me Kazan's omission of this key image.
7. Hervey, Higgins and Haywood define compensation as 'techniques of making up for the loss of important ST [source text] features through replicating ST effects approximately in the TT [target text] by means other than those used in the ST' (Hervey *et al.*, 1995: 28). For a discussion of censorship in Hollywood, see Maltby (1996). By the late 1950s, the Production Code had eased. Williams' *Suddenly Last Summer* (1959, dir. Joseph L. Mankiewicz, adapted by Gore Vidal and Williams), which also deals with homosexuality, was approved despite its themes of nymphomania and cannibalism. Erskine and Welsh report that the movie is 'praised as one of the best free adaptations of modern drama' (Erskine & Welsh, 2000: 332).

8. Luis Olmo's acclaimed 2003 revival of *Las bicicletas son para el verano* was not deliberately cinematic in staging like Plaza's production. For a comparison of the two productions, see my review in *Western European Stages* (Zatlin, 2003).
9. Sandra L. Richards describes Yoruba spectacles in these terms: 'In unmasking a transcendent reality, the spectacle strives to increase the collective life-force, or potentiality of all those present, by reasserting the link between the living community, departed ancestors, the yet-to-be-born, and the entire cosmos'' (Richards, 1992: 70).
10. Gómez also analyses how *Bwana* significantly changes the character of the mother, by making her less racist and comic and by drawing parallels between the subordinate status of Ombasi as a black man and of the mother as a woman in patriarchal society. There is almost no lapse in time between *Dark Man's Gaze* and this film version. More understandably Molina's *Esquilache* in 1988 presents a feminist perspective that would never have occurred to Buero-Vallejo when he wrote *Un soñador para un pueblo* 30 years earlier. For discussion of feminist rereadings of these texts, see Gómez's *Estreno* article on *Bwana* (Gómez, 2002) and my *Symposium* article on *Esquilache* (Zatlin, 1998).
11. In 2003, I posed the question directly to Ignacio del Moral, who is both playwright and screenwriter, and to José Luis Alonso de Santos, who has had three of his plays turned into movies. Alonso de Santos confirmed that he was less pleased with *Bajarse al moro* than with *La estanquera de Vallecas*, and totally at odds with the movie version of *Salvajes*. Alonso de Santos is credited with being a co-author, along with the respective directors and an additional writer, for the first two movies and was not involved in the third one. *La estanquera de Vallecas* (1986, dir. Fernando Colombo) is a faithful transformation, that makes predictable changes, including a softened ending. *Bajarse al moro* (1988, dir. Eloy de la Iglesia) adds some episodes that differ in tone and rhythm from the original, including an epilogue that significantly changes the ending. *Salvajes* (2001, dir. Carlos Molinero) adds episodes that emphasize sex and violence and thus alters the overall tone. The play and film script have been published together in an edition of the film bookstore in Madrid.
12. For a more complete analysis of the film adaptation of *Testament*, see my article in *ALEC* (Zatlin, 2001).
13. Harling wrote *Steel Magnolias* in memory of his sister, on whom the character of Shelby is based. In the play edition, he affirms that the action is remembered, rather than written. Some of the play's dialogue is carried over verbatim in the screenplay, which Harling also wrote.

References

Actrius. Dir. Ventura Pons, 1996.
Amic/Amat. Dir. Ventura Pons, 1998.
Aguilar, C. *Guía del Video-Cine*, 4th ed. Madrid: Cátedra, 1992.
Albee, E. *Who's Afraid of Virginia Woolf?* New York: Signet, 1983.
Alonso de Santos, J. L. E-mail, 2 April 2003.
Andrew, D. Adaptation. In Naremore, J., ed., *Film Adaptation*. New Brunswick, NJ: Rutgers University Press, 2000, 28–37.
baile, El. Dir. Edgar Neville, 1959.
Bajarse al moro. Dir. Fernando Colomo, 1988.

Bazin, A. Theatre and cinema. In G. Mast and M. Cohen, eds, *Film Theory and Criticism*, 3rd ed. New York and Oxford: Oxford University Press, 1985, 356–69.

Benet i Jornet, J. M. *E.R.* Barcelona: Edicions 62, 1994.

Benet i Jornet, J. M. *Legacy* (trans. J. DeCesaris). New Brunswick, NJ: ESTRENO Plays, 2000.

Besas, P. Rev. of *Las bicicletas son para el verano. Variety,* 8 February 1984: 20.

Besas, P. *Behind the Spanish Lens. Spanish Cinema under Fascism and Democracy.* Denver: Arden Press, 1985.

bicicletas son para el veranos, Las. Dir. Jaime Chávarri, 1984.

bicicletas son para el veranos, Las. By Fernando Fernán Gómez. Dir. Luis Olmos. La Latina Theatre, Madrid, 5 March 2003.

Bwana. Dir. Imanol Uribe, 1996.

Calle Mayor. Dir. Juan Antonio Bardem, 1956.

Carroll, N. *Mystifying Movies. Fads and Fallacies in Contemporary Film Theory.* New York: Columbia University Press, 1988.

Cartmell, D. *Interpreting Shakespeare on Screen.* New York: St. Martin's Press, 2000.

casa de Bernarda Alba, La. Dir. Mario Camus, 1987.

Chase, M. *Harvey* (illustrated by Blechman). New York: Oxford University Press, 1953.

Cyrano de Bergerac. Dir. Jean-Paul Rappeneau, 1990.

Death of a Salesman. Dir. Volker Schlöndorff, 1985.

del Moral, I. *La mirada del hombre oscuro.* Madrid: SGAE, 1992.

del Moral, I. Personal interview, Madrid, 6 March 2003.

Desire Under the Elms. Dir. Delbert Mann, 1958.

Erskine, T. L. and Welsh, J. M. *Video Versions. Film Adaptations of Plays on Video.* Westport, CT and London: Greenwood Press, 2000.

García-Abad García, T. Una Bernarda de cine: Lorca del papel a la pantalla. *Estreno* 27.2 (2001): 4–7.

George, D. From stage to screen: Sergi Belbel and Ventura Pons. *Anales de la Literatura Española Contemporánea.* 27.1 (2002): 89–102.

Gómez, M. A. *Del escenario a la pantalla. La adaptación cinematográfica del teatro español.* Chapel Hill: North Carolina Studies in the Romance Languages and Literatures, 2000.

Gómez, M. A. Subalternidad de raza y género en *La mirada del hombre oscuro* de Ignacio del Moral y *Bwana* de Imanol Uribe. *Estreno* 28.2 (2002): 28–33.

Gorina, A. Rev. of *La casa de Bernarda Alba. Guía del Ocio.* Barcelona (24–30 April 1987): 11.

Harling, R. *Steel Magnolias.* Garden City, NY: The Fireside Theatre, 1986.

Harvey. Dir. Henry Koster, 1950.

Hervey, S., Higgins, I. and Haywood, L. M. *Thinking Spanish Translation. A Course in Translation Method: Spanish to English.* London and New York: Routledge, 1995.

Hueso, A. L. El referente teatral en la evolución histórica del cine. *Anales de la Literatura Española Contemporánea.* 26.1 (2001): 45–61.

Jackson, R., ed. *The Cambridge Companion to Shakespeare on Film.* Cambridge: Cambridge University Press, 2000.

Mains sales, Les. Dir. Fernand Rivers, 1951.

Maltby, R. Censorship and self-regulation. In G. Nowell-Smith, ed., *The Oxford History of World Cinema*. Oxford: Oxford University Press, 1996, 235–48.

Martin, M. and Porter, M. *Video Movie Guide 1999*. New York: Ballantine Books, 1998.

Mast, G. Literature and film. In: J.-P. Barricelli and J. Gibaldi, eds, *Interrelations of Literature*. New York: The Modern Language Association of America, 1982, 278–306.

Mast, G. and Cohen, M., eds. *Film Theory and Criticism*, 3rd ed. New York and Oxford: Oxford University Press, 1985.

Midsummer's Night Dream. Dir. Michael Hoffman, 1999.

Miller, A. *Death of a Salesman*. New York: Penguin, 1976.

Neubert, A. Text-bound translation teaching. In W. Wilss and G. Thome, eds, *Die Theorie des Ubersetzens und ihr Aufschlusswert für die Ubersetzungs-und-Dolmetsch-didaktik*. Tübingen: Gunter Narr Verlag, 1984, 61–70.

Newmark, P. *Approaches to Translation*. Oxford and New York: Pergamon Press, 1981.

Nieva de la Paz, P. Pilar Miró ante el teatro clásico. *Anales de la Literatura Española Contemporánea*. 26.1 (2001): 255–76.

Odd Couple, The. Dir. Gene Saks, 1968.

Pérez Bowie, J. A. Teatro en verso y cine: Una relación conflictiva. *Anales de la Literatura Española Contemporánea*. 26.1 (2001): 317–35.

perro del hortelano, El. Dir. Pilar Miró, 1996.

Podol, P. *La casa de Bernarda Alba in performance: Three productions in three media*. *Estreno* 21.2 (1995): 42–44.

Richards, S. L. Under the 'Trickster's' sign: Toward a reading of Ntozake Shange and Femi Osofisan. In J. G. Reinelt and J. R. Roach, eds, *Critical Theory and Performance*. Ann Arbor: The University of Michigan Press, 1992, 65–78.

Ríos Carratalá, J. A. *El teatro en el cine español*. Alicante: Instituto de Cultura Juan Gil Albert, 1999.

Roberts, S. In search of a new Spanish realism: Bardem's *Calle Mayor* (1956). In P. W. Evans, ed., *Spanish Cinema. The Auteurist Tradition*. Oxford and New York: Oxford University Press, 1999, 19–37.

Salvajes. Dir. Carlos Molinero, 2001.

Salvajes. Movie script by Jorge Juan Martínez, Carlos Molinero, Clara Pérez Escrivá and Salvador Maldonado. Play text by José Luis Alonso de Santos. Madrid: Ocho y Medio, Libros de Cine, 2001.

Seger, L. *The Art of Adaptation: Turning Fact and Fiction into Film*. New York: Henry Holt, 1992.

señorita de Trevélez, La. Dir. Gabriel Ibáñez. 1984.

Songe d'une nuit d'été, Un. By William Shakespeare. Dir. Jorge Lavelli. Comédie Française, Paris, 29 May 1988.

Sontag, S. Film and theatre. In G. Mast and M. Cohen, eds, *Film Theory and Criticism*, 1985, 340–55.

Steel Magnolias. Dir. Herbert Ross, 1989.

Streetcar Named Desire, A. Dir. Elia Kazan, 1951.

Vázquez-Ayora, G. *Introducción a la traductología*. Washington, DC: Georgetown University Press, 1977.

Wagner, G. *The Novel and the Cinema.* Cranford, NJ: Associated University Presses, Inc.; London: The Tantivy Press, 1975.

Who's Afraid of Virginia Woolf? Dir. Mike Nichols, 1966.

Williams, T. *A Streetcar Named Desire*, 25th anniversary edition. New York: New American Library, 1972.

Zatlin, P. Josefina Molina's *Esquilache*: Example of feminist film transformation? *Symposium.* 52.2 (1998): 104–15.

Zatlin, P. From stage to screen: *Amic/Amat. Anales de la Literatura Española Contemporánea.* 26.1 (2001): 239–53.

Zatlin, P. Valle-Inclán and Fernán Gómez: Major revivals in Madrid, 2003. *Western European Stages* 15.2 (2003): 11–14.

Questionnaire for Theatrical Translators

(1) From what language or languages do you translate plays?

(2) Approximately how many plays have you translated and over what period of time?

   If you have translated many plays over a long period, please feel free to limit your answers below to the most recent 8–10 plays or the most recent 10–12 years and indicate here that you are doing so.

(3) Do you always translate directly from a language you know well?

   If you have ever worked through someone else's translation rather than an original play, please identify the text involved and how well you thought the process worked.

(4) Do you have an agent for handling your theatrical translations?

   If yes, how successful has your agent been in getting your work performed?

   If no, have you ever tried to get an agent, and why were your efforts unsuccessful?

(5) Do you belong to The Dramatists Guild? (NOTE: Question was modified for other countries, e.g. Sociedad General de Autores y Editores, Société des Auteurs et Compositeurs Dramatiques.)

   If yes, how does the Guild help you?

(6) Have you ever translated plays at the specific invitation of directors or theatres?

   If these commissioned translations have been staged, please list below the plays and, if the information is not in your cv, when and where they were first performed.

If any of your commissioned/invited translations were subsequently NOT performed as expected, please explain what
happened.

(7) Have you translated plays, of your own choosing, on your own
initiative?

If these self-generated translations have been staged, please list
below the plays and, if the information is not in your cv, when
and where they were first performed:

By what means were you able to achieve these productions?

(8) Have you ever had the opportunity to work on the first production
of a translation in any way, polishing with the actors or working
with the director?

If yes, please comment on the impact you feel this collaboration
had on the quality of your translation and of the production
itself.

(9) Have you ever had problems getting rights to translate a play,
or problems getting rights to have a play translation published or
performed?

If yes, please describe the circumstances.

(10) Have any of your play translations been published?

If yes, and the information is not in your cv, please list plays and
bibliographic data here.

By what means were you able to achieve these publications?

(11) To what extent do you believe that your theatrical translations need
to be adapted for your target audience in order to have them staged
successfully? (In other words, how familiar is your target audience
with the culture of your source text?)

Please cite specific examples of aspects of a play that you have felt
obliged to adapt.

(12) Please identify one or two plays that you found relatively easy to
translate and explain why.

(13) Please identify one or two plays that you found relatively difficult to
translate and explain why.

(14)   In general terms, what factors can help a theatrical translator meet with success in having play translations performed?

(15)   In general terms, what factors hinder theatrical translators from having play translations performed?

(16)   In a nutshell, what advice do you have for aspiring theatrical translators who wish to get started in the field?

(17)   Have you also translated other literary genres?

If yes, how does that experience compare with translating plays?

(18)   I intend to include in my acknowledgements a list of translators who have kindly shared their insights with me. Additionally, may I quote freely from all your answers in my writing on the subject of theatrical translation?

If not, please indicate what specific answers you do not want attributed to you by name.

Bibliography

Aaltonen, S. *Time-Sharing on Stage. Drama Translation in Theatre and Society.* Clevedon: Multilingual Matters, Topics in Translation 17, 2000.

Bassnett, S. *Translation Studies,* 3rd ed. London and New York: Routledge, 2002.

Bassnett, S. and Lefevere, A. *Constructing Cultures. Essays in Literary Translation.* Clevedon, Philadelphia, Toronto, Sydney and Johannesburg: Multilingual Matters, Topics in Translation 11, 1998.

Buhler, S. M. *Shakespeare in the Cinema. Ocular Proof.* Albany, NY: State University of New York Press, 2002.

Cartmell, D. *Interpreting Shakespeare on Screen.* New York: St. Martin's Press, 2000.

Cary, E. (adopted name of Cyrille Znosko-Borovski, died 1966). *Comment faut-il traduire?* Introduction Michel Ballard. Presses Universitaires de Lille, 1986.

Coursen, H. R. *Shakespeare in Space. Recent Shakespeare Productions on Screen.* New York: Peter Lang, 2002.

Erskine, T. L. and Welsh, J. M. *Video Versions. Film Adaptations of Plays on Video.* With John C. Tibbetts and Tony Williams. Westport, CT, and London: Greenwood Press, 2000.

García Lorenzo, L., ed. *Traducir a los clásicos.* Teatro Cuadernos no. 4. Madrid: Ministerio de Cultura, Instituto Nacional de los Artes Escénicos y de la Música, 1989.

Gómez, M. A. *Del escenario a la pantalla. La adaptación cinematográfica del teatro español.* Chapel Hill: North Carolina Studies in the Romance Languages and Literatures, 2000.

Jackson, R., ed. *The Cambridge Companion to Shakespeare on Film.* Cambridge: Cambridge University Press, 2000.

Johnston, D., ed. *Stages of Translation.* Bath, England: Absolute Classics, 1996.

Merino Álvarez, R. *Traducción, tradición y manipulación. Teatro inglés en España 1950–1990.* León: Universidad de León, 1994.

Naremore, J., ed. *Film Adaptation.* New Brunswick, NJ: Rutgers University Press, 2000.

Picon-Vallin, B., ed. *Le Film de théâtre.* Avant-propos by Élie Konigson. Paris: CNRS Éditions, Arts du Spectacle, 1997.

Ríos Carratalá, J. A. *El teatro en el cine español.* Alicante: Instituto de Cultura Juan Gil Albert, 1999.

Scolnicov, H. and Holland, P., eds. *The Play Out of Context. Transferring Plays from Culture to Culture.* Cambridge and New York: Cambridge University Press, 1989.

Thomas, A. and Blostein, D., eds. Special issue on translations. *Modern Drama.* 41.1 (Spring 1998).

Upton, C.-A., ed. *Moving Target. Theatre Translation and Cultural Relocation.* Manchester, UK and Northampton, MA: St. Jerome Publishing, 2000.

Vilches de Frutos, M. F., ed. *Teatro y cine: La búsqueda de nuevos lenguajes expresivos.* Special issues of *Anales de la Literatura Española Contemporánea.* 26.1 (2001) and 27.1 (2002).

Zuber, O. *The Languages of Theatre. Problems in the Translation and Transposition of Drama.* Oxford and New York: Pergamon Press, 1980.

Zuber-Skerritt, O., ed. *Page to Stage. Theatre as Translation.* Amsterdam: Rodopi, 1984.

Index

Escudé i Gallès, Beth, 7; *El color del gos quan
    fuig* (*Killing Time*) 7, 97
Espasa, Eva, 27, 51
Esperet, Núria, 177
Esslin, Martin, 159, 166
Estreno, x, 11
ESTRENO Plays, viii, x, 7, 33, 36, 46, 47, 51,
    59, 66, 74, 98, 143
Estudios de Doblaje Sonoblok (Barcelona),
    141
Everett, Rupert, 180
Europe, viii, 15, 39, 43, 108, 111, 120, 145,
    161, 163; Northern Europe, 76;
    European, 6, 12, 13, 53, 58, 81, 125, 126,
    131, 133, 160, 193; Eastern European, 117
European Translation Workshop, *See*
    Atelier Européen de la Traduction
European Union, 2, 19, 57, 63
Evans-Corrales, Carys, 49, 98
Ewans, Michael, 97-98, 99
Eye, The, 128

Farrell, Joseph, 27, 51, 141-42, 148
Fassbinder, Rainer Werner: *Müll die Stadt
    und der Tod, Der* (*Ordures la ville et la
    mort, Les*), 78
Faulkner, Sally, 166
Feingold, Michael, 165
Feldman, Sharon, 32, 46, 49, 91-92
Fellini, Federico, 131; *8 1/2*, 160
Fennario, David: *Balconville*, 109-10
Fernán-Gómez, Fernando, 161, 163, 186;
    bicicletas son para el verano, Las, 177,
    185-87, 199, 200; *viaje a ninguna parte, El*,
    161
Fernandez, Manny, 16
Fernández Pérez, Antonio, 55
Fernández-Tiscornia, Nelly: *Made in Lanús*,
    189
Ferrá, Max, 30
Ferrer, José, 179
Ferrero, Carmen, 82, 84
festivals, film: 127, 162, 163, 172, 179, 190,
    193, 198; theatre: 34, 41, 54, 55, 56, 59,
    137
Feydeau, Georges: *Dormez, je le veux!*
    (*Caught with His Trance Down*), 96; *Fil à
    la patte, Un* (*Not by Bed Alone*), 96
fidelity, 2, 5, 7, 26, 29, 81, 140, 153, 154, 155,
    171, 175, 181, 184, 189
Field, Sally, 193
Field, Syd, 165
filmed theatre, *See* canned theatre
Findlay, Bill, 83, 84, 99

Finland, 130; Finnish, 124
Firth, Patti, 114-15, 121
Flaubert, Gustave, 87
Flockhart, Calista, 180
Floeck, Wilfried, 48
Florida International University, 98
Flotats, Josep Maria, 15
Fo, Dario, 29-30; *Non si paga*, 29; *Sopa de mijo
    para cenar*, 29-30
Foote, Horton, 161
format (for playscript), 67-68
Formosa, Feliu, 23, 51, 78, 100
Fornés, María Irene: *Fefu and Her Friends*
    (*Fefu y sus amigas*), 28
Fosse, Bob: *All That Jazz*, 150, *Chicago*, 150
France, 2, 15, 18, 24, 25, 31, 34, 35, 36-37, 40,
    41, 42, 45, 47, 49, 51, 53-59, 61, 64, 65, 69,
    70, 106, 118, 120, 124, 125, 126, 127, 130,
    131-32, 140, 162, 179
France, Peter, 13, 19
Franco, Francisco, 28, 55, 129, 161, 163, 187,
    188; Francoist Spain, 173
Francophone, 23, 46, 110, 113
Frankfurt (Germany), 44, 132, 144-45, 146
Frayn, Michael, 4, 26-27, 34; *Benefactors*, 93,
    100; *Copenhagen*, 1; *Copenhague*, 19
Freiburg (Germany), 18
French, vii, viii, x, 2, 7, 13, 14, 22-28, 31, 32,
    34, 35, 41, 43-46, 48, 49, 51, 53-59, 60-62,
    64, 65, 68, 70, 72-76, 78, 79, 80, 81, 88, 90,
    91, 95-96, 98, 108, 109-13, 114, 116, 117,
    124-27, 130, 131, 137, 138, 140, 142, 145,
    162, 180, 188, 189
French Canada, 130; French-Canadian, 117,
    136
Fricke, Almuth, 28, 33, 41-42, 44, 49, 50, 59,
    138, 147, 148
Frisch, Max, 64
Fuentes, Carlos, 40
Fukushima, Tatsuya and David L. Major,
    127, 134, 146, 148
Fundamentos (publishing house), 45, 97

Gaard, David, 36
Galán, Eduardo and Javier Garcimartín:
    posada del Arenal, La (*Inn Discretions*), 95
Galantière, Lewis, 79
Galicia (Northwest Spain), 69, 80
Galin, Alexander, 29
Garci, José Luis: *abuelo, El*, 163
García, Rodrigo, 44; *Notas de cocina I*, 56
García, William, 11, 19
García-Abad García, Teresa, 164, 166, 173,
    200

National Drama Prize (Spain), 123
National Endowment for the Arts, 8
National Theatre Prize (Spain), 175
National Theatre Studio (London), 21,
61-62, 66
National Translation Prize (Spain), 45
naturalistic, *See* realism/naturalism
Nazi, 108; neo-Nazism, 109, 190
NDiaye, Marie, 61
Neruda, Pablo, 161-62, 189
Netherlands, 125-26
networking, 39, 47, 48, 53-65
Neubert, Albrecht, 198, 201
Neville, Edgar, 163, 199; *baile, El,* 174-76,
177, 181, 182; *vida en un hilo, La,* 163
New Brunswick (New Jersey), 138-40
New Jersey, 12, 127-28, 144-45
New Jersey Repertory, 93
New Jersey Shakespeare Festival, *See*
Shakespeare Theatre of New Jersey, The
New Orleans (US), 70, 183-84
New Theatre Publications, 44
New York City, 8, 10, 13, 30, 36, 38, 46, 50,
79, 83, 85, 96, 103, 113, 114, 127, 128, 146,
170, 181-82
New York City Opera (CONY), 138, 147
New York Times, 4, 5
New Zealand, 130
Newmark, Peter, 95, 97, 98, 101, 198, 201
Nice (France), 70
Nichols, Mike: *Who's Afraid of Virginia
Woolf?,* 191-93, 202
Nick Hern (publishing house), 39, 44, 46, 47
Nicoll, Allardyce, 157-58, 167
Nida, Eugene, 153
Nieva de la Paz, Pilar, 178, 201
Nigro, Kirsten, 34, 52
Nobel Prize, 161, 189
Noiret, Philippe, 162
Norwegian, 70, 124, 126
Nosotros Theater (Los Angeles), 120
Nottage, Lynn: *Poof!,* 82, 83
Notting Hill, *See* Gate Theatre
Nouvelles Scènes Hispaniques, 56
Nowell-Smith, Geoffrey, 165, 167
Nowhere in Africa, 127-28
Nowra, Luis, 69, 88, 101

Oberon Books, 60, 63
obscenity, 92, 112-13, 142
O'Casey, Sean: *Juno and the Paycock,* 71
O'Connor, Patricia W., x, 7, 41, 46-47, 49, 51,
101
Odd Couple: Together Again, The, 152

Odéon Theatre (Paris), 138
Odets, Clifford, 34
Odashima, Koshi, 22, 26-27
Officiel des Spectacles, L' (Paris), 131
Offstage Theatre and Film Bookshop
(London), 14
Ohio Wesleyan University, 11
O'Horgan, Tom, 30
Olivero, Francisco, 82, 83
Olmo, Luis, 199
O'Neill, Eugene: *Desire Under the Elms,* 192,
200; *Long Day's Journey into Night,* 70
opera, viii, 125, 137-38, 145, 146, 147
Opéra de Monte-Carlo, 137
Orlean, Susan: *The Orchid Thief,* 150
Oscar (Academy Award), 127, 150, 161, 162,
163, 179, 183, 190, 191
over-translation, 70-72, 97
*Oxford Guide to Literature in English
Translation, The,* 13-14, 18

Pace University (Manhattan), x, 11, 69, 85,
93
Pajares, Andrés, 196
Palestine, 63
Pallín, Yolanda: *Luna de miel (Honeymoon),*
85, 94-95, 98, 101
Panofsky, Erwin, 158
Paraguay, 42
Paramount, 165
Paris, 2, 22, 28, 30, 31, 38, 42, 48, 49, 50, 56,
65, 69, 74, 81, 93, 131, 138, 144-45, 161,
188; Parisian, 53
Parkert, Cecilia: *Witness,* 63
Parton, Dolly, 193
Pascual, Itziar: *Meowless,* 11-12
Paso, Alfonso, 50
Pasqual, Lluís, 29
Patriot, The, 136-37, 142
Paugam, Pascale, 31, 33, 39, 45, 49, 53, 80-81
Paviot, Hugo, 25-26, 32, 41, 45, 48, 49, 52, 90
Pavis, Patrice, 5, 6, 7, 9, 20, 84, 97, 101
Peck, Gregory, 161
Pedrero, Paloma, 8, 36, 69, 85-86; *Color of
August, The,* 10-11; *estrella, Una,* 8; *First
Star and The Railing,* 20; *llamada de
Lauren, La,* 80-81; *Night Divided, A,* 93;
Parting Gestures, 69; *Wolf Kisses,* 36
Penn State University, 30, 46, 73
Pérez Bowie, José Antonio, 179, 201
Pérez-Firmat, Gustavo, 105
Pérez Galdós, Benito, 162; *abuelo, El,* 162-63
Pérez Gómez, Ángel A. and José L.
Martínez Montalban, 163, 167

151-52, 153, 155, 164, 181-82; *Odd Couple II*, 152; *Oscar and Felix: A New Look at the Odd Couple*, 152
simultaneous translation (in theatre), 125, 143-44
Sirera, Rodolf: *Plany en la mort d'Enric Ribera*, 144
Skármeta, Antonio, 189; *Ardiente paciencia*, 161-62, 189-90; *Burning Patience*, 38, 161-62, 165; *cartero de Neruda, El*, 162
slang, *See* colloquial language
Slovak, 57
small-cast play (adapted for film), 191-97
Smith and Kraus (publishing house), 46
Snows of Kilimanjaro, The, 129
Sociedad de Teatro y Medios de Latinoamérica, *See* Theater – und Mediengesellshaft Lateinamerika
Sociedad General de Autores y Editores (SGAE), 34, 36-37, 48, 50, 52, 190
Société del Auteurs et Compositeurs Dramatiques (SACD), 34, 35, 36-37, 49-50, 56-57, 65
Society of Authors (UK), 36-37, 50
Solanas, Charo, 4
Solano, Bernardo: *Entries*, 143
Somigli, Luca, 151, 168
song (as intertext), ix, 6, 25, 49, 74, 90-91, 96
Sontag, Susan, 156, 158, 159, 168, 173, 197, 201
soundtrack, 124, 130, 141, 143, 145, 175, 181
South (of US), 8
South America, *See* Latin America
South Coast Repertory (California theatre), 26
Southern Cone (of South America), 14
Soviet Union, 9
Spain, 11, 15, 18, 24, 26, 28-29, 34, 35, 36, 39, 41, 44, 46, 47, 48, 54, 55, 56, 58, 59, 71, 72, 73-74, 76, 81, 85, 87, 97, 103, 107, 109, 115, 120, 124, 129-30, 131, 138, 141, 161, 162, 166, 173, 178, 190, 197; Spaniard, 54, 98, 190
Spanish, vii, viii, x, 2, 7, 13, 14, 15, 22, 23, 24, 25, 26, 28, 29, 30, 31, 35, 38, 41, 45, 46, 47, 49, 50, 53, 54, 55, 57, 58, 59, 65, 67-68, 69, 70, 75-76, 79-80, 81, 82, 83, 84, 85, 87, 91, 96, 98, 103-09, 111-17, 118-19, 120, 123, 124, 125, 127, 129-30, 136, 138-40, 141, 145, 146, 153, 160, 162-63, 164, 173, 174, 185-88, 191, 198
Spanish America, *See* Latin America
Spencer, David, 67, 101
Sproul, Atlee, 47

Staatschauspiel (Dresden), 50
Staatstheater Kassel, 50
Stadttheatre Konstanz, 50
stage directions, 10, 67-68, 74, 80, 82, 103-04, 117, 170, 183
stageworthy, 53, 77
Stam, Robert, 150, 153, 154, 168
Stepun, Fedor, 166
Stewart, Jimmy, 183
Stoppard, Tom, 34, 61
Storer, Edward, 35
Stranger, The, 155
street language, *See* colloquial language
Strindberg, Johan August, 37; *Fröken Julie (Miss Julie)*, 95
Struthers, Sally, 152
Stuttgart (Germany), 25, 59
Suarez, Dorothée, 57, 66
Suárez, Emma, 178
subtitle, defined, 123-24, 128, 133; guidelines, 132-36, 138, 139
Surbezy, Angès, 97
survey, *See* questionnaire
Svich, Caridad, 6, 20, 32, 37, 46, 49, 59-60, 66, 97; *Alchemy of Desire/Dead-Man's Blues*, 97; *Iphigenia Crash Land Falls on the Neon Shell That Was Once Her Heart*, 97
Swahili, 127
Sweden, 31, 131, 189; Swedish, 7, 24, 25, 63, 95, 124, 131, 146
Sweet Bird of Youth, 164
Switzerland, 120
Szanto, George, 188
Szel, Elisabeth: *casa de las Chivas, La*, 161

Tandy, Jessica, 183
Taylor, Elizabeth, 191-92
Teatro Avante (Florida), 137, 138, 140
Teatro Cervantes (Buenos Aires), 120
Teatro Hispano Gala (Washington, D.C.), 143-44
Teatro Rodante Puertorriqueño (New York City), 36
Teatro de la Luna (Washington, D.C.), 143
television, ix, 15, 31, 39, 78, 123, 125-26, 131, 132, 133, 134, 135, 137, 144, 145-47, 151-52, 156, 160, 161, 164, 165, 169-71, 172, 174, 181, 198
Templer, Sally, 141-42, 149
Tepperman, Shelley, 17
Texas, 13
Thai, 128
Theater – und Mediengesellshaft Lateinamerika, 44, 48, 59, 66